C H SPURGEON'S FORGOTTEN EARLY SERMONS

A companion to the New
Park Street Pulpit

*Twenty-eight sermons compiled from the
Sword and the Trowel by Terence Peter Crosby*

DayOne

© Day One Publications 2010
First printed 2010

ISBN 978–1–84625–202–0

British Library Cataloguing in Publication Data available

Unless otherwise indicated, Scripture quotations in this publication are from the
Authorized (King James) Version (AV), Crown copyright

Published by Day One Publications
Ryelands Road, Leominster, HR6 8NZ
☎ 01568 613 740 FAX 01568 611 473
email—sales@dayone.co.uk
web site—www.dayone.co.uk
North American—e-mail—sales@dayonebookstore.com
North American—web site—www.dayonebookstore.com

Cover design by Wayne McMaster
Printed by Thomson Litho, East Kilbride

Contents

Contents

L overs of Spurgeon's preaching have always had a special affection for the sermons of his New Park Street years, with their youthful vibrancy and freshness, but, when compared with their more numerous Metropolitan Tabernacle successors, a far lower percentage of these actually reached publication. Of the sermons preached mostly on Sundays and Thursdays an average of roughly one hundred and five per year are extant for the thirty years of his Metropolitan Tabernacle ministry, but an average of only about seventy per year for his seven New Park Street years. The purpose of this volume is to reintroduce some twenty-eight of these early gems which appeared in *The Sword and the Trowel,* all but one after his death.

The New Park Street Pulpit

The first of Spurgeon's sermons in print appeared in 1854 in the *Penny Pulpit* series; these and others reappeared in the first two volumes of his *Pulpit Library.* At the start of 1855 Spurgeon began his own *New Park Street Pulpit,* which ran to three hundred and sixty-eight weekly numbers in six and a quarter annual volumes before the move to the Metropolitan Tabernacle. Some misconceptions need to be corrected. Firstly, there were only three hundred and fifty-four sermons involved, as nine long sermons produced double numbers with or without other material attached and two special meetings took up a further five numbers. Secondly, of the three hundred and fifty-four only ninety-eight were actually preached at New Park Street Chapel, the size of which was soon inadequate for the rapidly growing congregations. As a result a further ninety-two *New Park Street Pulpit* sermons relate to two series of services at Exeter Hall and as many as one hundred and fifty-six to the famous series at the Surrey Gardens Music Hall.

The Metropolitan Tabernacle Pulpit

After Spurgeon's death at the start of 1892 the publishers continued to concentrate on sermons preached at the Metropolitan Tabernacle, but two individual sermons from the New Park Street years appeared towards the end of Volumes 40 and 41 (1894–5). Then from Volume 44 (1898) to Volume 48 (1902) it became the practice to publish a New Park Street sermon on a monthly basis. After that a few more early sermons were to appear in Volumes 49, 50, 53, 54 and 55, the last in 1909. In all eighty-eight sermons were involved, this time all but five having been preached at New Park Street Chapel itself. Of these eighty-eight, sixty-three had appeared in the monthly magazine *The Baptist Messenger*, nineteen in the first two volumes of Spurgeon's *Pulpit Library* and three in both sources.

Sermons from the New Park Street years published posthumously in The *Metropolitan Tabernacle Pulpit,* showing volume and sermon numbers:

Vol. 40: 2392

Vol. 41: 2443

Vol. 44: 2554, 2558, 2562, 2563, 2567, 2572, 2576, 2581, 2585, 2589, 2594, 2598, 2602

Vol. 45: 2607, 2611, 2615, 2616, 2621, 2625, 2629, 2634, 2639, 2642, 2647, 2651

Vol. 46: 2656, 2660, 2664, 2668, 2673, 2677, 2681, 2686, 2690, 2695, 2700, 2703, 2707

Vol. 47: 2711, 2715, 2720, 2724, 2728, 2733, 2737, 2741, 2746, 2750, 2754, 2759

Vol. 48: 2763, 2766, 2772, 2776, 2780, 2785, 2789, 2794, 2798, 2802, 2807, 2811

Vol. 49: 2815, 2836

Vol. 50: 2875, 2896, 2908, 2915

Vol. 53: 3036, 3042, 3048, 3054, 3060, 3066

Vol. 54: 3077, 3081, 3087, 3093, 3100, 3105, 3108, 3114, 3120

Vol. 55: 3126, 3133, 3139

Other Publications

The *New Park Street* and *Metropolitan Tabernacle Pulpit* volumes are by no means the only places where sermons from Spurgeon's New Park Street years are to be found. A few others appeared only in the *Penny Pulpit* and *The Baptist Messenger* while the two sermons preached on his first visit to New Park Street Chapel on 18 December 1853 were included in his *Autobiography*. But the other main source of material is of course the magazine Spurgeon started himself, *The Sword and the Trowel*, which was the source of over sixty of the sermons published in *The Metropolitan Tabernacle Pulpit* after Spurgeon's death. Some fifteen of these were roughly dated according to the year and issue of the magazine in which they had first appeared.

Posthumous *Metropolitan Tabernacle Pulpit* sermons showing original years of publication in The Sword and the Trowel:
1866: 2970
1867: 2982
1869: 2976, 2999, 3014, 3028
1870: 2990, 2995, 3007, 3021, 3034
1871: 3040, 3046, 3052, 3064, 3070
1872: 3075, 3083, 3089, 3101, 3129
1873: 3107, 3112, 3118, 3124, 3135
1874: 3143, 3149, 3155, 3156
1875: 3161, 3165, 3168
1876: 3174, 3181, 3187, 3193, 3199
1877: 3205, 3211, 3217, 3231, 3237(a), 3237(b)
1878: 3243, 3283
1879: 3249
1880: 3255, 3261, 3267
1881: 3153, 3273
1882: 3279
1883: 3289, 3295, 3301, 3307, 3313, 3319
1884: 3330, 3340
1885: 3345
1887: 3350, 3479
1890: 2645
1891: 3175

The Sword and the Trowel
In addition to these sermons from the Metropolitan Tabernacle years, *The Sword and the Trowel* provided the bulk (in some cases all) of the material in other compilations of Spurgeon's sermons and writings.

This was the case with *An All-Round Ministry* (twelve of the Presidential addresses at the Annual Conference of the Pastors' College—the 1876 address had already reappeared in *Lectures to my Students* instead), *Only A Prayer Meeting* (forty addresses at the Monday evening Prayer Meeting), *Pictures from Pilgrim's Progress* (apparently also addresses at Monday evening Prayer Meetings), *Till He Come* (twenty-one Communion meditations and addresses) and *The Treasury of David* (expositions of all 150 Psalms), all reprinted by Pilgrim Publications. More recently Eric Hayden compiled a volume entitled *C. H. Spurgeon's Sermons Preached on Unusual Occasions* (Pilgrim Publications, 1978), a collection of forty-four sermons and addresses of various kinds first published in *The Sword and the Trowel* between 1869 and 1901. A few more addresses from *The Sword and the Trowel* are to be found in *Classic Counsels* (The Wakeman Trust, 2003) and *Sunlight for Cloudy Days* (The Wakeman Trust, 2010), both edited by Peter Masters. Some of the sermons in these three recent collections are also to be found in the posthumous volumes of the *Metropolitan Tabernacle Pulpit*.

The Forgotten Sermons

For a number of years after Spurgeon's death (to 1905 at least) the compilers of the monthly periodical included in the annual volume an updated 'INDEX OF TEXTS OF SERMONS, OUTLINES, ETC., BY C. H. SPURGEON, IN "THE SWORD AND THE TROWEL"'. Though a few texts are omitted and there is of course no place for articles and addresses which appeared without texts, this index is a valuable tool and reveals that there is much other material by Spurgeon in *The Sword and the Trowel*. This includes articles, expositions, lectures to students of the Pastor's College, further Presidential and Prayer Meeting addresses, Communion addresses at Mentone, and almost a hundred of his first and last sermon outlines (from 1851 onwards and during his final illness in 1891–2). Pilgrim Publications have gone some way towards filling the gap by reprinting Spurgeon's own contributions to *The Sword and the Trowel*, currently covering its first twenty-two years (1865–1886). However, there are many other items which are yet to be reprinted including a number of early sermons from Spurgeon's New Park Street years, the vast majority of which were either reported or forwarded by Pastor Thomas Medhurst, who had been Spurgeon's first pastoral student. Usually items in *The Sword and the Trowel* were undated, but here there is sufficient information to indicate that there are thirty-seven such sermons, published between 1889 and 1902. Nine of these have already been reprinted and are therefore omitted from this volume. They are as follows:—

IN *ONLY A PRAYER MEETING:*

1. 'Honey out of the Rock' (Psalm 81:16—a Prayer Meeting address at New Park Street Chapel on Monday evening 8 June 1857)

IN *C. H. SPURGEON'S SERMONS PREACHED ON UNUSUAL OCCASIONS:*

2. The Saving Name of Jesus (Matthew 1:21—preached in a tent at Ross, Herefordshire, on Thursday 3 September 1857)

3. Comfort in Trouble (Psalm 88:3—preached at The Piece Hall, Halifax, on Wednesday afternoon 7 April 1858)

4. Revival Work (Habakkuk 3:2—preached at The Piece Hall, Halifax, on Wednesday evening 7 April 1858)

5. A Sermon on Clapham Common (Luke 12:40—preached on Sunday afternoon 10 July 1859)

6. Earnestness (an address to the missionaries of the London City Mission on Tuesday morning 1 January 1861) [Also in *Speeches at Home and Abroad*]

IN *CLASSIC COUNSELS:*

7. Clear the Way [retitled Clear away the Obstacles] (Isaiah 57:14— preached on a weeknight in 1856)

IN *C H SPURGEON'S SERMONS BEYOND VOLUME 63* (DAYONE, 2009—BOTH OF THESE SERMONS APPEARED FIRST IN *THE BAPTIST MESSENGER*):

8. The Dew of Blessing (Hosea 14:5–7—preached at New Park Street Chapel in 1856)

9. The Trowel and the Sword (Nehemiah 4:18—preached at New Park Street Chapel in late August 1859)

Sermons in this volume showing original years of publication in *The Sword and the Trowel*

1889
1. p. 537 The coming day (Romans 13:12—preached at the Independent Chapel, Wivenhoe, near Colchester, on Wednesday evening 18 April 1855)

1893
2. p. 370 Unpublished notes of New Park Street sermons no.1 (James 1:12—preached on Thursday evening 11 September 1856)
3. p. 430 Unpublished notes of New Park Street sermons no.2 (Psalm 51:10—preached on Thursday evening 18 September 1856)
4. p. 504 Unpublished notes of New Park Street sermons no.3 (Isaiah 53:5—preached on Thursday evening 16 October 1856)
5. p. 558 Unpublished notes of New Park Street sermons no.4 (Psalm 101:1—preached on Thursday evening 13 November 1856)

1894
6. p. 11 Unpublished notes of New Park Street sermons no.5 (Daniel 5:6—preached on Sunday evening 16 November 1856)
7. p. 216 Unpublished notes of New Park Street sermons no.6 (Proverbs 8:17—preached on Thursday evening 11 December 1856)
8. p. 361 Unpublished notes of New Park Street sermons no.7 (Matthew 7:24–27—preached on Monday evening 11 May 1857)
9. p. 491 Unpublished notes of New Park Street sermons no.8 (Romans 5:6—preached on Thursday evening 14 May 1857)

1895
10. p. 12 Unpublished notes of New Park Street sermons no.9 (John 14:6—preached on a Lord's Day evening 1856)
11. p. 127 Unpublished notes of New Park Street sermons no.10 (Psalm 73:28—preached in 1856)

12. p. 221 Unpublished notes of New Park Street sermons no. 11 (1 Peter 3:18—preached in 1859)

13. p. 477 Jesus—Saviour (unpublished notes—Matthew 1:21—preached in the Botanic Gardens, Belfast between 15 & 22 August 1858)

1896

14. p. 1 Lessons from Mount Nebo (Deuteronomy 32:48–50—preached at New Park Street Chapel on a Lord's Day evening 1855)

15. p. 109 An eternal distinction (Matthew 25:46—preached at New Park Street Chapel '40 years ago')

16. p. 421 Jesus Christ—the Breaker (Micah 2:13—preached at Queen's Square Chapel, Brighton, on Wednesday evening 23 April 1856)

1897

17. p. 59 The death of Moses (Deuteronomy 34:5—a short sermon written 'more than 40 years ago')

18. p. 121 Come ye children (Psalm 34:11—preached to Sunday-school teachers at The Temple, St Mary Cray, Kent, on Wednesday afternoon 20 February 1856)

19. p. 512 Seest thou this woman? (Luke 7:44—preached at St Martin's Hall, Long Acre, on Wednesday evening 3 September 1856)

1898

20. p. 492 C. H. Spurgeon's most striking sermons no.9 (unpublished notes—Matthew 28:5—preached at Castleton (between Newport and Cardiff) on Wednesday morning 20 July 1859)

1899

21. pp. 577 & 625 (2 parts) A Visit to Calvary (John 19:5—preached at The Hanover Square Rooms on 14 March 1856 on behalf of the Exeter Buildings' Ragged School) [N.B. Incomplete in C. H. *Spurgeon's Sermons Preached on Unusual Occasions*]

1900

22. pp. 49 & 105 (2 parts) Christ the rock (1 Corinthians 10:4—preached at New Park Street Chapel in 1856)

23. pp. 337 & 405 (2 parts) The deaf and the dumb (Mark 7:32–35—preached at Westbourne Grove Chapel on Friday morning 5 February 1858)

24. p. 473 Jesus communicating his riches (2 Corinthians 8:9—an early meditation)

25. p. 521 Christ glorified in his people (John 17:10—an early sermon)

26. pp. 569 & 617 (2 parts) Four most gracious things (Isaiah 55:1–3—an early sermon)

1901

27. pp. 49 & 109 (2 parts) Spiritual Samsons (Judges 16:6—an early sermon)

28. pp. 325 & 393 (2 parts) Inward fears (2 Corinthians 7:5—preached at Brighton 'more than 40 years ago')

Acknowledgements

I am, once again, grateful to Judy Powles, Librarian of Spurgeon's College, for granting access to the original materials, to Digby James, for his photographic and computing skills, and to Trudy Kinloch, for her editorial skills, all of whom have made this volume possible.

Index of texts (* = not represented elsewhere in Spurgeon's sermons)

The coming day*

A sermon, delivered 18 April 1855, by C. H. Spurgeon, pastor of New Park Street Chapel, Southwark, at the Independent Chapel, Wivenhoe, near Colchester.†

'The night is far spent, the day is at hand.'—Romans 13:12.

T HESE are short words, but full of meaning. He who lieth tossing on his weary couch at midnight is glad when he seeth the coming morn. The warder on the castle top, who all night long keeps sentinel with the stars, rejoiceth when he finds that 'the night is far spent, and the day is at hand.' 'The morning cometh' is a gospel to a fainting spirit.

I shall speak, first, of *the night of the heart*; secondly, of *the night of the world*; and thirdly, of *the night of our existence as to time*.

First, THE NIGHT OF THE HEART. The heart is a little world in itself; it has its days and nights, its summers and winters. I shall speak of that dark night through which the Christian has to pass when conviction throws its dark shadow over his heart. When the Lord begins to deal with a sinner, he takes away all his boasted self-righteousness, and often brings him into such a low and desponding state that he loathes his very existence. I do not believe in a man's being born again without pain. Many of us passed through great distress and affliction before we knew that our sins were pardoned. For months I wished I had been born a dog instead of a man, whilst my sins made midnight in my soul. It is not every convert who has to go through the same burning fiery furnace, but every person has, in a measure, to pass through the dark night of conviction. We must all feel that godly sorrow which needeth not to be repented of; otherwise we shall know nothing of the saving power of Christ. There may be persons here present who are passing through the state I have just mentioned. You are beginning to feel a night in your heart. It was all light a little while ago, when you felt you were as good as other people; and if I had called you a sinner, you would have said, 'and so is everybody else'; but you did not consider yourself much to blame. Now you feel that all the Bible says of you is true, and that you are worse than you could have imagined. You fear that you will be lost for ever: you feel yourself to be so vile. Yet your self-despair and bitter grief are not evidences of eternal darkness, but the rather they are tokens that 'the night is far spent, the day is at hand.' I would say to every poor creature groaning under corruption, and bowed down with heaviness by reason of sin, 'The night is far spent, the day is at hand.'

You say, 'How am I to know this?' I will give you three or four signs by which you may tell when your night is nearly over, and your day is coming. When your night is far spent, *it is the darkest with you*. They tell us that the darkest part of the night is that which precedes the dawning of the day. I know it is so in the heart. Are you getting worse than you were? Do you feel yourselves more deeply lost than ever? Man's extremity is God's opportunity. Therefore, despair not, thou trembling one. Say not that God will not have mercy upon you. When you are cast down, God will help you up. If you are brought down to self-despair, now is the day of deliverance. When the iron enters into thy soul, then shalt thou come forth from the prison-house. Some have gone so far in despair, that they have been ready to destroy themselves; and yet they have been saved. I beseech you, never listen to the suggestion of the foul spirit, who is both a liar and a murderer: keep your hands off your own life, and believe that the despair which now makes existence itself a burden is meant to drive you to the Saviour.

Another sign that 'the night is far spent, the day is at hand,' is when *your candle is burning out*. I was hesitating one night about a text, and I sat up late, when I noticed that my candle was dying down, and flickering in the socket; then these words forcibly struck me as most appropriate, 'The night is far spent, the day is at hand'! If I were to question the people of Wivenhoe as to their spiritual state and condition, they would probably say, 'We are as good as other people. We pay twenty shillings in the pound, and hope to go to heaven.' What is this but trusting to your own righteousness? Have you not discovered that, though you may be as good as other people, you will not be measured by them, but by the standard of the Bible. If you have found out your true condition, your candle is not quite so bright as you thought it was; in fact, it is burning low. Once your character shone like the stars; but now its glory has departed, and your own esteem is lost in darkness. Is the candle of your righteousness burned out? If so, 'the night is far spent, the day is at hand'; and it will not be long before you will rejoice with God's people.

Another sign by which you may tell when the morning is coming, is *you will see the morning star*. The morning star! What is that? Jesus Christ is the Morning Star! Poor sinner! hast thou had a glimpse of Jesus? Hast thou had a sight of the bleeding Saviour? If you have seen the Morning Star, the day has come. That man who puts his trust in Jesus is saved. The gospel is simply, 'Look unto me, and be ye saved, all the ends of the earth.' There is nothing to do but look; look, and be saved. I lately saw a fine picture representing Moses lifting up the serpent in the wilderness. He held up the brazen serpent with one hand, and pointed to it with the other, and cried to the wounded Israelites, 'Look! look! and live.' A poor man lay before him with his arms encircled with serpents; but as he was looking at the brazen serpent, the venomous reptiles were falling off him. Another man was trying, with all his might, to untwist the serpents which had fastened around his body; but they were twisting themselves around him all the tighter for his efforts. A poor mother was holding an infant in her arms over the tops of people's heads, to let it see the brazen serpent, whilst she was gazing at it most earnestly herself. O mother, hold up your child to let it look to the cross, for there is life for your child as well as for you! It is 'look,' my brethren. Have you seen enough of Christ to rely upon his virtue and merits? Can you put your trust in his power? Can you venture to repose wholly upon him? If you can, 'the night is far spent, the day is at hand.'

In the country, we can tell when the morning cometh *by the twittering of the birds around our window*. When little-faith cries, 'cheer up, cheer up,' and faith sings its carol, and love gives forth its note, the morning has come. The devil has been a liar from the beginning, and is so tonight, for he tells you that you are hopelessly lost in darkness. Tell him, no; you have a little hope yet, and will have more by-and-by, for 'the night is far spent, the day is at hand.' I fear there are some here who no more understand what I am saying than if I spoke to them in an unknown tongue. With all solemnity, let me tell you that, if you have never been convinced of sin, of righteousness, and of judgment to come—if you have never been ploughed in conscience by the Spirit, never wounded by the sword of the Lord, you have neither part nor lot in this matter, and are in the gall of bitterness and the bonds of iniquity. May God, in his mercy, send you a night of darkness, that you may long for a morning with Jesus! 'The evening and the morning were the first day'; and if you have no evening, no morning will come to you. With this part of the subject I have done.

Secondly, THE NIGHT OF THE WORLD. O poor world! thou hast had a long, long night since the time when mother Eve stretched out her hand, and plucked the fruit of the tree.

'Oh, what a fall was there, my brethren!
Then you, and I, and all of us, fell down,
While sin and Satan triumphed over us!'

From that moment the sun of earth's true light was quenched, and its heaven was veiled in darkness. Since that time darkness has covered the earth, and thick darkness the people. We see in various directions Romanism, Mahommedanism, and Paganism in their thousand forms, making night hideous. It is enough to make a Christian weep tears of blood to think how long this world's night has lasted. He who feels aright will feel the deepest woe at heart when he thinks of the sad consequences to his fellow-creatures of these ages of midnight. Since the days of Noah, how many millions of men have been swept into eternity without hope! O night of sin, dark thou art! But my text says, 'The night is far spent, the day is at hand.' Let us hope that the night of the world is nearly spent, and that a glorious day is dawning. The Psalmist tells us of the beasts of the forest, that 'The sun ariseth, they gather themselves together, and lay them down in their dens. Man goeth forth unto his work and to his labour until the evening.'

These are two signs which show us that the day is coming. *The beasts are lying down.* The Church of Rome has, in many places, lost its former power: it has no such sway as it had before the Reformation. It may roar as it pleases, but its power is broken wherever the gospel is faithfully preached. It can make no progress where there is light; and to me it seems to be making for its den. Soon, by God's command, the angel will cast the millstone into the flood, and Babylon the great shall be fallen.‡

Once Mahommedanism could have caused ten thousand scimitars to flash from their scabbards, and strike deep for the false prophet; but now Islam is as a wolf which would raven if it could; but its teeth are drawn. Where are the gods of the heathen? Are they not falling? True, Juggernaut may still stand up, but not in its former honour. The beasts are hastening to their lairs. Take courage, Christians, for 'the night is far spent, the day is at hand,' and the latter-day glory will speedily come!

The church is assuredly going forth to her labour. There never was a time when God's church was doing more than now, although it is still doing little enough. Christians have too often been a lazy set, and the conduct of some of them is enough to make observers infidels. I recollect hearing of a colloquy between an infidel and a Christian minister, who were in the constant habit of passing each other. 'Do you preach the gospel?' asked the infidel, one day, of the Christian. 'I do,' replied the latter. 'And do you believe there is a hell?' 'Most certainly I do,' rejoined the Christian. 'Then how is it,' said the infidel, 'that you have been in the habit of seeing me every day for many years, and have never once warned me of it?' What a question to answer! Might it not be put to some of you? We have a great deal of profession, but where is the power of religion? Think of the days of Whitefield and Wesley; there were giants in those days; twenty modern Christians tied up in a bundle would not make one of them. Dealing with Christian professors in masses, have we not reason to be disgusted with them, and, most of all, with ourselves? Yet the church was never more active than now; and, save in apostolic times, never was more accomplished. Fifty years ago, where were our Missionary Societies, our Sunday-schools, Ragged-schools, Tract Societies, and Bible Societies? There were but faint foreshadowings of them. It was a happy day when the sun began to shine, and saints began to quit their couches, and go forth to serve their Lord. Blessed is the prophecy which lies within foreign missions. Our Sabbath-schools are also most hopeful signs. I am no fortune-teller, neither do I profess, like some popular preachers, to predict the end of the world, or to know the date of the second coming of our Lord. There are so many opinions about it that I dare not venture a new one; but I do venture to hope that the general activity of the church of God is a sign that the day of the Lord is drawing nigh. There are many other hopeful signs. Christian people are working together, and more unity is seen. The church is awaking, and we hope it cannot be long ere travailing Zion shall bring forth her children. Oh, that the nations of the earth may bow before Jesus, and rejoice in his marvellous light! 'The night is far spent, the day is at hand.'

In a happy, hopeful frame of mind, we may feel like the Greek soldiers returning from the Persian wars, when at last they beheld the sea which washed the shores of their beloved country. They clapped their hands, and, with loud voices, cried, 'The sea! the sea!' I see the waters of that great sea of glory which will spread from pole to pole. I hope to live to see Christ in his glory yet upon the earth, and to hear the song, 'The kingdoms of this world have become the kingdoms of our God, and of his Christ.' May revolving years prove that we are right in the hope that 'the night is far spent, the day is at hand'!

If I had time tonight, I would give you three or four proofs of the fulfilment of the prophecies, and show you that the glories of the latter day are hastening on. The prophecies of God are the figures upon the clock of time. In the times of our Lord a star pointed out the place of his nativity; and now a star of promise may be seen moving towards the hour of his glory. If you are a reader of the prophecies, and a watcher of events, you will be apprehensive that the Lord is coming quickly. 'The night is far spent, the day is at hand.' Cast your eyes over the world, and in every country you will see stars of hope. When we look at China, we cannot help saying, 'Verily, the night is far spent, the day is at hand.' Keep on with your gifts, and labours, and prayers, and hopes. Although the vision tarry, it must come at last.¶

Thirdly, THE NIGHT OF OUR EXISTENCE IN THIS DYING WORLD IS FAR SPENT, and the day is at hand. In a certain sense, while we live upon this earth, we are all in the night. This time-state is, comparatively, darkness. Here we have nights of sickness, care, trial, and weariness. This life is, indeed, to many, a dreary night. Still, it is not altogether night, for—

Chapter 1

'The men of grace have found
Glory begun below.'

This world is a howling wilderness to those who go howling through it; but the wilderness and the solitary place rejoice and blossom as the rose when faith is in full exercise. The believer is happy; but still, as compared with the glory to be revealed hereafter, his present life is a night. The night with many is far spent, and the day is at hand. May I not say to many a grey-headed sire, 'Brother, thy night is far spent, and thy day is at hand'? I am afraid that, to some, the grey head, instead of being a crown of glory, is only a fool's cap. I once heard Mr Jay say that, if a man had lived sixty or seventy years, and not loved Jesus, nor made his heaven secure, to call him a fool was to call him by his right name. I recollect reading of a certain fool who was kept in a nobleman's palace, and because he was so clever, his lordship gave him a walking-stick, and told him that whenever he found a bigger fool than himself, he was to give him that stick. Some time after, his lordship was taken dangerously ill, and calling the fool to his bed-side, he said, 'I am going to die.' 'And what provision have you made for your long journey?' said the fool. 'None at all,' said his master. 'Have you a home in the other country?' asked the fool. 'No,' replied his lordship. 'Then take this stick: whenever I go a journey, I make provision for it.' I tell you, friends, if your silver locks are not a crown of glory, they accuse you of gross folly. If you are saved in the Lord, I would willingly change places with you, because you are nearer to the eternal day; but if you are not in Christ, I feel a trembling compassion for you. To die in the Lord is sweet; but to die without hope, how terrible! May you all be ready for the eternal morning!

To certain others 'the night is far spent, the day is at hand,' not because of age, but because of illness. She whose cheek is blanched with fell disease, upon whose face there comes the hectic flush, the faint memory of health; she has the token of the rising sun, if she be the Lord's daughter. Glory shines in those eyes. She is melting away into the eternal. To her 'the night is far spent, the day is at hand.' He who has long nursed a cancer near his heart, or whose languid frame shows that death has marked him for its own, if he be a believer, may congratulate himself upon the speedy coming of the glorious morrow. But let us all look to ourselves, my friends, and recollect that, if we are Christians, we are nearer to the land of the unfading day than we may think. O man, dost thou think that thy bones are iron, and thy ribs steel? No, thou art dust, and unto dust thou shalt return. Perhaps before another week has tried us, we may have entered upon the endless Sabbath! Young as we are, we may have passed beyond the region of clouds and gloom before another year begins. How bright will be the day! Oh, if we could see a day in heaven! It is a day at which the sun might turn pale with envy. A day with Jesus—what felicity! 'There shall be no night there'—no night of fear, no night of sorrow, no night of death. There they neither see mattock, nor shroud, nor coffin, nor hearse. Let us rejoice that every hour shortens the night, and hastens on the day. Let us triumph in the prospect of life's new morning. 'The night is far spent, the day is at hand.'

With some of you, your present night is far spent, and no morning is coming! Would to God that this were not so! Must I, my Lord, at last speak like Boanerges, when I would sooner be a Barnabas? Must I close with anathemas? Must I speak to those who love not the Lord Jesus? Help me, O Lord, to speak with power! Some of you may expect no day when you die, but a dark and endless night. You may die in a moment! O sinners, you are standing over the mouth of hell upon a single plank, and that plank is rotten! You are hanging over a yawning gulf, by a single rope, and the strands of that rope are snapping! You are in awful danger—in danger of eternal destruction—and yet you make mirth! You will go away tonight, and the wind will blow away from you what I have said; and every warning will be forgotten. But, mark my words, the hour will come when you and I shall meet again. You say, 'When shall we meet again?' Beware of the judgment!

At the bar of God I shall confront you; before the judgment-seat of Christ I shall meet you. The thought staggers me! I shall have to stand in the witness-box against your souls, and say, 'I warned them, but they would not hear. I bade them fly to Jesus, but they refused.' If I am unfaithful you will lay your blood at my door, and I shall sink with you to well-deserved perdition. I cannot bear it! If you are lost, it shall not be for want of calling upon you to repent of your sins, and to believe in Jesus for salvation. It shall not be for want of telling you that the wages of sin is death, but the gift of

God is eternal life through Jesus Christ our Lord. Drunkard, is thy cup so sweet that thou wilt drain it to the dregs? O thou filthy man, is there anything so sweet in thy lasciviousness as to make thee barter away thy soul and heaven for ever? O thou miser, idolizing thy gold, is it more precious than the bliss of heaven? And thou, young man, without a thought of God, will you venture thus to die? Will you dare to die without a refuge to flee to in the great and terrible day of the Lord? 'Turn ye, turn ye, for why will ye die, O house of Israel?' God's power alone will turn you from your evil ways. If you heave a sigh to the Lord Jesus, he will come and save you. He who lifts up his soul to God, and cries, 'Lord, save me, or I perish,' shall be heard and answered. It matters not that words fail you; only tell the Lord that you are a wretch undone, and that if you perish, you are resolved to perish at the foot of the cross of Christ, and you shall never be cast out.

I have heard that when Mrs Ryland was dying she was in great darkness of soul. Her quaint husband, John Ryland, went to her bedside, and said to her, 'You are going to heaven, my dear.' 'No,' cried she, 'I am going down to hell.' 'And what will you do when you get there? Do you think you will pray there?' She replied, 'I am sure I shall pray as long as I exist.' 'Why, then,' said her husband, 'if you pray in hell, they will say, "Here is praying Betty Ryland come here; we cannot have praying people here; turn her out."' It is impossible for a praying soul to be lost; for a praying soul has a measure of faith, and faith saves. A praying heart is a token that for you there is day coming, and not night.

Behold, at this very hour, Jesus cries again to sinners upon earth, 'Come unto me, all ye that labour and are heavy laden, and I will give you rest.' May God, in his infinite mercy, lead you to the only true rest—rest in Jesus! May the good Spirit apply these rambling remarks to all your souls, and may the seafaring men of Wivenhoe find a port in Jesus, when all the night is over, and the day of glory dawns upon us in Immanuel's land! Amen.

Notes

* Published in *The Sword and the Trowel*, October 1889.

† 'We met with the following report of a sermon preached by us more than thirty-four years

ago. It was taken down by a local reporter, and has remained buried among our old papers. It may be viewed as a curiosity of youthful preaching, and therefore we print it.'

‡ 'We should hardly speak in this fashion now. Romanism is crippled, but the essential doctrines of Popery are spreading in the Church of England, and elsewhere.'

¶ 'To the ungodly the day of the Lord will be darkness, and not light. The signs of the Lord's coming which we would now mention lie rather in the deepening darkness than in any growing light. This is a deep subject, for it is not for us to know the times and the seasons; but yet there are reasons for cheering expectation.'

Unpublished notes of C.H. Spurgeon's New Park Street Sermons, no. 1

Preached on Thursday evening, 11 September 1856

REPORTED BY PASTOR T. W. MEDHURST, CARDIFF

'Blessed is the man that endureth temptation: for when he is tried, he shall receive the crown of life, which the Lord hath promised to them that love him.'—James 1:12.

NOTE here, first, *The character of this man:* 'The man that endureth temptation.' Second, *The condition of this man:* 'Blessed.' Third, *The prospect before this man:* 'When he is tried, he shall receive the crown of life.' Fourth, *The reason for this man's hope:* 'Which the Lord hath promised to them that love him.'

I. THE CHARACTER OF THIS MAN: '*The man that endureth temptation.*'

Temptation from God is with a view to test and try our faith. In one sense, God never tempts any man. 'Let no man say when he is tempted, I am tempted of God: for God cannot be tempted with evil, neither tempteth he any man: but every man is tempted, when he is drawn away of his own lust, and enticed.' When the word tempt is connected with sin, it can never belong to God; but only when the word tempt means to try, to test, which it frequently does. In the case of Abraham, it is said, that 'God did tempt Abraham' (Genesis 22:1). In Hebrews 11:17, this word tempt is explained: 'By faith, Abraham, when he was *tried*.' Thus, then, when the word tempt means to test or try, it can very properly be applied to God, for he tries the hearts of the children of men.

Temptation, when it comes from Satan, is not to try us, but is with a view of destroying us. View the word 'temptation' in whatever sense you please, the blessing is contained in the word '*endureth*.' It is not, 'Blessed are they who suffer,' but, 'Blessed are they who endure temptation.' Let us take care to distinguish between temptation and enduring temptation. It is not, 'Blessed is the man who *escapes* temptation.' If the Christian escapes the trouble, he misses the blessing. It is not, 'Blessed is the man who tries to *avoid* temptation, or trouble, by getting out of the way of it.' Never try to avoid trouble for the sake of being free from trial. If you can sing God's praises in the furnace, keep in the furnace. If you find that you can serve God best in your present condition, though it be a painful one, it is at your peril that you will seek to change your state. It is not the temptation that makes me a Christian; I am not a child of God because I suffer trouble. 'Man is born unto trouble, as the sparks fly upward.' It is not the temptation that brings the blessing; it is the enduring of it. Enduring is looking up, and saying, 'My God hath sent these trials, and by his grace I will take them and bear them all for him,'

II. THE CONDITION OF THIS MAN: '*Blessed*.'

The enduring Christians are sure to be blessed, because for certain if they can endure temptation, they are the children of God. The devil says it is an evident sign of perdition that you are so troubled. The next time he tells you that you are not blessed because you endure temptation, tell him to read the twelfth chapter of the Epistle to the Hebrews. The devil reads the Bible sometimes, I can tell you. You are not only blessed in your condition, but in being allowed to suffer for Christ. There is one man of whom I read in the Bible whom I envy. It is Simon, the Cyrenian, because he was privileged to carry Christ's cross after him. I can never sing that hymn which speaks of drinking drops out of Christ's bitter cup. No man could do that; it would be all too strong for human flesh to bear. No man could drink damnation, as Christ did for his people. But there have been moments when I have thought that to suffer with Christ must be the highest honour that can possibly be put upon a Christian.

Not only are we blessed in the honour of being permitted to endure temptation, but I know the saints will bear me witness that it is true, when I say, 'We are blessed in our feelings also.' If you are a child of God, your troubles will make you go oftener to your Father. The more you are troubled, the more you are brought near to God. No one knows all the depths of the meaning of this word 'blessed'; it is such a great word. Blessed! Blessed!! Blessed!!!

III. THE PROSPECT BEFORE THIS MAN: '*When he is tried, he shall receive the crown of life.*'

There is heaven before the tried believer. The believer, when he is tried, shall receive the crown of life, not because of his doings or his sufferings; all Christians know better than to think that. God has promised the crown of life to them that love him. 'What shall be done unto the man whom the King delighteth to honour?' He is to be crowned. Cheer up then, believer; in a little while thou mayest be walking the golden streets. Thy head shall wear a crown. Thy hand shall wave a palm. Thou shalt be happy for ever.

IV. THE REASON FOR THIS MAN'S HOPE: '*Which the Lord hath promised to them that love him.*'

The Christian's only hope is in the promise of God. The only hook on which a poor sinner can hang his hope of heaven is the promise of God. Every believer knows that he shall receive the crown of life at last, because God has promised it to them that love him. When the world frowns and threatens, remember what God has promised. God has promised the crown of life 'to them that love him.' If I love him, he has promised the crown of life to me. There are some who say they may be believers one day, and unbelievers the next; but if they are good at the end, if they happen to die on a day when they are believers, it will be all right with them. I rejoice that the promise is not made to those who are good at the end. It is promised to those who love God, to those who love God at any time; and I take it that those who love God at any time, love him at all times. If I love God, he will keep me to the end; and at the last he will give me the crown of life; for, if I love him, he has promised the crown of life to me. '*The crown of life,*'—*of life,* by which is meant, not mere existence; existence will be given to all men, whether they be in heaven or in hell. 'The crown of life' means, life in all the enjoyments of life, life in all its glories, the very cream of life. Sometimes we have the milk of life here, in those sweet moments of nearness to Jesus, and of communion with him. By-and-by we shall have

26 C H Spurgeon's forgotten early sermons

the cream of life. 'We shall receive the crown of life,' for so hath the Lord 'promised to them that love him.'

Chapter 3

Unpublished notes of C. H. Spurgeon's New Park Street Sermons, no. 2

Preached on Thursday evening, 18 September 1856

REPORTED BY PASTOR T. W. MEDHURST, CARDIFF

'Renew a right spirit within me.'—Psalm 51:10.

THE spirit here meant, I take it, is that spirit which we refer to when we say, 'such a man is of a bad spirit.' We mean that he is of a bad disposition, and that he has certain evil qualities dwelling within him. David prays that he may have '*a right spirit*' renewed within him, that is, a right disposition for spiritual things.

'A right spirit' may be judged of by its desires after God. It cannot rest if it has not communion with Jesus. It longs and pants after nearness to the Saviour. It is a spirit that prizes the Saviour above everything. If it speaks of him, it piles words upon words in his praise. It feels that half his worth can never be told. Among the ten thousand, he is the chief. If he is lovely, 'He is altogether lovely.' 'A right spirit' can never make enough of the Lord Jesus. If it has lost his sweet presence, it groans, and moans, and is miserable, until his presence is recovered.

'A right spirit' is *a loving spirit*. 'A right spirit' is *a meek and quiet spirit*. It is a spirit that will not murmur against God. It keeps silence. Though its bones wax old through its roaring all the day long, yet it murmurs not against its God. 'A right spirit' is *a humble spirit*. It never takes any honour to itself; but gives it all to God, to whom all honour belongs. 'A right spirit' is *a forgiving spirit*. It turns the other cheek to him who has smitten the one. It would bear all injuries rather than inflict one.

'A right spirit' may be judged by its breathings after THE HOLY SPIRIT. It is attentive to the softest whisper of the Spirit. The instant the Spirit of God points to a particular path of duty, the 'right spirit' goes in that path. Even if there be no footing, it plants its foot in the sea, and believes that it shall stand firm, even as Peter did while his Master held him up. The 'right spirit' cannot rest unless it feels the constant communications of the Holy Spirit putting into it sweet thoughts and holy desires. If it cannot feel the promise applied, it groans over the promise. If it cannot pray, it groans over prayer.

Have we this 'right spirit'? I think most of us have need to pray this prayer, 'Renew a right spirit within me,' for we are none of us perfect in this matter, I fear.

I. First, then, we have here A SAD AND LAMENTABLE FACT IMPLIED. There are many persons who require a renewal of 'a right spirit.'

There are many whom we will not be so uncharitable as to call hypocrites, who yet by *their conduct* give us very grave reasons to suspect their Christianity. There are some Christians, at least they call themselves such, who can do many an act as un-Christian as it can possibly be. They come to chapel, and say they enjoy the sermon; they even sit down at the ordinance of the Lord's supper. They are all in white then, they are so amiable! But when they go from chapel to their homes, or their business, then they are not at all in white. They can lie and cheat, even as do others who make no profession. Such persons require a renewal of the 'right spirit.'

There are others whose conduct before the world is irreproachable; but *their conversation* in private is not consistent. If I were to tell you how some of our hearers spend their Sunday afternoons, you would perhaps laugh, but you would have more need to cry. They begin on this wise, 'Did you see Mrs So-and-so? She has a new bonnet today,' or, 'Mr Somebody-else was away, I wonder what is the matter?' Or, if there be anything peculiar in the appearance of the minister, that is discussed; but the precious things of which he has been speaking are quite forgotten. Much of the Sunday talk, the table talk, ay, and the parlour talk, too, is quite inconsistent with the profession of many Christian professors. Surely such persons need a renewal of the 'right spirit.'

II. We have here, in the second place, A HAPPY CIRCUMSTANCE SUPPOSED. It is supposed that the person groans over his wrong spirit. He cannot bear it any longer. He feels he is not like what once he used to be, that he has not that warmth and fervour he once had. He knows his loss, he feels it, and he groans in consequence. To be in a 'lukewarm' state, to know it, and yet not to feel it, not to groan over it, is worse by far. A person whose limb is mortifying feels no pain. Bless God then, if you can feel, if you can groan.

Praying times will become groaning times with the Christian when he is not in a 'right spirit.' Ah! we try to pray sometimes; but we cannot; we rise from our knees cold and miserable; and then again we say, 'Satan shall not cheat us of our time of prayer.' We try once more to pray; perhaps it may be better than it was before, yet still we are not refreshed. Prayer has become a labour, not a privilege, as it once was; it has become a time of groaning. Yet if you can cry and groan over your prayers, thank God that you can do so.

Ordinances, too, will be seasons of crying and sighing. You will remember what delight you used to experience at the ordinances; but now, alas! it is not so with you. 'The fault is in myself,' you say, 'I know the river is not dry; but I cannot bathe myself in its waters, and be refreshed from my fatigue, as once I used to do. I know the food is still there on my Lord's table, and it is as sweet as ever; I know it is there, but I cannot partake of it.' You go from the house of your God groaning, 'My leanness, my leanness, woe unto me!'

They are groaning times with the Christian, when he remembers *former favours,* the years of the right hand of the most High. 'Oh!' he says, 'Those Bethel visits, those sweet love-tokens, those blessed manifestations I used to have, where are they now?'

The Christian, *when he has lost the company of Jesus,* begins to mourn. Just as the dove mourns for its mate, so does the Christian mourn for his Lord. He is miserable, and cannot be happy, seeing he has lost his 'right spirit.' He will never think of his loss without groaning. If he can, depend upon it, he is in a very wrong spirit.

III. We have here, in the last place, A NECESSARY PETITION TO BE PRESENTED. 'Create in me a clean heart, O God; and renew a right spirit within me,' or, as it is in the margin, '*a constant spirit.*'

What resolves you have made sometimes! You have said, 'Now, I will live close to Jesus today; I will be more earnest; my minister shall not have to speak so pointedly to me again about my lukewarmness; I will now climb to the tops of the Delectable Mountains.' But did you ever climb to the summits of the Delectable Mountains for all your resolves? I know I have often made similar resolutions, but woe is me! they have been destroyed as easily as a cobweb is when you set your foot upon it in walking down your garden.

David did not make any such resolves. He began at the right place. 'Lord, do thou do this for me. Do thou renew a right spirit within me.' You cannot manufacture grace; God must give it to you. There are some who are groaning, and they mean still to continue to groan. They think it is a high attainment to be always groaning; I do not think so. You may prefer Egypt if you like; but I prefer Canaan much more. Praying is better than groaning. When we feel a desire in our hearts for spiritual things, or for an increased nearness to Jesus, the best way is not to feed the desire, but to strike it with prayer, and to do it at once; not to begin to trifle with it, and to put off decision. A trifling spirit is next door to a sinning spirit. I never knew a person yet, who was too light and careless, but he became too sinful; or a person who was too confident, who did not become too bold and presumptuous. Pray until your desire after 'a right spirit' becomes, not 'the spirit of fear; but of power, and of love, and of a sound mind' (2 Timothy 1:7).

How important it is that we should all pray this prayer! If those who are in the right road have need to be careful, how much more need have they to take heed to their feet who are in the wrong road! 'And if the righteous scarcely be saved, where shall the ungodly and the sinner appear?'

Unpublished notes of C. H. Spurgeon's New Park Street Sermons, no. 3

Preached on Thursday evening, 16 October 1856

REPORTED BY PASTOR T. W. MEDHURST, CARDIFF

'He was wounded for our transgressions.'—Isaiah 53:5.

THERE are six words in the text, and there also *six wonders*. There are four wonders upon the surface of the text, and two wonders hidden beneath, or within the text.

I. The first wonder is, THE SAVIOUR HIMSELF: 'HE.'

Consider who the Redeemer is, and you will wonder. He is 'the mighty God' (Isaiah 9:6), of whom it is written, 'In the beginning was the Word, and the Word was with God, and the Word was God' (John 1:1). He by whom all things do exist and consist, he before whom angels veil their faces, he who holdeth creation 'in the hollow of his hand' (Isaiah 40:12), he who is the Son of God by eternal filiation, he is our Saviour, and 'He was wounded for our transgressions.' Dost thou not wonder when thou considerest who is thy Redeemer? Think, those hands which were fixed to the cross by cruel nails, could have hurled thunderbolts; those lips could have been the doors of thunder; those feet which were nailed to the tree, trod upon the boisterous waves, and they shall one day tread upon this earth in kingly majesty. Is it not a wonder of wonders that he should have been 'wounded for our transgressions'?

It is wonderful that he should have taken human form at all; it is much more wonderful that he should have been *wounded* for us. Thou canst never tell how deep was that condescension which stooped to redeem *thee*. *H*ere is hope for a poor, trembling sinner. If an angel had asked you to commit your soul to his keeping, you would have done well to refuse him, for you could not trust your soul to the keeping of an angel. But you need not be afraid to trust your soul with this wondrous Saviour. 'No,' sayest thou; 'if I had a million souls, I would trust them all with him.'

II. The second wonder is, THE SAVIOUR'S SUFFERINGS: 'He was *wounded* for our transgressions.'

'He was wounded' not only in his mortal frame, but in his spirit, *in his soul*. We are apt to judge of Christ's sufferings more by his bodily wounding than by his soul-wounding. The Holy Spirit, in sacred Scripture, dwells more upon the Saviour's bodily sufferings for this reason, because we can more easily understand them. We can comprehend them better than we can his soul-sufferings. Nevertheless, we are told that his soul was 'exceeding sorrowful, even unto death' (Matthew 26:38): for though the soul is immortal, the Redeemer's soul felt as though its very immortality were in danger of becoming extinct through the greatness of the sufferings. 'A wounded spirit who can bear?'

The Saviour 'was wounded' *in his reputation. He* was cruelly slandered. They who had professed friendship toward him, turned round against him. He that ate bread with him lifted up his heel against him. He knows what a broken heart means, for his heart was broken and crushed. He himself was the very fountain of grief. His sorrows were as a sea without a shore, an abyss without a bottom, and as darkness without light. But it is vain to attempt to describe the sorrows of Jesus, for they surpass all description. It is better to be silent concerning them; to describe them is an impossibility. 'He was wounded,' tormented, bruised, crushed, 'for our transgressions.'

III. The third wonder is, THE SINNERS FOR WHOM THE SAVIOUR WAS WOUNDED. 'He was wounded for *our* transgressions.'

Not for his friends, but for his enemies was he wounded.

'Thou, O my Jesus, thou didst me
    Upon the cross embrace;
For me didst bear the nails and spear,
    And manifold disgrace.

'And griefs and torments numberless,
 And sweat of agony;
Yea, death itself; and all for me,
 Who was thine enemy.'

It would have been wonderful had Jesus been wounded for an angel; but he did not die to save angels, he died to save sinful men. He gave himself a sacrifice on account of our transgressions, even for us who are among the very vilest. Lay the emphasis upon the pronouns, '*Our* griefs, *our* sorrows, *our* transgressions, *our* iniquities, *our* peace,—with his stripes *we* are healed,'—and see with what force and beauty the Scripture reads. It is a wonder that Jesus Christ should have died for anyone; but when we think that he died for *us,* it does indeed appear exceeding wonderful. It is a wonder of wonders to every Christian when he thinks that Jesus died for *him.* It seems easier for him to believe that Jesus died for everyone else than for him; to him it is indeed a miracle of miracles that he should be saved. 'He was wounded for *our* transgressions.' Christ Jesus died for none else but sinners. It might have been written over the cross of Christ, 'He that is not a sinner hath no part here.' In the roll of life there is not to be found the name of one person who was sinless; they are all sinners saved by blood.

'Round the altar priests confess,
If their robes are white as snow,
'Twas the Saviour's righteousness,
And his blood that made them so.'

IV. The fourth wonder is, THE SUBSTITUTION OF THE INNOCENT ONE FOR VILE TRANSGRESSORS: 'He was wounded *for our transgressions.*'

To a great degree, the word substitution is the pith and marrow of the gospel. If I were asked to give a description of the gospel as nearly as I could in one word, I should say, 'Substitution.' Think believer, is it not a wonder that Christ should have died for you, in your stead? Is it not a wonder to see Jesus, the innocent Son of God, judged at the bar of God as though he were the sinner? He was not actually so, but by imputation he was reckoned the sinner. Is it not wonderful to see the sinner at the foot of the throne of God pardoned, justified, not for anything which he has done, but because of what Jesus has done for him? He who knows what it is to see Christ in his rags, and himself in the robes of Christ, understands the gospel. What a wonderful doctrine is that of substitution! Trace the Saviour from Gethsemane to Calvary, and remember that all he suffered was for thee, believer, and then thou wilt be filled with wonder.

V. The fifth wonder is a hidden wonder, and it is this, THAT ALL THIS WAS A SECRET UNKNOWN TO THE JEWS.

They thought Jesus could not be the Son of God, because he was such a sufferer. They would not receive him as the Messiah, because he was 'a man of sorrows, and acquainted with grief.' The prophet seems to speak of it as a wonder; 'Surely,' saith he, 'He hath borne our griefs, and carried our sorrows: yet we did esteem him stricken, smitten of God, and afflicted. But he was wounded for our transgressions.'

And is it not a wonder to us that we did not know the Saviour before? Some of my friends say sometimes, 'How foolish I was not to know the Saviour; the gospel is so plain, that he that runs may read, and he that reads may run; and yet I did not understand it!' Yes, the fountain was filled with blood to wash away your sins, and yet you thought it was empty. The manna was lying all around your door, and you could not see it. Verily, it is a marvel to us that we saw not this wondrous sight sooner, that he 'was wounded for our transgressions.'

VI. The sixth wonder, and this also is a hidden wonder, is, THE SUFFICIENCY OF THE SUFFERINGS OF JESUS CHRIST.

It is wonderful that his blood should take away the sins of one sinner; how much more wonderful is it that it takes away the sins of so many! It is all-sufficient to cleanse away the foulest transgressions. Christ's precious blood cleanses from all sin each and every one of all his people. Do you not wonder that Christ's blood should wash such a wretch as you are, you, who are covered with sins? Yet Jesus' blood is sufficient to cleanse even you. Let me ask you, 'Do you desire a greater Saviour than the one I have to preach to you?' 'No,' you say, 'I do not, indeed.' Possibly, someone says, 'May I believe that Jesus died for me?' Answer me these questions. Do you feel your need of a Saviour? Are you brought to hate sin? Do you feel that in yourself you are lost and ruined? Are you really seeking after Jesus? If so, you may believe that Jesus died for you, for he is even now your Saviour.

One or two hints. If 'He was wounded for our transgressions,' how foolish is self-confidence! It is in vain that you trust in your own works, they can never save you. How wicked is self-love! If you set yourself, or anything else, before Christ, you are not much like him. He loved his enemies, and died to save them. How great and how glorious, then, is the security of every believer, since Jesus the Substitute was 'wounded for our transgressions'! When Satan tells you of your manifold sins, tell him that Christ Jesus was wounded for your *'transgressions'*; not for one sin merely, but for all. 'He was wounded for our transgressions.' Let us all say with Joseph Hart,—

'Lord, we fain would trust thee solely;
　'Twas for us thy blood was spilt,
Bruisèd Bridegroom, take us wholly;
　Take and make us what thou wilt.
Thou hast borne the bitter sentence
　Pass'd on man's devoted race;
True belief and true repentance
　Are thy gifts, thou God of grace.'

Unpublished notes of C. H. Spurgeon's New Park Street Sermons, no. 4

Preached on Thursday evening, 13 November 1856

REPORTED BY PASTOR T. W. MEDHURST, CARDIFF

'I will sing of mercy and judgment: unto thee, O LORD, will I sing.'—Psalm 101:1.

GOD has designed various ways by which men may express their feelings. Is the heart sorrowful? The tear seems the sign by which the sorrows of the heart are manifested. Are we joyful? Singing appears to be the mode by which God would have us express our joy. As joy is a great part of the Christian religion, we may conclude that to be the reason why God has said so much in his Word about praise. He seems to have honoured praise even more than he has honoured prayer; he has given praise a place in heaven, but we read not that he has so honoured prayer. Prayer rises like sweet incense to the skies; but praise needeth not to be burned on earth before it can enter heaven, for it is there already.

Our subject for tonight shall be singing. We mean not so much the singing of the lips, as the singing of the heart. 'Singing and making melody in your heart to the Lord,' as Paul says, in Ephesians 5:19.

First, a Christian ought to *sing with his face*. If your heart be sorrowful, yet let not your countenance be sad. Have a smile on your face, even though there be a sigh in your breast. Remember our Saviour's words, 'Moreover when ye fast, be not, as the hypocrites, of a sad countenance: for they disfigure their faces, that they may appear unto men to fast. Verily I say unto you, They have their reward. But thou, when thou fastest, anoint thine head, and wash thy face; that thou appear not unto men to fast, but unto thy Father which is in secret: and thy Father, which seeth in secret, shall reward thee openly' (Matthew 6:16–18).

If you are sorrowful, let not the world know it. Sigh unto God. Let your closet be witness to your sighings and tears; but let not the world see them. People naturally dislike to be unhappy; and if they see a Christian always looking melancholy, they say they will have nothing to do with a religion that makes men so miserable. I believe a Christian, who walks through the world miserable and melancholy, dishonours his God. I try to think of this whenever I am depressed. I know it is a very difficult thing to appear happy and cheerful when the heart is heavy and sorrowful. There will be times when you will not be able to do so, that I know full well; still, the Christian ought so to live before the world as far as he can. It is true that your Master wore a sorrowful countenance; but remember that he had your sins upon his shoulders, he was suffering for you. He was sorrowful that you might not be so. He does not wish you to imitate him in his sorrowfulness. You are commanded to be joyous. 'Rejoice in the Lord alway: and again I say, Rejoice.' 'Rejoice evermore. Pray without ceasing. In every thing give thanks: for this is the will of God in Christ Jesus concerning you.'

Having a melancholy countenance will not recommend your religion. You will not be able to draw young converts to Christ if you frown at them. He who is cheerful and happy in his religion, is the man whom God will use to bring young converts to himself.

Christians can afford to be cheerful and rejoice, seeing their sins are all pardoned. Seek to recommend religion by a happy mode of living, by being always cheerful.

A Christian should, also, *sing with his voice*. Do not adopt a sanctimonious and whining tone, or that kind of voice which affects solemnity without while there is no solemnity felt within. He that feels solemnity in his heart will speak in a solemn manner, without affectation. I do not believe there is any religious *twang* that the Saviour would have us adopt. When we speak concerning religious topics, we should speak with our natural voice.

Let the words of the sweet poets of Zion be frequently in your lips. Sing and make melody with your voice, as well as in your hearts, unto the Lord. Though there will be sighs and groans on account of indwelling sin, yet the believer in Jesus ought to sing, because his sins are all forgiven him for his name's sake. There is no reason at all why the Christian should not keep on singing from the day of his conversion until the day that he enters into Paradise.

The subject of the psalmist's song is twofold. '*I will sing of mercy and judgment.*' Speak we of *mercy?* Have you nothing to sing about? Has today been a day without mercies? No, I know it has not. A day without mercies would be a day in hell! What, nothing to sing about? You are not houseless, are you? You are not destitute of clothing. You are not foodless. You have your health, or, if not health, you have your life; you are not in hell! Then I am sure you have something to sing about, if you are not there. Glory be to God's sovereign grace, there are many here, who not only know they are not in hell, but they are assured they never shall be cast into the regions of eternal woe; surely they will not say they have no song to sing. Is there not a whole sonnet in that sweet word ELECTION?

'Sing ye loud, whose holy calling
    Your election plainly shows.'

Is there not enough to sing about in JUSTIFICATION, and ADOPTION, and FINAL PERSEVERANCE? Ay, you can sing of that grace which broke the power of sin, which has kept you from sin, which will preserve you unto the end, and which will, at last, land you safe in heaven!

The Christian has to sing of *judgment* as well as mercy. There is the difficulty, to sing of judgment. To sing of mercy is easy; who could not sing of mercy? But they who are taught of God, know how to sing of *judgment* as well as mercy. I dare say there are some who could wish the word 'judgment' were left out, because it is such a hard word. Yet, beloved, be ye well assured, there are some lessons which we could never learn to spell with the letters which make up the word 'mercy.' It must be a song of '*mercy and judgment.*' Are you bereft of your friends? Is not Christ better to you than all your earthly friends? You still have Jesus. You have not lost your Saviour. Are you poor and destitute? Is not Christ better to you than all earthly comforts? Is he not your 'all, and in all'? If we never walked in the darkness, we should not prize the light so much as we do. If we never mourned an absent God, perhaps we should not set such a high value upon communion with Jesus. If our Father were never to frown, we might not prize his smiles so highly as we do now.

'I will sing of mercy and judgment.' What a chequered path is human life! It is like unto Joseph's coat of many colours. There are blacks and whites in our lives; there are ups and downs, there are hills and dales, there are smiles and frowns, there is 'mercy and judgment'; and yet, how safe a path it is that leads to glory!

Here we have not all mercy, lest we should say, 'This is my rest, here I would for ever dwell.' God himself says, 'This is not your rest;' therefore, he gives us judgment as well as mercy, that we should feel that this is not our rest, and should desire more earnestly the rest that remaineth to the people of God, in the land that is above.

Neither have we here all judgment; but 'mercy and judgment.' Some have had smiles lately, and they can sing of mercy. Others have had frowns, and they can sing of judgment. Others have had smiles and frowns, and they can 'sing of mercy and judgment.'

This song belongs to Christians only. The unsaved sinner will have judgment; but it will be 'judgment without mercy.' It will be a terrible thing to the sinner if he dies in his present condition, and, without mercy, enters into eternity.

Unpublished notes of C. H. Spurgeon's New Park Street Sermons, no. 5

Preached on Lord's-day evening, 16 November 1856

REPORTED BY PASTOR T. W. MEDHURST, CARDIFF

'His thoughts troubled him.'—Daniel 5:6.

THOUGHT, to the Christian, is a thing of delight. He can look back into *the past,* even into the ages of eternity, and see in the mind of God eternal thoughts of love towards him, and this causes him to exclaim with wonder, 'How precious also are thy thoughts unto me, O God! how great is the sum of them!' The believer can think of Calvary, where the Saviour made a complete atonement for all his sins, and satisfied all the demands of justice on his behalf; and as he thinks, he sings, 'Who loved me, and gave himself for me.' The Christian can think of *the present,* and rejoice in his Saviour's love with joy unspeakable; he can think of the present with something more than complacence, even with ineffable delight, and adoring gratitude. He can think of *the future,* of the confusion and destruction of all worlds, without any fear, for all will be well with the man who is in Christ. He sings,—

'What cheering words are these!
    Their sweetness who can tell?
In time, and to eternal days,
    'Tis with the righteous well.'

Thought, to the Christian, is a source of joy; but thought, to the unpardoned sinner, is a source of trouble and sorrow. Any thought that is at all serious, or that is worth a thought at all, is a trouble to the sinner, so that he seeks to drown himself in thoughtlessness. He endeavours to drive dull care away, so he says, and this is only another name for driving his thoughts away.

In considering our text, let us notice,—

I. THE NATURE OF TROUBLOUS THOUGHTS: 'His thoughts troubled him.'

I beg the sinner to think tonight of *the past*. I know he will not think, if he can help it; but by the help of my God I will compel him to think, as for a little while I now address myself to his case.

May the Holy Spirit now cause thee to think of the past! Let thine eyes turn back, and look along the years thou hast lived. Let thy memory even now conjure up thy sins; thy sins against thy God, thy sins against thy fellow-men, the sins of thy lips, the sins of thy heart. Darest thou think of thy guilty past without horror? Art thou not filled with dread when thou rememberest that God will bring thee into judgment for every evil thing that thou hast done, unless thou dost repent and forsake thy sins?

May the Good Spirit now lead thee to think of thy privileges! Thou hast had pious parents; thou wast early instructed in the Holy Scriptures, and taught in the Sabbath-school; thou hast often seen thy mother's tears on thy behalf; thou hast many times heard thy father pray for thee, that thou mightest give thine heart to Jesus. Yet, alas! thou art still persevering in thy sins.

May the Gracious Spirit now call back to thy memory the many strivings thy conscience has had with thee! How thou didst tremble as thou didst listen to a powerful sermon! How often thou hast wiped the tear away, and yet returned to thy sins! Thou hast sinned against thy privileges; thou hast foully wronged thy conscience. Dost thou not even now recall the memory of thy friends who have gone, with whom thou didst join in sinning? Whither have they gone? Why art thou spared? Think!

May the Blessed Spirit now help thee to think of *the present!* Some of you have sat under the sound of the gospel for a long time. Sometimes you weep; but you brush the tears away speedily, and are still careless. I could weep for some of you, because you leave off weeping for yourselves. You have heard many solemn warnings, yet are you sinning still against the Lord. Take heed. There may come a day, and that day may come soon, wherein you would give worlds for a tear; but no tear of true repentance shall then be given you. It were better for some of you that you had been in Sodom and Gomorrah, than to have been where you are, and what you are. They will have the lowest place in hell who have sat beneath the faithful ministry of the Word, and yet have continued hardened in sin. Beware, lest God say of any of you, 'Let him alone; he shall die in his sins, he shall likewise perish.'

Now may the Convincing Spirit lead you to think of *the future!* The future! That word to some of you is as a roll of lamentations, written within and without. What have you to expect in the future? In an instant, your soul may leave your body, and you will then, face to face, meet him whom you have despised, and whose mercy you have rejected. How dreadful will then be your doom! Remember that, after death, there will be the judgment; and after the judgment will be pronounced those terrible words, 'Depart from me, ye cursed, into everlasting fire, prepared for the devil and his angels.' May none of you, my dear hearers, ever know the full meaning of those awful words!

Look up now. Darest thou think of God, even now, without terror, when thou rememberest how thou hast rebelled against him? 'God is good,' sayest thou? Yes, God *is* good; but he is, nevertheless, inflexible in justice. God is merciful; but he will not be merciful at the expense of righteousness. God is powerful, and he will execute his vengeance upon all who reject his Son, Jesus Christ. Does not that thought fill thee with fear? God is true; and because he is true, thou wilt be lost eternally unless thou wilt fly to Jesus for salvation from the wrath to come. Thou mayest well let thy thoughts trouble thee, if thou art living without Christ.

'I believe in no God, and in no future state,' thou sayest. 'The fool hath said in his heart, There is no God;' but because 'the fool hath said, No God,' does that prove that there is no God? Certainly not; it only proves that the man is a 'fool', or he would not speak so foolishly and so falsely. The wicked man wishes there were no God, and therefore he says, 'There is no God.' Let thy thoughts trouble thee, sinner, while I tell thee that there is a God, and that he is angry with the wicked every day. There is a heaven;

but thou wilt never be found there, unless here thou dost repent of sin, and dost believe on the Lord Jesus Christ. There is a hell; and into that hell thou wilt surely be cast, if thou dost wilfully reject Jesus, and dost refuse his salvation. If thou art unconverted, I pray that thy thoughts may trouble thee, as Belshazzar's thoughts troubled him.

II. THE DESIGN OF TROUBLOUS THOUGHTS: 'His thoughts troubled him.'

Some troublous thoughts are *the harbingers of mercy*. May it prove so in your case, my hearer! Usually, before a man is savingly brought to Christ, he is greatly troubled on account of his sins. Before the Lord fills a man, he empties him of all his fancied self-righteousness, he makes him realize his lost state by nature, and by practice, too. Are you very sad because you are thus troubled? If so, I rejoice for you; for such troublous thoughts are the heralds of salvation. Hast thou a wounded spirit? Let nothing be used for the healing of thy wounds but the precious blood of Jesus. Nature possesses no balsam for the curing of sin-sick souls. Think not that it will suffice for thee to reform thyself; that, by leaving off certain sins, thou wilt thereby obtain peace with God. Perhaps thou sayest, 'I will leave off drinking and swearing, and then I shall have peace.' Bethink thee, my friend, there are very many who were never drunkards or swearers, yet they had no peace with God until the blood of Jesus was applied to their broken hearts. Seek healing for thy wounded and troubled spirit in the blood of Jesus; but seek it nowhere else. If thy thoughts now trouble thee, so that thou art cast down on account of sin, yet if thou wilt trust in the Lord Jesus, thou shalt soon rejoice. Every saint who is now in heaven had his castings down on account of sin when here below. Thy troublous thoughts are the forerunners of Jesus as thy Saviour.

Some troublous thoughts are *the heralds of justice,* the messengers of vengeance, the officers of judgment. I have seen some such cases when men, on their death-beds, had troublous thoughts indeed. The groans and moans they uttered were truly awful to hear. I have talked to them of mercy and of Jesus; but they have replied, 'It is too late now to think of Jesus and of mercy, they are nothing to us now; it is too late, it is too late!' How terrible to feel remorse, but not repentance! To know the horrors of despair, but to be strangers to true penitence! How horrible, when the poor soul stands upon the brink of eternity, to be, at last, forced to leap into the future state, with all its sins unforgiven!

Do your thoughts trouble you now? Then flee to Jesus. The remedy for troublous thoughts is in Jesus alone. The only way for you to get quit of the thoughts that trouble you, is to seek that the blood of Jesus Christ may be applied to your conscience by the Spirit of God. That is a never-failing, an infallible cure.

'Come, ye souls by sin afflicted,
  Bowed with fruitless sorrow down;
By the broken law convicted,
  Through the cross behold the crown.
    Look to Jesus—
  Mercy flows through him alone.'

Unpublished notes of C. H. Spurgeon's New Park Street Sermons, no. 6

Preached on Thursday evening, 11 December 1856

REPORTED BY PASTOR T. W. MEDHURST, CARDIFF

'I love them that love me; and those that seek me early shall find me.'—Proverbs 8:17.

HERE is sweetest comfort for both saints and seekers, for those who love God, and those who are seeking after God. Solomon was truly wise when he wrote these words on God's behalf; but we must understand this text, not merely as the utterance of Solomon, but as the language of Divine Wisdom. These are the words spoken by Almighty God, concerning all those who '*love*' him, and all those who '*seek*' him.

Here is, first, *Comfort for doubting saints*; and, secondly, *Encouragement for earnest seekers*.

I. First, here is COMFORT FOR DOUBTING SAINTS: 'I love them that love me.'

One of the principal things which often makes a Christian doubt is this, he is afraid that God does not love him. 'Does God love me?' is the question he often asks himself. 'Does God stand to me in the relationship of a Father?' 'Am I a special partaker of his affections?' 'Does he look upon me with eyes of love?' These are questions which often perplex the true children of God, and they tremble lest they should not be recipients of that love which God has for all his chosen people. A true believer may sometimes very properly sing that verse which many have condemned,—

> "'Tis a point I long to know,
> Oft it causes anxious thought,
> Do I love the Lord, or no?
> Am I his, or am I not?'

That question may be easily answered, your fear may be at once quashed, and you may give up all your perplexity. If you love God, you may be sure that God loves you.

There are certain times when we are apt to doubt and to call in question the love of God toward us. Sometimes, it is *when we have a vivid sight of our own unworthiness*, when we make a fresh discovery of our own depravity, when filth and corruption rise up within, and we have revealed to us how vile we are. Then, looking at our own worthless condition, we say, 'Is it possible that God can love such depraved beings as we feel ourselves to be?' God is so holy, so pure, and so good, that I cannot help loving him; but can so holy a God love me? Can a God so pure regard me with affection? How dare I expect that he will look upon me with any other than eyes of wrath, and anger, and indignation? That the good God can love sinful me, seems too great a miracle of mercy. But if thou canst say, 'I love God,' thine unworthiness is no argument against thee with God. Confess thine unworthiness, weep over thy vileness, be ashamed of thy guiltiness, and repent of thy sinfulness before God. Yet, if thou canst say, after all that, 'I love God,' thou mayest look back into eternity, and say with the poet,—

> 'In the mind of God I see
> Eternal thoughts of love to me.'

If we love God, 'we love him because he first loved us' (1 John 4:19).

Providential reverses and afflictions will sometimes cause us to call in question the love of God toward us. 'There,' says the poor Christian, 'my wife has been snatched away by death, my children, too, are laid in the grave, my house has been given to the flames, my character has been blasted by the breath of calumny; yea, more, even God himself seems to rise up against me, and to shut out my prayer, when I cry unto him. Can I believe that God loves me? Are these his methods of dealing with his children? I see the wicked prospering, they are fat and flourishing, they are not in trouble as other men. Can it be possible that God loves me, and yet I am so tried?' Yes, poor tempted, troubled one, be assured that God does love thee, that he sees thy tears, and hears thy sighs; he will not forsake thee, though he may seem to be long in coming to thy deliverance. God's tarryings are often tests for his people's faith. If thou canst truly say, 'I love God,' be assured that it is a fact that God loves thee. Notwithstanding all thy troubles, and all thy afflictions, he loves thee, even thee. This requires a high degree of faith; but it is a faith we all should have, if we love God.

Sometimes Satan, by *most blasphemous temptations,* tries to make us believe we are not the children of God. There are times when the old lion of the pit roars at us so terribly that we can scarcely tell our own names, and much less can we tell that we are the children of the Living God. Satan besets us with such vile insinuations and such horribly blasphemous thoughts, that we are filled with terrors. I well remember the time when I was communing with my God, and, all on a sudden, such a torrent of the most horrible and blasphemous thoughts rolled through my brain; the most awful words,—I had never heard the like, even from the most profane,—rushed to my mind, though, blessed be God, they did not pass my lips! I shall never forget how I stood, with my hand upon my mouth, lest I should give utterance to one of those terrible words. Then, in that lovely lane, I fell down on my knees, and implored God to deliver me from those vile thoughts. They were not my own, I knew full well, for I hated them with an intense hatred; I knew it was the devil who was pouring the foul stream into my soul. Satan first insinuates these abominations, and then he tells us that we cannot be the children of God, or we should not have such thoughts as these. Now, at such times, let none of us think that God does not regard the cry of his children. They are fiercely, terribly, horribly tempted; but, glory be to God, he hears their sighs, and counts their tears, and he will lift up their heads!

Though the child of God may be sorely beset with terrible temptations, yet, if he can say, amidst them all, that he loves God, he may rest assured that God loves him. 'Ah!' but sayest thou, 'there is the point, I am afraid I do not love God'? Art thou thus afraid? Then let me try and test thee. Thou sayest thou hast no hope in the Lord, and no love to him. What, my friend, wilt thou take for thy hope? 'Take for my hope?' thou exclaimest, 'why I would not sell it for worlds!' Dear friend, if you do not love God, do not go to his house any more, tarry at home instead. You quickly answer, 'What, sir, not go to the house of God any more? I must go; I love to go.

'"There my best friends, my kindred dwell,
    There God my Saviour reigns."'

Oh, but I thought you said you did not love God! You are a strange creature. You do not love the Lord, and yet you love to go to his house! You are a contradiction to yourself.

If you do not love God, then give up reading the Bible. 'What did you say? Oh, sir, I could not give up reading my Bible; I must read it, I love to read it, it is the Word of my God!' There is another contradiction.

Well, now, here is another test. Suppose, when you are in the midst of all your sorrows, someone should come to you, and say, 'Now, curse God and die,' would you curse him? I know your answer. 'Oh, no, no, a thousand times no, sir; I would not curse him for all the world! What, sir, speak ill of him? Why, he is all goodness; I can find no fault with him! I could not speak ill of him, for I love him.' Ah, the truth will come out somehow; you do love the Lord after all. Poor soul, if thou hast but a spark of love to God, if it be real, genuine love, then remember that what God says is truth, and he says, '*I love them that love me.*' Let not thy sins, or thy trials, or Satan's temptations, make thee think God does not love thee. He does and ever will love all those who love him.

II. Secondly, here is ENCOURAGEMENT FOR EARNEST SEEKERS: 'Those that seek me early shall find me.'

To seek God is to *desire* him. Do you really and truly desire God, not with that faint desire which will vanish as soon as you go home; but with that living desire which will never rest satisfied till it finds the Saviour? If so, thou art seeking him in truth. If thou art saying, 'My highest and best desire is to be one with Christ, to be regenerated by the Holy Spirit, to be free from sin, and to live unto God,' then thou art a true seeker, and soon thou shalt be a finder. Desires are the truest seekings in the world.

But such seeking always implies *praying*. No one can be a sincere seeker who has desires, yet never puts his desires into words. Spiritual desires will be thrust out into the world as it were naked, in the form of sighs, and groans, and tears, as the poet says,—

'Pray if thou canst or canst not speak.'

Spiritual desires often burst out thus, 'Oh! Oh, that! Oh, that I could! Oh, that I might!' You cannot make much out of those expressions, can you? But our gracious God understands their meaning. He knows what 'Oh!' means when it comes from a contrite heart. He knows what 'Oh, that!' means, and 'Oh, that I could!' 'O God,' the poor soul would say, 'Oh, that I could love thee!' 'Oh, that I could be holy!' 'Oh, that I might be regenerate!' Alas! often the poor seeking soul can get no further than 'Oh, that!' John Bunyan has pictured this case very well somewhat after this fashion. A man, sent on an errand by his master, is riding on a horse that will not go quickly enough, so the man is belabouring him to make him go faster, because he is anxious speedily to perform his errand; and the master, seeing that it is so, takes the will for the deed, he reckons the man's obedience by his willingness, and not according to the horse's slowness. That is just how our God does with poor sinners. He knows what they would say, and what they mean, though they cannot express their desires in words; and he takes the will for the deed. I like what a brother said, one evening in prayer, when he had stuck fast, and could go no further. 'O Lord,' he cried, 'Thou knowest what I mean, though I cannot tell thee, and so it does not matter, for thou knowest!' That is just it; those sighs and broken sentences are real prayers, and God accepts them as such.

A seeking soul will search for God *in the use of the means of grace,* in his house, and in his Word. He who is earnestly seeking after his God will go anywhere to find him; he will attend all the services of the sanctuary in order that he may find Christ; he will be like the spouse of old, not able to find rest till Jesus is found. The bride said, 'By night on my bed I sought him whom my soul loveth: I sought him, but I found him not. I will rise now, and go about the city in the streets, and in the broad ways I will seek him whom my soul loveth.' So with all true seekers after Jesus; they will seek for him in his Word and in his ordinances. They know that Jesus 'feedeth among the lilies,' and so they search among the lilies of his Word to discover him there, and they will use every means to find him. I remember that my grandfather was once explaining to me the way of salvation, and he said, 'You must use the means as if your salvation wholly depended upon them, and then you must go to God as though you had done nothing at all, and trust wholly and entirely in Christ Jesus for salvation.' A true seeker will employ the means, but will put no dependence whatever upon them.

Earnest seeking will also take place at *the specified time:* 'those that seek me *early.*'

This implies that some will seek God, but they shall not find him. Jesus said, 'Strive to enter in at the strait gate: for many, I say unto you, will seek to enter in, and shall not be able; when once the master of the house is risen up, and hath shut to the door' (Luke 13:24–25). Many persons, when they come to their death-bed, appear to seek for Jesus; but it is not the real, earnest seeking of a truly-awakened soul. Through terror they seem to seek; but the day of grace with them has passed; it is now for them too late. When once a soul is really convinced of sin by the Holy Ghost, that soul will seek God 'early'; early in the use of means, and early in the diligent use of all opportunities. I take this word 'early' to mean *earnestly.* The convinced soul will be in thorough earnest in seeking after God.

'Those that seek me early' are those who seek the Lord early in life. The children's hymn well puts it,—

''Twill save us from a thousand snares,
To mind religion young.'

I have met with some elderly Christians who despise early piety. 'What,' say they, 'why, he is only a child!' I am thankful that there are so many grey heads among my members; but my crown and rejoicing I must say is, that there are so many boys and girls who are members of this church. Why, a child is the most likely person to find God! He has not such an accumulation of guilt to clog him as the man who has lived thirty or forty years before he began to seek after his God. The child has not learned to reason and speculate about the Word of God. The child reads the Bible, and believes it. The child reads the 'faithful saying, and worthy of all acceptation, that Christ Jesus came into the world to save sinners,' he knows that he is a sinner, and just believes that Jesus Christ died to save him. He has the simplicity of faith, and so knows that he is saved.

Earnest seeking, also, has *a glorious promise* attached to it: 'those that seek me early *shall find me.*'

Oh, to find God! Then, thou hast found a Father! Then, thou hast found happiness on earth, and endless pleasures and fulness of delights in heaven above! Thou hast found the way to escape from hell, and to get to heaven. All thou canst even wish for, and more than that, is to be had for the seeking; but, alas! alas! such is the brutality, yea, such is the devilry of man, that he would rather be damned than be saved, unless God, by his Spirit, makes him willing in the day of his power! Blessed be his name, he has said, his people *shall* be willing in the day of his power! Our text says, 'I love them that love me; and those that seek me early *shall* find me.' Then, 'Seek *ye* the Lord while he may be found, call *ye* upon him while he is near' (Isaiah 55:6), for 'If *ye* seek him, he will be found of *you*' (2 Chronicles 15:2).

Unpublished notes of C. H. Spurgeon's New Park Street Sermons, no. 7

Address delivered on Monday evening, 11 May 1857

REPORTED BY PASTOR T. W. MEDHURST, CARDIFF

'Therefore whosoever heareth these sayings of mine, and doeth them, I will liken him unto a wise man which built his house upon a rock: and the rain descended, and the floods came, and the winds blew, and beat upon that house; and it fell not: for it was founded upon a rock. And every one that heareth these sayings of mine, aud doeth them not, shall be likened unto a foolish man, which built his house upon the sand: and the rain descended, and the floods came, and the winds blew, and beat upon that house; and it fell: and great was the fall of it.'—Matthew 7:24–27.

CHRIST gives us here two parables; the first concerning 'a wise man, which built his house upon a rock,' the second, concerning 'a foolish man, which built his house upon the sand.' The same storm came upon both houses; one house stood fast, because 'it was founded upon a rock,' while the other house, whose foundations were on the sand, fell. The wise man represents the saint, and the foolish man represents the sinner.

I. We learn from these two parables that, IN GOD'S PROVIDENCE, THE SAME TRIALS BEFALL THE SAINT AND THE SINNER.

If a man be troubled, that alone is no proof that he is a Christian. A saint or a sinner cannot be known by his outward circumstances. In one instance, the saint may be poor and the sinner may be rich; in another, the saint may be rich, and the sinner may be poor. The same trials in providence happen to both; but the one wadeth through much tribulation to the kingdom of heaven, while the other wadeth through much tribulation to the kingdom of hell.

We notice here that *the trials were the same*. The same rain descended, the same floods came, and the same winds blew and beat upon both houses. The reason why the wise man's house fell not was because it was built upon a rock.

The trials of a believer are many. 'The rain descended,' not merely a shower, but shower after shower descended. 'The floods came,' not one flood, but floods, flood upon flood. 'The winds blew,' winds of trouble, not one trouble alone, but many troubles. One would have thought that the rains alone were enough; but no, the rains are succeeded by floods, and by winds, too. The Christian will never be free from trouble till he sets his foot upon Canaan's land.

Note, too, that *the troubles came from different sources.* There was the rain from above, the floods from beneath, and the winds from we know not where. The Christian's trials and troubles are various. There are trials from above; the hiding of his Father's face. Clouds come between himself and his Saviour; he loses the sweet sense of communion. He has floods from beneath, temptations and trials from hell, and from the world. The winds, too, blow upon him, troubles from he knows not where; something weighs down his spirits, he can hardly tell what it is, a depression of mind he cannot account for, presses him to the very dust.

Note, again, *there were troubles for every part of the house.* Rain for the roof, floods for the foundation, and winds for the walls. So the believer must expect troubles from all quarters. He will have troubles in his head; Satan will seek to lead him astray in his thoughts, and will tempt him to forget God. He will have troubles from his own heart; sin and corruption will arise, and sorely distress him. Believers must expect trouble. The rain will descend, the floods will come, the winds will blow; but if our foundation is on the Rock, Christ Jesus, we shall not be swept away.

II. Secondly, notice THE SECURITY OF THE BELIEVER, AND THE CAUSE OF HIS SECURITY.

All these troubles came upon that house, yet 'it fell not: for *it was founded upon a rock.*' I dare say it trembled beneath the violence of the storm, and probably the poor inhabitant trembled, too. Possibly he may have said to himself, when the rain was pouring down, 'The roof must fall in, surely the next flood will destroy my house.' Ah, this is just the case with us! We think we shall surely fall, we are afraid the storm will overwhelm us; but we do not fall, the believer is always secure, he is as safe in the storm as in the calm.

'Oh!' says one, 'I am afraid my faith will fail.' Well, beloved, *it* may fail; but your security does not depend upon your faith, though your comfort may. Christ does not say that the house fell not, because it had strong pillars in it, or because of the thickness of the walls; but it fell not because it was built upon a rock. Now, your faith is not the house; it may be a pillar in it, and though that may fail, you will not be destroyed. 'If we believe not, yet he abideth faithful.'

'But I am afraid I shall lose the perceptible feeling of Christ's love toward me.' Well, we may lose this, too; but when faith is weak, and I have lost the sensible enjoyment of Christ's love, can I even then say,—'Nothing in my hand I bring, simply to thy Cross I cling'? Can I sing of Jesu's blood and righteousness alone, without anything of my own? Can I feel that Christ is my only hope? When my eye of faith is dim, can I cast myself on Jesus, sink or swim? Then, beloved, if you can do that, you are on the Rock, and you are safe. Though the pillar of your faith may fail, your house cannot fall; for you are secure in Christ Jesus your Lord. He is your Rock, and he is your Refuge, too.

Note yet once more, we are only told that the house fell not; we are not told that the house received no damage from the storm. Possibly, the dweller in the house had been tricking out his windows a bit, and had put some decorative work there, and some fine ornamentation on the roof, too. Well, these may have been washed away by the violence of the storm. Just so is it often with the Christian. He is not really damaged by trouble; but he may lose many of his comforts and enjoyments. The rain descends upon our comforts, and dissolves them; poor sugary things they are, they soon melt.

But though the ornamental part may have been carried away, the house stood firm. I dare say, when the storm was over, the poor man came out to see what loss he had sustained; and when he looked around, and saw one house here in ruins, and another yonder razed to the ground, he lifted up his hands in astonishment, and exclaimed, 'What a firm rock this must be on which my house is built! What a solid rock it must be to endure such a storm!' God delights to make his children wonder sometimes. If you have been a believer long, you have no doubt often been made to marvel. Can you not look back with astonishment, and wonder how it was that you escaped out of the mouth of the dragon? Do you not often lift up your hands in amazement and gratitude? Can you not even now sing the high praises of your great Deliverer? Will you not unceasingly sing of Christ Jesus, who is your Rock, and your Fortress, and your High Tower? The house 'fell not: for it was founded upon a rock.' This is the reason of your security, believer; for you are on the Rock of Ages, Christ Jesus the Lord.

'When storms of wrath around prevail,
Whirlwind and thunder, fire and hail,
'Tis here our trembling souls shall hide,
And here securely they abide.

'We own the work of sovereign love;
Nor death nor hell our hopes shall move,
Which fix'd on this Foundation stand,
Laid by God's own almighty hand.'

Unpublished notes of C. H. Spurgeon's New Park Street Sermons, no. 8

Delivered on Thursday evening, 14 May 1857

REPORTED BY PASTOR T. W. MEDHURST, CARDIFF

'Christ died for the ungodly.'—Romans 5:6.

CONSCIENCE in every man must tell him that God is just, and, as a necessary consequence, that God must punish sin. Then comes the question,—How can God be just, and yet the justifier of the ungodly? The answer is,—There is redemption in Christ Jesus. God is 'just, and the justifier of him which believeth in Jesus.' Believers are 'now justified by his blood.' In Jesus, God's justice is vindicated to the very utmost, and yet his mercy shines forth in all its glory. The religion which denies the doctrine of the atonement is not of God, and never can succeed. It may hold together the few, who affect to be intellectual, because they are ignorant. The doctrine of the substitutionary sacrifice of our Lord Jesus Christ is the fundamental principle of the Christian religion. This is the only doctrine that teaches how justice can have its full dominion, and yet mercy exercise its sway. Here we have a full-orbed mercy and a fullorbed justice; and neither of them eclipses or casts a shadow over the other. All God's attributes are at one at Calvary. We must stem the torrent of error by preaching 'Jesus Christ and him crucified.' As we clearly proclaim the gospel, 'as the truth is in Jesus,' we shall undermine every citadel of error and falsehood; and we must often preach the great central truths of the gospel, such as this, 'In due time Christ died for the ungodly.' 'While we

Chapter 9

were yet sinners, Christ died for us.' 'For Christ also hath once suffered for sins, the just for the unjust, that he might bring us to God.'

I. Consider, first, THE PERSON OF THE SUBSTITUTE: '*Christ* died for the ungodly.'

He was *Man,* and yet he was *God. He* who suffered in the room, place, and stead of the ungodly, was *Man. He* partook of the weaknesses of humanity. He was the perfect Man; the only Man in whom there never dwelt sin. Christ never fell in Adam. He was 'the Seed of the woman'— 'made of a woman.' His life was blameless. From his eye there never flashed the fire of unhallowed anger. On his lip there never rested the word of deceit. His soul never knew an imagination of evil. The prince of this world had nothing in him. He knew no sin, he did not sin, he could not sin. He was pure, perfect, spotless, holy, acceptable unto God. His sufferings must have power to bless others, for they were not necessary for himself. There was no reason in himself why he should ever know pain, heave a sigh, or experience a sorrow. All his sufferings had reference to his people. His object in dying was to secure their salvation.

Christ was very *Man,* he was also very *God.* The humanity of Christ did not lower his divinity; the divinity was undiluted and infinite. Christ was 'very God of very God'; he possessed all the attributes of the Eternal One. He who hung upon the cross was the great Creator who made all worlds. We know nothing of a human atonement apart from a Divine Sufferer. None but the shoulders of God could sustain the stupendous burden of the mountains of our guilt, and bear it all away. We must have a Divine Sacrifice. It is our joy to know that we have it in the person of our Lord Jesus Christ, who 'died for the ungodly.' The bleeding body of Jesus was in alliance with the unsuffering Deity. The wounds of Jesus, his streaming, spear-rent side, were taken into union with the nature of the Ever-living and Eternal God. What an infinite merit the Godhead must have imparted to the sufferings of the Manhood of Christ! It is not possible that your sins or mine can ever have exceeded the merit of the blood of Christ. Who can limit the efficacy of his precious blood?

II. Secondly, think of THE SUFFERINGS OF THE SUBSTITUTE: 'Christ *died* for the ungodly.'

These sufferings were endured on behalf of all who believe. They had two creditors,—God and man. The great Creditor, God, and the lesser creditor, man, have received payment in full for all their debts. Christ perfectly loved both God and man. When 'Christ died for the ungodly,' he endured the wrath of God against sin. In his sufferings on the cross, he looked up towards heaven for relief; but heaven was dark, and the sun was eclipsed. He looked down for sympathy; but he had to give it, not to receive it. A sorrowful mother needed his care; she could not afford him a word of consolation.

Within the great Substitute's soul there was an agony such as we can never know. Above, there were the swelling waves of Almighty wrath covering his soul. Listen to that dreadful, soul-piercing cry, 'My God, my God, why hast thou forsaken me?' It seems to be the gathering up of all his griefs into one expression. Like some vast lake, which receives the torrents of a thousand mountain streams, and holds all within its banks, so does that sentence seem to grasp all Christ's woes, and express them all, '*Why hast* thou *forsaken* me?'

At length, he bowed his head, and gave up his spirit. He had suffered all that we ought to have suffered; he had given to God a full recompense for all our sins; he had presented on our behalf a complete atonement,—

'And, to the utmost farthing paid
Whate'er his people owed.'

We were ungodly. 'Christ died *for the ungodly.*' What joy it is to think that we have such a perfect atonement to rest upon! If there were one sin Christ did not carry on the tree, or one evil thought of one of his people that he did not bear, we could not be saved. But Christ has borne the whole. He has obeyed, and rendered satisfaction for the jots and the tittles, as well as the great and weighty things, of the whole law of God. He has gone to 'the end of the law for righteousness'—not merely half way,—but all the way: not near to its boundary, but even to its very end, for 'every one that believeth.' He not merely sipped the cup of wrath, and drank a portion of its bitter draught; but he drained it to the very dregs; and, ere he died, he turned the cup bottom upwards; and, when he saw there was not a single black drop trembling on its brim, he exclaimed, '*It is finished.*' He had drunk the whole. Glory in this, ye living people of the living Christ! 'Christ died for the ungodly,' even for you. He has offered for you a complete sacrifice, acceptable unto his Father.

III. Now, note THE ACCEPTANCE OF THE SUBSTITUTE'S SACRIFICE. To all who believe in the name of the Only-begotten Son of God, the Lord has given a full discharge for all their sins. If we believe in Jesus Christ, there is a certainty afforded that God is well content with what Christ has offered, has done, has suffered. That receipt was given when Christ who 'died for the ungodly,' rose again from the dead for their justification.

Christ paid the full redemption price, the ransom was presented before the Father's judgment throne, the Eternal Father looked at the price, his dear Son's precious blood, and he was well content. The atonement was fully accepted.

'If Jesus ne'er had paid the debt,
He ne'er had been at freedom set.'

But, seeing he was set at liberty, and rose again from the dead, that is God's proof that Christ has done all that was necessary to be done. Thou blessed Lamb of God! I see thee rising from thy tomb, in splendour ineffable, dazzling the eyes of the guards, and making them flee away in terror! And when I see thee risen from the dead, I see myself accepted, and all thy redeemed people fully delivered, and permitted to go free, never to be arrested for their sins, and never to be banished for their iniquities.

Now, poor trembling seeker, what sayest thou? Thou hast been saying, 'I cannot rest on Christ.' Soul, hear me! God is satisfied with Christ; art thou dissatisfied? God thought him enough; dost thou think him too little? Did the Lord, the King, against whom thou hast offended, accept the sacrifice of Jesus, and dost thou unbelievingly and distrustfully say, 'He is not enough for me'? Cast away such guilty, Christ-dishonouring fears, I beseech thee. Oh, may the blessed Comforter enable thee now to say,—

'Just as I am—without one plea
But that thy blood was shed for me,

And that thou bidd'st me come to thee,
  O Lamb of God, I come!'

Is it possible that you can have a view of Jesus Christ dying on the cross 'for the ungodly,' and yet your heart will not believe? Can it be that you see him nailed to the tree, and yet your heart wants something else to rest upon beside that cross? Surely it is because you do not know Jesus Christ, that you cannot trust him. Oh, may the Holy Spirit now show you Christ, and so reveal him unto you, that you may at once cry out, 'My Jesus, my Christ, my Lord and Master, forgive my doubts; my faith now casts itself on thee once for all,—sink or swim, thou art now my only hope, all my stay, and wholly my confidence.'

  Sinner, thou must be saved by faith in Christ, and by faith alone. Salvation consists in simply casting thyself down on Christ. '*Christ died for the ungodly.*' Do not rely upon anything thou canst do, or thou canst think, or thou canst say, or thou canst know; rest alone on Christ, and thou art safe. Rest anywhere else, and thou art lost. Be thou who thou mayest, and what thou mayest, though thou wert the worst sinner out of hell, yet if thou art brought to trust in the Christ who 'died for the ungodly,' thou art safe from that very hour, and thou art safe eternally. But, be thou warned, be thy feelings the best, thy sentiments the most orthodox, thy experience the most savoury, thy deeds the most moral, out of Christ, thou art out of grace, and thou shalt be shut out of heaven to all eternity.

  Dost thou say, 'My sins are many'? The atonement of Christ is wondrous. Dost thou cry, 'My heart is hard'? Jesus can soften the hardest heart. Dost thou say, 'Alas! I am so unworthy'? Christ died for the unworthy. Dost thou say, 'I am so vile'? Jesus Christ came to save the vilest. Down with thee, sinner; down, down with thyself, and up with Christ.

  Now, turn thine eye towards Christ Jesus. Look to him. He suffers, he bleeds, he dies, he is buried, he rises again, he ascends on high. TRUST HIM, and thou art safe. Give up all other trusts, and rely on him, and thou shalt pass 'from death unto life.' This is the sure sign, the certain evidence of the Spirit's indwelling, of the Father's election, of the Son's redemption, when the heart is brought simply and solely to rest and trust in the Christ, 'who died for the ungodly.'

Chapter 9

'So great, so vast a sacrifice
   May well my hope revive:
If God's own Son thus bleeds and dies,
   The sinner sure may live.'

Unpublished notes of C. H. Spurgeon's New Park Street Sermons, no. 9

Delivered on a Lord's-day evening in 1856

REPORTED BY PASTOR T. W. MEDHURST, CARDIFF

'Jesus saith unto him, I am the way, ... no man cometh unto the Father, but by me.'—John 14:6.

WHAT can be more plain, not to say homely, than these words, '*I am the way*'? If we have lost our way, we want a plain direction if we are to find it again. So, when we preach to sinners concerning the 'way' of salvation, we cannot be too simple. Those preachers who have been the most successful soul-winners have been the most easily understood by their hearers. We need ministers who will compel us to use our Bible, not our dictionary. Our aim must ever be to bring sinners to Christ. I will this evening show you the way to heaven as plainly as I can.

I. JESUS IS THE ONLY WAY OF SALVATION.

Jesus is the way to holiness, to acceptance, to God, to heaven. There is a glorious intolerance in the text: 'No man cometh unto the Father, but by me.' 'There is none other name under heaven given among men, whereby we must be saved.' 'He that believeth and is baptized shall be saved.' What about the man who does not believe? May there not be another way whereby he may be saved? Here is Christ's answer: 'He that believeth not shall be damned.' It is the best of all charity to be honest; our Lord and Master would never have pandered to the modern spurious charity, there is nothing like that in his teaching. Jesus ever denounced the wrong as loudly as he commended the right. He did not say, 'Well done, Scribes and Pharisees, you do your best, and you will be all right.' No, he righteously condemned them, and cried, 'Woe unto you!' He preached against every doctrine except that which he himself taught.

There seems to be growing up amongst us an idea that a man is of a persecuting spirit if he does not think that the one who flatly contradicts him is as right as himself. If we do as some wish, we shall in time reach that blessed state of charity which had been attained by the courtiers of the Sultan, who, when he said, *at midday,* 'It is midnight,' replied, 'Yes, sire, there is the moon, and there are the stars.' Today, we are expected not to protest against Popery, lest we should be considered bigots; we must subscribe to all that men teach, if only they are sincere. Suppose a man, travelling due North, was sincere in thinking he would get to the South, do you think his sincerity would bring him to the desired destination? If a man was sincere in thinking that prussic acid was a wholesome food, would the poison do him no injury? If a man starved himself while he sincerely believed he was feasting, how long would it take him to get fat? You say, 'These things are contrary to the laws of nature.' Just so, and the laws of God's gospel are as fixed and true as are the laws of nature. If you are honest and sincere in keeping to the road of ruin, you will reach the natural end of that road, eternal destruction. Sincerity in believing a lie does not change the lie to the truth. There is but one way to heaven; there is only one Saviour, Jesus Christ is exclusively 'the way.' This excludes all by-paths, all cross-roads, and all short cuts. Scripture knows nothing of the new theory, that we may be all right though we are in direct opposition to the Word of God.

The way of good works does not lead to heaven. We must still have decided, faithful preaching upon justification by faith. There is as much need today for us to declare this elementary doctrine of the Christian religion as there was in the days of Martin Luther. We must explain, and expound, and enforce, the doctrines of grace, and the absolute necessity of trust in the finished work of the Lord Jesus Christ. We must be saved by *his* doing and dying, and not by anything of our own; we must be justified by *his* righteousness, and not by our own, for indeed, we have none. The canker of self-righteousness is everywhere. As ministers of Christ, it is necessary for us to come back to the old cry, 'Salvation is not of ourselves. Salvation is of the Lord. Jesus is the only way; there is none other.' Jesus Christ is the Substitute of his people. He bore their sins in his own body on the tree; and now, those who are 'his people' are saved by him 'from their sins.' Their sins were laid on Jesus; and that which he did on their behalf, saves them; not anything they can do. We might as well expect to sail to America on a millstone, as expect to go to glory by our own doings. There is no way to heaven other than Jesus, trusting his merits, resting on his atoning sacrifice.

The way of salvation is not partly of works and partly of grace. The way of salvation is all of grace. None can assist Christ in the work of saving guilty men. God does not take a composition from bankrupt debtors, and then let his Son, Jesus Christ, make up the deficiency. Who helped the Eternal Jehovah when he made the heavens? Who was with God when he raised the arches of azure? Who, beside the Lord Jehovah, poured out the wide and open sea into its mighty channels? Is there a single flower that had an angel to help God to make it? Can you find even one blade of grass that owes its origin partly to the divine and partly to the human? Never! God was alone in creation. Even so, God is alone in the greater work of salvation and redemption.

Who helps the Almighty God in providence? Those ponderous wheels that are so high, and terrible, are ever rolling on; who is it that makes their axles stand fast, and guides the wheels in their wondrous revolutions? Is there any man who controls the clouds? Have you heard of any king or potentate who manages the storms? Is not the Eternal the only One who puts a bit between the teeth of the winds, and stands as the Almighty Charioteer who can rein them up at will? Will he let a puny creature, whom he has made, take part with him in the workings of providence?

Is it likely that he will suffer a sinner to become a shareholder in the mightier work of grace and salvation? No. The Messiah comes alone from the winepress, with his garments red with his own blood, 'travelling in the greatness of his strength.' He that speaks in righteousness, 'mighty to save,' trod the winepress alone; and of the people there was none with him. Upon Calvary's cross, no other blood than that of Jesus Christ contributed to his people's redemption. The glorious Lord will not yoke himself with thee, sinner, in order to secure thy salvation. Yoke an angel with an emmet, link an archangel with the tiniest gnat which ever fluttered in a summer's eve; but never think of joining the Omnipotent Jehovah with man's nothingness. The Almighty God yoked with the sinner's feebleness, the Everlasting, the Infinite Maker of all, to be simply a co-worker with us, and we labouring together with him, and helping him to do what he could not do without us in procuring our salvation;—is not the very thought arrant blasphemy?

Even ordinances which God himself ordained must never be trusted to as a means of salvation. Jesus Christ is 'the way', not baptism; not the Lord's supper. As for those things which God did not ordain,—infant sprinkling, human ceremonies, Ritualistic observances, confirmation of the ungodly, wax images, gilt crosses, artificial flowers, fine music, intoning, fasting communions, and so on,—these are sins in God's sight; put instead of Christ's work, they are idolatry. You might as well trust to the ordinances of an old hag as to the ordinances of any priest, Romish or Anglican, who pretends that he has more power with God than you have yourself. We are all alike in the sight of God in this respect; if we come before him as sinners, he accepts us in Christ. If any assume priestly power over their fellow-sinners, let such men tremble for themselves, and remember the fate of Korah, Dathan, and Abiram. He who talks about conferring salvation on others, should look at the dreadful condemnation which awaits his own soul, unless he repents of his great sin. God will yet cause his judgments to come forth, and utterly destroy those who would trench upon the priestly prerogatives of the one and only Great High Priest, our Lord and Saviour Jesus Christ.

He who rests upon his feelings will be as much deceived, as he who rests upon his works. The blood of Jesus saves; not my sense of guilt, nor my consciousness of depravity, nor all my knowledge of my guilt. Salvation is all in Christ Jesus from first to last; putting his pierced hand on all our doing, believing, seeing, feeling, experiencing, he covers it all up, and says, 'I am the way.' Therefore, I must rely on Christ alone, for—

'None but Jesus, none but Jesus,
Can do helpless sinners good.'

II. JESUS IS THE PERSONAL WAY OF SALVATION: 'I am the way.' The way of salvation rests entirely upon the person of our Lord Jesus Christ. We do not think enough, honour enough, preach enough, about the person of Christ. We must be clear about the merit of the precious blood of Christ; we do well to meditate much upon the sponge, the vinegar, the nails, the five wounds, the bleeding side, the dying cry, 'It is finished,' the resurrection, and the ascension of our Lord; but we must not forget 'Jesus Christ himself.' We want not so much doctrine about Christ, as Christ himself. Doctrine is the throne on which Christ sits; but we must have Christ upon the throne. If we are to have our churches full of life and power, we must have more preaching of Christ, talking of him, dwelling with him,—a bleeding Saviour visibly crucified among the people.

We want the Incarnate God, the real Christ; we do not want a picture of the crucifixion on the wall, we want Christ in the heart. We do not want the portrait of the Saviour on stained-glass windows; but we do want the image of Christ portrayed in living lines upon our souls. We must have the blessed person of Christ, the real, living Christ, still giving the shout of a King in the midst of the camp of Israel. This is the power to save the soul, this is the power to move the world. When we live, it must be Christ living in us. When we are fed, it must be upon Christ, the Bread of God coming down from heaven. When we reach heaven, it will be to be where Christ is, beholding his glory. Our pardon comes from Christ Jesus the Lord. We are accepted in Christ, the Beloved. Our salvation is all in Christ; Christ our wisdom, Christ our righteousness, Christ our redemption, Christ our sanctification. The very real, personal Christ must be our Saviour. '*I am the way.*' Jesus Christ did all that was necessary for the salvation of all sinners who trust him. The blood which streamed from his veins, from his heart, cleanses from all sin. The perfect righteousness of Jesus is the believer's justification. Christ is all believing sinners need.

III. JESUS IS THE PERFECT WAY OF SALVATION.

He is not part of the way, but he is the whole of the way. Christ is the way from the place where the sinner is, as a sinner, right up to heaven. Jesus Christ comes to the sinner just where he is; he is to the sinner, as a sinner, where he is, an all-sufficient Saviour, to bring the guilty one to glory. As a sinner, hopeless, senseless, dead, you are to believe that Jesus Christ is the

Saviour for just such as you are. The way to heaven is the way which begins from where you are, and goes straight to heaven. 'Believe on the Lord Jesus Christ, and thou shalt be saved.' 'He that believeth on the Son hath everlasting life,'—insurance against sin, and insurance against terror. They who believe on Christ shall hold on their way, and in Christ the righteous shall wax stronger and stronger. The believer is really, vitally, personally, and spiritually, one with the Lord Jesus Christ.

IV. JESUS IS THE PRESENT WAY OF SALVATION.

Jesus does not say, 'I will be the way.' He says, 'I am the way.' Not, I may be, but 'I am.' That is, presentness. You have not to feel your need before you come to Christ. Come to Christ, and you shall feel all you need to feel afterwards. The whole of salvation is in Christ; thy sense of need must come from him, and thou must trust him to give thee a sense of need. Thou sayest, 'But my heart is so hard.' Yes; but it is Christ's work by his Spirit to soften thy hard heart. It is salvation to trust Christ; thou must trust to Christ for all, and he will do everything. The only qualification for mercy is guilt; the only qualification for washing is filth; the only qualification for salvation is that thou art a lost, ruined, helpless, undone sinner.

Trust Jesus Christ now, and thou shalt be saved. Come to Christ without anything of thine own, resting wholly on what the Lord Jesus Christ has done; and, thus coming, Christ will in no wise cast thee out. Soul, let me put it thus. If thou wilt throw thyself flat on Christ, and trust wholly in his atonement, if thou dost perish, thus coming to Christ, I shall perish, too, for I have no other hope of salvation than this which I preach to you. What can you want more? Here is a God to trust to; here is a Man who has finished transgression, and made an end of sin, and he takes thee, and does everything that is necessary for thy salvation. It is not what thou art, but what he has been, and what he now is, that saves the guilty. Jesus does not want thee to bring the price of a rusty nail's worth of merit; but he wants thee to come empty-handed, with nothing of thine own. Away with even thy mouldy crusts, and thy counterfeit farthings; and come to Jesus just as thou art, saying,—

'Just as I am,—without one plea
But that thy blood was shed for me,

And that thou bidd'st me come to thee,
    O Lamb of God, I come!'

May the Holy Spirit take these words, and open them up to thine understanding, and give them an abiding place in thy heart, and lead thee to Jesus Christ who is 'the way' of salvation! Amen.

Unpublished notes of C. H. Spurgeon's New Park Street Sermons, no. 10

Delivered in 1856

REPORTED BY PASTOR T. W. MEDHURST, CARDIFF

'But it is good for me to draw near to God: I have put my trust in the Lord GOD, that I may declare all thy works.'—Psalm 73:28.

I T is to the first part of this text that your attention is directed. They that are far from God shall perish; God will surely destroy all those who depart from him. 'But,' says the psalmist, 'it is good for me to draw near to God.'

There are many ways in which a true believer draws near to God. He does so in the secret place of communion, in the quiet retirement of fellowship, and in the chamber of meditation. Believers draw near to God when they commune together at the table of their Lord, where they commemorate his death, and anticipate his second coming. We frequently draw near to God when we search the Scriptures, and delight ourselves in the precious promises of the sure Word, when our hearts receive the promises as being 'yea and amen in Christ Jesus.'

We 'draw near to God' in the most blessed manner when we bow the knee in prayer. It is then that we find our God and our heaven; it is then that we tell our secrets into the ear of our Father, and he reveals to us the secrets of his own eternal love. So we will, at the present time, limit our text to the blessedness of drawing near to God in prayer. To the child of God, prayer is always good. We who have known the need of prayer, who have tried the power of prayer, and who have proved its efficacy in times of trouble, can bear this as our solemn, yet withal, cheerful testimony, 'It is good for me to draw near to God.'

I. LET US EMPLOY OUR TEXT AS A TEST.

If our prayers are true and acceptable, by them we 'draw near to God.' Unless we 'draw near to God,' we do not pray. Repeating mere forms of prayer is neither profitable in the utterance, nor shall it return in blessings upon us from the throne of God. In all true prayer, we must have God before our eyes; we must believe God to be present, hearkening to our petitions, hearing our every word, and listening to our every sigh; and we must also know that God is granting our requests, and sending the answer of peace and assurance into our souls. All true prayer is put into the hands of Christ, who is our Representative before the throne of God. Looking up, through faith, we see him taking our petitions within the veil, sprinkling them with his blood, putting them into his censer, and letting the incense of his intercession ascend with them before the throne of the Most High. The essence of prayer is thus drawing near unto God, drawing near to God through Christ, realizing the actual presence of God as we are addressing him.

There are degrees in thus drawing nigh unto God. Some draw nigh to God, though their souls are filled with solemn awe, while they are overwhelmed with an awful sense of his sublimity and majesty. They have no feeling of delight or confidence; but simply a sense of being in the presence of 'the High and Lofty One, that inhabiteth eternity.' Subdued by a sense of his splendour, sinking under a dread of the terror of his justice, awed by the majesty of his power, and of his spotless purity, the soul falls prostrate in speechless confusion before the throne, and can scarcely give utterance to a single word.

There are others, who, having a clear consciousness that their sins are pardoned, can read their title clear to mansions in the skies, and are enabled to walk amid the glories of Deity, crying, 'Holy! Holy! Holy!'— though awed, yet not overwhelmed with solemn fear and dread. These see, not so much the majestic greatness of God, as his goodness; they discern his love more than his justice. They seem to speak with God face to face; they come up close to him, tell out their wants into his ear, breathe out their desires before his heavenly face, and look up with confidence expecting an answer.

There are others of the children of God, who are enabled to take a supreme delight in their Heavenly Father's splendour and majesty. They so rely upon the blood and righteousness of Christ as to have no fear or apprehension. They behold upon the throne their Father and their God; and, as children, in the confidence of love, they draw nigh. They lay hold of the knee of the Eternal Jehovah, they grasp the arm of the Omnipotent One; they plead with God as dear children, and prevail. They understand the language of the psalmist, when he said, 'My heart and my flesh crieth out for the living God.' Not all saints attain unto this degree of drawing near to God; but there must be a drawing nigh to God in some degree, or else there is no sincerity in your prayer; there is nothing in it acceptable unto God, or profitable to your own soul.

II. LET US USE OUR TEXT TO EXCITE OUR DESIRES IN PRAYER.

'It is good for me to draw near to God.' Let me, then, stir up my soul to earnestness of supplication. The great want of the Church today is fervency of prayer. We seem to believe more in preaching than in praying; we come together on Sundays to hear preaching, we stay away on Mondays when the saints are gathered together praying. We seem to put the mercy-seat *underneath* the pulpit. We long for the coming day,—and it will come,—when we shall *ascend* from the pulpit to the mercy-seat, and shall prove the united prayers of the Church of Christ to be as mighty a power for the conversion of sinners as the preaching and expounding of the Word of God.

It is good to draw near to God, because prayer explains many difficulties. The psalmist had been in great perplexity. He was full of trouble about the affairs of this world, he saw the godly in distress, and the wicked prospering. He tried to reconcile this strange providence with the goodness of God. He failed in solving the mystery, until he 'went into the sanctuary of God'; but there he understood the explanation of the whole difficulty. There are many enigmas in providence, and many mysteries in Scripture, which we shall never comprehend until we learn their solution on our knees. The best student in divinity is not the one who reads most, but the one who prays most. We must take the Word of God, and look alone to the Great Illuminator of our souls, the Holy Ghost, seeking his teaching by daily, earnest, believing prayer. Prayer will expound Scripture and explain providence. Ask in prayer, and God will give you an insight into the meaning of mysteries. Keep your eye fixed on Christ; he is in the centre of every maze. Fall on your knees and pray, and God will clear away all difficulties from your path or enable you to surmount them. Prayer will quickly end all controversy between you and God.

It is good to draw near to God because prayer is the mother of deliverances. If we are in any trouble or trial, let us present ourselves at the mercy-seat, and we shall soon discover a way of escape.

'Prayer makes the darken'd cloud withdraw,
Prayer climbs the ladder Jacob saw,
Gives exercise to faith and love,
Brings every blessing from above.'

Prayer, and faith, and sincerity, and importunity, will deliver thee, no matter how many or how mighty are thine enemies.

It is good to draw near to God, because prayers obtain promises. This is one of the blessings of faith, and it is also one of the blessings of prayer; they both obtain promises. Every answered prayer is a new promise. Plead the promise thou hast, and God will fulfil the promise, and hand it back to thee to plead again. Thou canst never exhaust the promise of God. It will multiply as thou pleadest it before the throne of God, even as the loaves and fishes multiplied when Jesus gave them to the disciples to feed the multitude. Be diligent in prayer, or thou wilt lose the promise, because it will be unfulfilled. Be much in prayer, often in thy closet, much on thy knees, fervent in thy supplications, because it is in answer to prayer that God fulfils his promises.

It is an evil thing not to draw near to God. Alas! there are some men and women who live without prayer. Such have never been regenerated by the Holy Ghost. They have never really felt their need of a Saviour; they have never poured out their hearts before the throne of God; they have never known the token of the Lord's favour in the gift of faith in Jesus Christ, the Son of God. My hearers, let me address you solemnly, and remind you that *a prayerless soul is a Christless soul, and a soul that is without Christ is a lost soul!* He who has never sought mercy, has certainly never obtained mercy. Be assured that you, who never bend your knees in prayer, who never draw near to God in supplication, are in the gall of bitterness, and in the bonds of iniquity, and that the wrath of God abideth on you, because you do not believe on Jesus Christ, the Son of God. Take heed unto yourselves, lest hereafter ye lift up your eyes in that place where hope can never come. It is probable that, in this great assembly, there are not many who are addicted to such gross iniquities as drunkenness, debauchery, lying, and the like; but there are many here who waste their time in worldly amusements that are questionable in character. Poor butterflies, who have no worthy aim in life, and who live only to get rid of time, regardless of eternity! Oh, precious time, for one hour of which they would hereafter give ten times the world's weight in gold, were it in their possession! How solemn a thing it is, that men and women should be spending all their time in doing nothing for eternity! How many waste more hours in dressing their poor bodies, in vain decorations of their empty heads, in frivolous conversation and silly amusements, than they employ in the affairs of their immortal souls! You may treat these matters lightly and carelessly now; but the day will surely come, when, on that bed of sickness, just entering the eternal world, these little things, as you regard them now, will assume their real size, and you will find how awful a thing it was for the soul immortal to be wasting all its moments in empty show and vain frivolity. May God grant you his grace to begin to live in earnest! May the Holy Spirit quicken you, that you may seek a Saviour for your souls! And then, having found Jesus as your own Saviour, may you go abroad, to—

'Tell to sinners round,
What a dear Saviour you have found.'

May you go forth, attempting to pluck sinners as brands from the burning; never resting, never being content, unless each day shall be marked by the conversion of a soul through your instrumentality! May you, as you 'draw near to God' day by day, and year after year, be enabled to say, 'Thanks be unto God Almighty, he hath graciously blessed me, *even me*, and used me, and hath given unto me his choicest blessing in making me his instrument in the conversion of sinners.' God grant it, for Jesus Christ's sake! Amen.

Chapter 12

Unpublished notes of C. H. Spurgeon's New Park Street Sermons, no. 11

Delivered in 1859

REPORTED BY PASTOR T. W. MEDHURST, CARDIFF

'For Christ also hath once suffered for sins, the just for the unjust, that he might bring us to God.'—1 Peter 3:18.

G OD is just, and a just God must punish sin. The great question is, *'How can God be just, and yet the justifier of the ungodly?'* False religions endeavour to answer this question, but they completely fail. The poor heathen thinks he has found the answer in his own terrible sacrifices. He thinks he may give 'his first-born for his transgression, the fruit of his body for the sin of his soul.' The deluded Papist thinks he has found an answer to the question in his daily mass; he says that there is in it 'a propitiatory sacrifice for the quick and the dead.' It is not thus that God's justice is vindicated, neither is it thus that his mercy shines forth in its glory.

There is a cold, speculative theology, that seeks to put this question far away. There are a few men who scoff at the atonement, and reject the thought of sacrifice. These never will be more than a few; they never can be many. The heathen and the Romanist *may* impress the multitude; but that system which denies the doctrine of atonement by the blood of Jesus Christ, or which puts it in the background, never can succeed. Its adherents may profess to be intellectual, because they are ignorant; but they will never convince the masses. It is stamped on nature by God that every man feels in his conscience a craving after a reply to the question, 'How can the just God justly forgive me the sinner?' If that question be not answered in some way, so that it may be seen how God can save, and yet maintain his justice, no system of theology can by any possibility succeed.

We must resist the tendency that seems to be in the minds of some, to keep back this vital truth, the fundamental truth of the Christian religion, namely, the doctrine of the substitutionary sacrifice of our Lord and Saviour Jesus Christ. Let us not argue against this tendency; but let us rather destroy it by our own personal determination to preach more earnestly and more constantly 'Jesus Christ, and him crucified.' The quickest way to slay error is to proclaim the truth. The surest mode of extinguishing falsehood, is to boldly advocate Scripture doctrine upon Scripture principles. Scolding and protesting will not be so effectual in resisting the progress of error as the clear proclamation of the truth in Jesus.

Let me now try to preach the doctrine of substitution, which is the Scripture answer to the questions, 'How can God's justice have its full dominion, and yet God's mercy exercise its sway?'—'How can there be a full-orbed justice and a full-orbed mercy, and neither of them eclipse or cast a shadow over the other?'

I. BEHOLD THE PERSON OF THE SUFFERING SUBSTITUTE: 'CHRIST *also hath once suffered for sins, the* JUST *for the unjust, that* HE *might bring us to God.'*

The Substitute was *of complex nature. He* was truly man, and yet he was truly God. *Christ Jesus* who 'suffered' in the room, place, and stead of God's chosen people, *was man,* man of the substance of his mother, most surely man. He partook of all the weakness of humanity, and was in all respects, sin only excepted, tempted as we are; yea, he became 'bone of our bone, and flesh of our flesh.' He was the perfect man, the only man in whom there never dwelt sin. There was no sin in his nature. No taint of original depravity ran in his veins. In his human nature he was 'without spot or blemish.' Conceived in a miraculous manner, he partook not, in any degree, of that transgression which is transmitted to us; for we are born in sin, and shapen in iniquity.

Christ did not receive any of that imputed sin which has fallen upon the race from Adam. Christ never fell in Adam. He was 'the seed of the woman', but he never lay in the loins of Adam. As a private person, Christ never fell; by nature, he was not in any sense a participator or partaker in Adam's sin. Though, on the part of his people, Jesus took upon himself Adam's transgression, and bore it right away, he himself was, in his original, without the shadow of a spot, the immaculate, the perfect Lamb of God's passover.

The life of the man Christ Jesus was in every respect blameless. From his eye no fire of unhallowed anger ever flashed. On his lips the word of deceit never rested. His pure mind never knew an imagination of sin. Satan's sparks fell on Christ's soul like fire dropping into the ocean, and were quenched for ever. Hell's quiver of temptations was emptied upon him, but no single arrow ever stuck in his flesh and blood. He stood invincible and invulnerable. He could not be wounded by temptation. 'The prince of this world cometh, and hath nothing in me,' was his own triumphant declaration. Not only did Christ not sin, but he could not sin. *'He knew no sin.'* He had no acquaintance with sin, he was a stranger to sin, sin had no commerce with him, he had no dealings with sin personally. His head turned not dizzy when upon the pinnacle of the temple. When down in the depths of humiliation, no grief found expression void of completest resignation. He was ever pure, perfect, spotless, holy, acceptable unto God.

The sufferings of Jesus have power to bless others, seeing they were not necessary for himself. He had no need to suffer as the result of sin, nor yet that, by the discipline of suffering, he might be purged from its evil. There was no reason in himself why he should ever know pain, or heave a sigh. His sufferings all had reference to his people. His object in suffering, bleeding, dying, was to secure the salvation of his chosen. Our souls may now trust Jesus, the perfect man, with the utmost confidence.

Let us also ever bear in mind that, *while Christ was truly man, yet was he also very God.* We believe and must ever teach that the perfect humanity of Christ did not lower his perfect Deity; his Divinity was undiluted and infinite. He was 'Very God of very God,' possessing all the attributes of the eternal Jehovah. He, who did hang upon the cross, was the same God who made all worlds. The very Word, who did bear our sins in his own body on the tree, was that Word by whom all things were made, and without whom 'was not anything made that was made.' We know nothing of a human atonement apart from the Deity of Christ Jesus. We dare not trust our souls upon a saviour who is but a man. If all the men that have ever lived, and all the angels that exist, could have wrought together, and striven throughout eternity to offer a sacrifice that should be a propitiation for the sins of a single man, they must have failed. None but the shoulders of the Incarnate God could bear the stupendous burden. No hand but that which set fast the spheres could shake the mountains of our guilt, and bear them away. We must have a Divine Sacrifice, and it is our joy to know that we have this in the person of our Lord Jesus Christ.

As for those who do not believe in the Deity of Jesus Christ, let them go their way, and preach what they will, we cannot stay to enter into controversy with them. We would speak of them as Mr Gadsby did. A building where Unitarianism was taught was erected opposite the chapel in which William Gadsby preached the gospel of the grace of God. One asked Mr Gadsby, 'Do you not feel sad about this opposition?' He replied, '*Opposition,* man! I do not know of any opposition.' 'No opposition?' 'No, brother, none whatever. Suppose I kept a baker's shop, and sold good wheaten bread, and some man came and opened an ironmonger's shop opposite, would that be opposition?' 'No, that would be quite a different line of business.' 'So,' said Mr Gadsby, 'the Unitarian Chapel is no opposition to us; it is in a different line altogether. It is a different article they have to deal out. We deal with the gospel of our Lord and Saviour Jesus Christ, and on that a soul may rest for eternity; but they deal with "another gospel, which is not another," with that which can never bring peace on earth, or blessedness in the world to come. There is no opposition.' Of course, in another meaning of the word, there is the greatest possible 'opposition' between us and Unitarians; and we will pretend to no manner of union with them, for we can never give up our belief in the Divinity and Deity of our Lord and Saviour Jesus Christ, nor can we have any fellowship with those who reject that blessed truth.

Let us stand beneath the cross of Calvary, and behold our Lord Jesus hanging there, and remember that his bleeding body was in alliance with the unsuffering Deity. Those wounds of his, that streaming, spear-rent side, was taken into union with the nature of the living and eternal God.

The infinite merit of the Godhead was imparted to the sufferings of the manhood. Neither your sins nor mine can ever exceed the merit of the precious blood of Christ. If our sins be high as mountains, the ocean of his atonement, like Noah's flood, covers the utmost summits of the mountains. It prevails twenty cubits upwards, till all the highest mountains are covered. Though our sins be never so crimson, the blood of Jesus Christ is more crimson, and the one washes out the other. Though our iniquities be never so dark and bitter, his death was more bitter and dark, and the black bitterness of his death hath taken away the blackness and bitterness of our sins; and therefore it is that 'He is able to save them to the uttermost that come unto God by him.'

Sinner, look at Jesus Christ! There is power in his atoning blood to wash away all thy sins. None can limit the efficacy of the precious blood of Christ. No sins can be too black or too numerous for that precious blood to cleanse. The blood of Jesus Christ is sufficient to accomplish all that God has purposed to accomplish by its shedding. Christ shall never fail in any respect. His cross is a battering-ram against which nothing shall stand. Before the cross of Christ, the stupendous ramparts of our condemnation must rock to and fro even to their fall; and not one stone shall be left upon another that shall not be thrown down. We need a greater confidence in the cross of Jesus Christ, a surer rest evermore on that Rock of Ages cleft for us.

II. CONTEMPLATE THE SUFFERINGS OF THE SUBSTITUTE: 'Christ also hath once suffered for sins.' These were endured on behalf of all them that believe. See him in Gethsemane.

'Gethsemane, the olive-press!
(And why so called let Christians guess)
Fit name, fit place, where vengeance strove,
And griped and grappled hard with love.

''Twas here the Lord of life appear'd,
And sigh'd, and groan'd, and pray'd, and fear'd;
Bore all incarnate God could bear,
With strength enough, and none to spare.'

There, for us, Jesus sweated until his soul became so full of agony that the blood flushed the rivers of his veins, and at last burst the banks and overflowed. 'His head, his hair, his garments bloody were.' He was clad in a ruby robe of his own blood; and there he continued still wrestling, with his soul burdened, and 'sorrowful even unto death,' that he might prevail on his people's behalf, and that he might suffer the wrath of God for their sins.

He rose from the place where he had been pleading, renewed in strength, and went forth to meet his doom. He was betrayed by Judas, one of the twelve. His own familiar friend, whom he had trusted, who did eat of his bread, lifted up his heel against him. You who have been forsaken by your firmest friend in the hour of your direst need, you that have known a plighted troth broken, pretended love turned into a deadly hatred, you may guess, but you can only faintly guess, the tremendous sorrow that came into the Redeemer's soul when the traitor, Judas Iscariot, betrayed him.

They hurry the Saviour away to Annas, to Caiaphas, to Pilate, to Herod, then back again to Pilate, without any breathing time, without any respite. They accuse him of sedition. *The King of kings seditious!* They accuse him of blasphemy; as if *God* could blaspheme! They could find no witnesses against him, except the basest scum of the people, who were prepared to swear to any falsehood, and even these agreed not one with another. There stood the perfect man, the Son of God, accused and slandered by men who were not worthy to be spit upon.

They condemn the innocent, they mock him, they laugh at him, they jeer at his majesty, and torment his sacred person. He is given up to the tender mercies of the Roman soldiery. They set him in an old chair as though it were a throne. They had just before torn his back with scourges, till his bones stood up like white cliffs in a sea of blood. They crown him with thorns. They cast an old purple robe on his shoulders, they mock and deride him, as though he were a sham king. For a sceptre, they give him a reed; for homage, they give him spittle; for the kiss of salutation, they give him the lips of mockery. Instead of bowing before him as their King, they blindfold him, and smite him in the face.

Was ever grief like thine, thou King of sorrow, despised by thine own subjects? Thou, who didst give them breath, dost have that breath back again on thee in violent and blasphemous oaths! Thou didst give them life; and they spent that life in mocking thee!

Jesus is led forth to Calvary. He is nailed to the cross by cruel and wicked hands. The rude rabble jeer at his sufferings. Within his soul, there is an agony such as we cannot fathom. Above, there are the swelling waves of Almighty wrath against our sins, covering all his soul. Hark! that dreadful soul-piercing cry, 'My God, my God, why hast thou forsaken me?' It seems to be the gathering up of all his griefs, sorrows, and sufferings into one expression. Like some enormous lake, which receives the torrents of a thousand rivers, and holds all within its banks, so does that sentence seem to grasp all his woes, and express them all, 'My God, my God, *why* hast *thou* forsaken *me?*'

At last, he bows his head, and yields up his spirit! At one tremendous draught of love, the Lord hath drained destruction dry for all his people. He has 'suffered' all that they ought to have suffered. He hath given to the justice of God a full recompense for all their sins. He has on their behalf presented a complete atonement,—

'And, to the utmost farthing paid
Whate'er his people owed.'

What joy it is, believer, to think that thou hast such a perfect atonement to rest upon! If there were one sin Christ did not suffer for on the cross, or one evil thought of one of his people that he did not bear, we could not be saved. But he has 'finished' the whole of his people's transgression, he has made an end of all their sins, he has obeyed all the jots and the tittles, as well as the great and weighty things, of the law of God, he has magnified it, and made it honourable. He has gone to 'the end of the law for righteousness'— not half-way, but all the way; not near to its boundary, but even to its very end. He has not merely sipped from the cup of wrath, not merely tasted a portion of its bitter draught, but he has drained it to the very dregs. Ere he died, he turned the cup of wrath bottom upwards, for he had taken all it contained; and when he saw that there was not a single black drop trembling on its brim, he exclaimed, with the loud voice of triumph, 'It is finished!' He had drunk the whole. Glory in this, ye living people of the living Christ! He hath offered for you a complete sacrifice, acceptable unto his Father. Glory in this, ye chosen people of the living God, that 'Christ also hath once suffered for sins, the just for the unjust, that he might bring us to God.'

III. REJOICE IN THE RESULT OF THE SUBSTITUTION.

The sufferings are finished. The debt is paid. Justice is satisfied. The law is magnified. Righteousness is established. For all his people's sins Christ has made a complete atonement, and for their justification he has risen from the dead.

Now, poor trembling seeker, what sayest thou to this? Canst thou not now rest on Christ? God is satisfied with his Son's atoning sacrifice; canst thou be dissatisfied with it? God thinks Jesus enough; canst thou think him too little? Did the Lord, the King, against whom thou hast offended, accept the reconciliation; and dost thou unbelievingly and distrustfully say, 'I fear it is not sufficient'? Cast away thy guilty fears, I beseech thee. May the blessed Comforter enable thee now to say,—

'Just as I am—without one plea
But that thy blood was shed for me,
And that thou bidd'st me come to thee,
    O Lamb of God, I come!'

Thou art to be saved by faith in Christ, who 'hath once suffered for sins,' and in Christ alone. Do not seek to make a saviour of thine own feelings. Do not think thou must experience this, or that, before thou comest unto Jesus. Christ wants no preparation from thee. Salvation consists in simply casting thyself down on Christ. Cast thyself down on thy very face in the dust before him, and once for all have done with thine own wretched self. Rely not on anything thou canst do, or think, or say, or know; rest alone on Jesus only, and thou art saved. Be thou who thou mayest, and what thou mayest, though thou wert the very worst sinner out of hell, be thy soul the blackest, yet if thou wilt trust in Christ who 'hath once suffered for sins, the just for the unjust,' thou shalt be saved.

Trembling sinner, look to Jesus, and thou art saved. Dost thou say, 'My sins are many'? His atonement is wondrous. Dost thou cry, 'My heart is hard'? Jesus can soften it. Dost thou exclaim, 'Alas, I am so unworthy'? Jesus loves the unworthy. Dost thou feel, 'I am so vile'? It is the vile Jesus came to save. Down with thee, sinner; down, down with thyself, and up with Christ, who hath suffered for thy sins upon Calvary's cross. Turn thine eye thither; see Jesus only. He suffers. He bleeds. He dies. He is buried. He rises again. He ascends on high. Trust him, and thou art safe. Give up all other trusts, and rely on Jesus alone, alone on Jesus, and thou shalt pass from death unto life. This is the sure sign, the certain evidence of the Spirit's indwelling, of the Father's election, of the Son's redemption, when the soul is brought simply and wholly to rest and trust in Jesus Christ, who 'hath once suffered for sins, the just for the unjust, that he might bring us to God.'

May the Holy Ghost bless these words, and send them home with comfort to many hearts, for our Lord Jesus Christ's sake! Amen.

Jesus—Saviour

Unpublished notes of a sermon by C. H. Spurgeon, delivered in the Botanic Gardens, Belfast, in August, 1858 (when about 7,000 persons were present)*

REPORTED BY PASTOR T. W. MEDHURST, CARDIFF

'Thou shalt call his name JESUS: for he shall shall save his people from their sins.'—Matthew 1:21.

THE person of the Lord Jesus is exceedingly precious to all believers. So great is their estimation of him, that everything concerning him is interesting in their view. To them, all his 'garments smell of myrrh, and aloes, and cassia, out of the ivory palaces.' There is not a spot where his foot has trodden, nor a thing which his hand has touched, nor a word which his lips have spoken, which is not consecrated to every true Christian, from the very fact that it has had a connection with him. Words that were ordinary words before, become silvery words when applied to him. Talk of a shepherd, and there is lovely pastoral beauty; but talk of the GOOD SHEPHERD, and there is a marvellous and incomparable richness of beauty. Speak of a prophet, a priest, or a king, and these titles are suggestive; but speak of Jesus, the PRIEST, the PROPHET, the KING, and there is a fulness in each of these words that we never saw before. The very words that were rich as silver, become like fine gold when applied to Christ. Sweet is that word 'friend'; but sweeter far is that 'FRIEND that sticketh closer than a brother.' The name 'husband' is golden; but oh! far more golden is it when we read, 'Thy Maker is thine HUSBAND; the Lord of hosts is his name.' When we see the Saviour standing in that relationship to his Church, then, in very truth, we understand what that word husband means. The very name of Christ is as a sonnet to the believer; but if there be one name that is more precious than another, if there be one title of our blessed Lord which is more precious than any besides, it is the name JESUS. We must put that name first.

'JESUS, the name that charms our fears,
    That bids our sorrows cease,
'Tis music in the sinner's ears,
    'Tis life, and health and peace.'

There is the sweetest music in the name JESUS. You may utter that name again and again, and each time it sounds like the pealing of the bells of heaven. It is a sonnet in a word; it is an oratorio in two syllables; it is the eternal chorus of the angelic host in five letters. *Jesus!* JESUS! JESUS! Who does not love that charming name? Who among the followers of the Lamb does not dwell upon it with delight? I verily believe that this is the Name that sounds above all others in heaven itself.

'JESUS, the Lord, their harps employs;
    JESUS, my love, they sing!
JESUS, the life of all our joys,
    Sounds sweet from every string.'

My business at this time is to endeavour to explain the meaning of the name JESUS. It is very simple, it means SAVIOUR; yet it will take some time to show some of the saving works which Christ has done, whereby he has earned for himself the name of Saviour. You ask our Sunday-school children, 'What is meant by being saved?' and they answer, 'It is an escape from hell, and an entrance into heaven.' That is true, but it is not all the truth. Salvation means much more than escaping from hell, and entering into heaven. In fact, that is rather the effect of salvation than salvation itself. The word 'salvation' is a bigger word than that. It reaches not only from hell to heaven, but from the depths of the fall of Adam, to the very heights of the bliss and perfection of the Second Adam, unto whose image the saved are to be conformed. In trying to explain the meaning of salvation, we must begin at the beginning, and go on to the end. 'He shall save his people from their sins.'

I. First, HE SHALL SAVE HIS PEOPLE PROM THEIR DEATH IN SIN.

By nature, all men are dead in sin. They not merely live in sin, but they are 'dead in trespasses and sins.' They have neither the will nor the power to renounce sin, and lay hold on eternal life. We may preach to dead sinners all the thunders of the law, but we cannot make them alive, so that they should run to Christ for refuge. We may try to woo them, but we cannot win their hearts for Jesus Christ. If all the preachers in the world were to attempt to win a soul for God, apart from the quickening power of the Holy Spirit, they would find they had undertaken an impossible task. Man by nature is dead, incapable of doing anything for his own salvation, until first of all he has been quickened into spiritual life. Some say, 'If a sinner takes the first step, Christ will do the rest.' The Romanists boast that St Denis, after his head was cut off, picked it up, and walked two thousand miles. That would have been an easy matter if he could have taken the first step. It is just the same with the sinner. If the sinner can take the first step, he can take all the rest, for it is in the first step that the difficulty lies. If the sinner can, by nature, make himself willing to be saved, he has no need afterwards for the Holy Spirit, for the nature which gave him the first right thing can give him all other right things unto the end; but there never was found yet in actual experience one man who came to Christ of himself. All who love Jesus, love him because he first loved them. His sovereign power made them willing, or they had still remained strangers to him. Men, like sheep, wander of their own free will; but neither sheep nor men ever returned of their own free will. As long as the world standeth, and human nature is what it is, we shall all have to say when we are brought to accept Christ's salvation,—

'Why were we made to hear thy voice,
    And enter while there's room;
When thousands make a wretched choice,
    And rather starve than come?

''Twas the same love that spread the feast,
    That sweetly forced us in;
Else we had still refused to taste,
    And perished in our sin.'

We could not preach with any hope of success did we not believe that our Master's power is going forth with our preaching, to make men willing to receive salvation. If men's salvation depended upon their voluntary acceptance of the truth we preach, we are assured that all our preaching would be in vain. We do not ask your will when we come to preach to you the gospel of God's salvation. You may be ever so unwilling; it is ours still to preach the truth of God, and he who commands us to preach his gospel to every creature will, in his own time and by his own power, turn your will, and change your mind, so that you shall lay hold of the things you once despised, and highly prize the things you once hated. Jesus Christ has the key of man's will. He can put a bit into the jaws of the leviathan sinner. He can turn men's hearts by just lifting his finger. This, then, is the first work Jesus does for his people, he saves them from their death in sin.

II. Next, HE SHALL SAVE HIS PEOPLE FROM THE BONDAGE AND TERROR OF THEIR SINS.

As soon as the sinner is quickened and made alive, he becomes very miserable. The first effect of the entrance of divine life in the soul is pain. As long as the sinner is dead spiritually, conscience is quiet, and he is peaceful in his sin; but when God gives spiritual life, the man begins to be miserable and unhappy on account of his sin. Mark this, as sure as ever thou hast been made alive by Jesus Christ, thou hast had to feel the weight of thy sin. There is a dead man;—heap burdens upon him, pile on heavy weights, he has no feeling. If that man could be made alive, he would soon cry out on account of those great loads. While he was dead, he knew nothing of the weight; but now that he is alive, the burden is intolerable. Stab a dead man to the heart, and there is neither sigh, nor cry, nor groan. Stab a living man, and his wounds bleed, and he cries out on account of the pain. Even so is it with the quickened sinner; so soon as the Lord makes a man spiritually alive, he begins to cry out that the burden of his sin is unbearable, that the bonds of his iniquity are exceedingly painful. Then Jesus saves him from the bondage and terror of his sin.

Children of God, can you not bear witness to this fact? When convinced of sin, you were almost driven to despair. You went to Moses, and he said, 'Do good works.' You tried to obey him, but how you failed! You tried ceremonies, baptism, the so-called Sacrament, church-going; but you were none the better. What could you do? The ghosts of your old sins haunted you every day. By night you dreamed of them, and by day you seemed to feel the hell of which you had dreamed by night. Do you remember the time when the burden was lifted, and all your terrors were quieted? Was it not when you saw Jesus crucified for you,—when you saw Jesus bleeding, dying in your stead? Then you were set free, fully emancipated; then your every fetter was broken, then every bond was snapped; then, by the life and blood-shedding of the Lord Jesus Christ, you were delivered from terror and alarm. So Jesus saves his people from the terror of their sins.

III. Thirdly, HE SHALL SAVE HIS PEOPLE FROM THE GUILT OF SIN.

Jesus takes away not only terror, but the cause of terror; every kind of cause that might give the believer terror on account of his sin. No sooner does the sinner come to Christ, and cast himself entirely upon him, than the Saviour takes away from him every blot, and speck, and stain, that had made him black before. Marvellous though it be, yet it is nevertheless true, the blackest sinner, believing in Jesus, in one moment becomes white as the angels in heaven.

'The moment a sinner believes.
   And trusts in his crucified God,
His pardon at once he receives,
   Salvation in full through his blood.'

I know of a surety this day there is not a sin in God's Book against my soul. I know my sins were many and heinous and deserved eternal wrath; but in the moment I believed on Jesus, he made a clean sweep of my sins. His blood cleanseth from all sin. All the sins of all his people were charged to the account of Jesus. He bore the penalty of their sins. They are all gone, and the believer may now look up to heaven, and say, 'Great God, I am clean. Through Jesus' blood, I am clean.' O master-mercy! Is not this the very prince of blessings, that the guilty sinner should become innocent, that he should not only have pardon, but should actually be set free from guilt, that he should be so cleansed that in God's Book there should not be a solitary charge against him? Blessed Jesus, thou dost cleanse thy people from their sins. Notice the boldness of the apostle Paul; he looks up to heaven, nay, seems to mount up into heaven; he seems to stand before the throne of God himself, and looking at that great white throne, dazzling in its purity, he cries, 'Who shall lay anything to the charge of God's elect?' O impious man, surely a thunderbolt will crush thee! Will not God raise himself from his seat to dash thee into pieces? No, no; there stands the apostle, fearless and dauntless, and he exclaims, 'Who shall lay anything to the charge of God's elect?' and, instead of thunder, there is heard from the throne this sweet answer to the bold challenge, 'It is God that justifieth.' And now Paul lifts his voice again, and cries aloud, 'Who is he that condemneth?' And the answer comes, 'It is Christ that died.' And you may even picture the apostle doing something beside this; he comes to earth, and cries, 'Who shall lay anything to the charge of God's elect? Who is he that condemneth?' And then he seems to go down to the lowest shades of hell, and marching through the ranks of the demons, he cries, 'Who shall separate us from the love of Christ?' and meeting grim death, and him that had the power of death, that is, the devil, he shouts in their face, 'For I am persuaded, that neither death, nor life, nor angels, nor principalities, nor powers, nor things present, nor things to come, nor height, nor depth, nor any other creature, shall be able to separate us from the love of God, which is in Christ Jesus our Lord.' Christ so completely saveth his people from their sins, that, before God, men, and devils, they can plead perfect innocence; there is nothing that can be laid to their charge.

IV. Again, HE SHALL SAVE HIS PEOPLE FROM THE POWER OF SIN IN THEIR LIVES.

We have in England a class of people who like good high Calvinistic doctrines, but who do not set much value on good, high, and holy living. With this class I have no sympathy; I detest above all things the Antinomianism which leads people to prate about being secure in Christ while they are living in sin. In my young days, I knew one man who stood on a public-house table, with a glass of gin in his hand, and said he was one of God's elect. They kicked him out of the place, and said they did not want any such elect people there; and they treated him as he deserved to be treated. There are some men who can live in sin, and drink and swear, and yet say they are God's elect people. I heard one man say,—and he was a very bad living man,—'I know I am one of God's dear people.' 'So you are,'

I said, 'dear at any price, either to be given or to be thrown away.' He did not like my plain speaking, but it was true. We cannot be saved by or for our good works, neither can we be saved without good works. Christ never will save any of his people *in* their sins; he saves his people *from* their sins. If a man is not desiring to live a holy life in the sight of God, with the help of the Holy Spirit, he is still 'in the gall of bitterness, and in the bond of iniquity.'

I understand you have very little of that error of doctrine in Ireland, but I fear you have something of its practice. Alas, that it should be so anywhere! Believe me, whatever else you are right in, if you are wrong in your *practice*, you are wholly wrong. By your fruits we must judge of you. If you bring forth the sour grapes of Sodom, depend upon it you are a Sodomite. You are not of Eshcol if you bring not forth the fruits of Eshcol. The thing we want in these times is practical piety. I heard a man talking, the other day, about '*saving faith.*' He was living in sin, and I could not make out what he meant. When, however, the collection was taken, and I noticed him carefully put his finger-nail round a threepenny piece for fear lest it should be a fourpenny, then I understood what *he* meant by '*saving* faith.' But the idea of 'saving faith' apart from good works, is just ridiculous. Jesus Christ saves his people *from* not *in* their sins. The saved man is not a perfect man; but his heart's desire is to become perfect, he is always panting after perfection, and the day will come when he will be perfected, after the image of his once crucified and now glorified Saviour, in knowledge and true holiness.

V. Lastly, HE SHALL SAVE HIS PEOPLE FROM FALLING INTO SIN SO AS TO PERISH ETERNALLY.

Those who are saved by Jesus are so saved that they can never be lost. They who are the children of God, are the children of God for ever. They are eternally dear to the heart of the Father, and accepted through the well-beloved Son. I never can understand how a man can be a child of God one day and a child of the devil the next. This I do know that, whatever my children may do, so long as they are alive, they will have a right to call me father, and I believe it will be utterly impossible for them by any means whatever to lose the rights of childhood. So, let a man be a child of God, and he is, he shall be, and he must be, everlastingly, a child of God, and an heir of the heavenly inheritance. Is God less loving than an earthly parent? I believe that God has more love in his heart than the fondest mothers have for their children; *they may forget,* but God will never forget his children. They shall be kept by his power through faith unto salvation. They shall hold on their way through flood or flame; they shall still be led through life; and they shall be safely guided through the iron gates of death; and at last they shall sing a loud triumphant song of hallelujah unto him who hath loved them, and who hath borne them safely home. Jesus Christ does not half save his people, he saves them from their sins wholly, completely, entirely. They shall never perish, neither shall anyone pluck them out of their Saviour's hands.

Now, my hearers, having described the salvation of Jesus, I have to urge you to lay hold on him, who is the sinner's only hope and refuge. Jesus Christ alone is the Saviour of his people from their sins. He alone can save. Am I this day addressing one man, or one woman, who is conscious of the weight of great guilt? Art thou saying, 'I am too guilty to be forgiven, I have gone too far astray ever to find mercy'? Come, I beseech thee, and hear words of comfort. Jesus Christ is able to save unto the uttermost all that come unto God by him. No sinner can be too great a sinner for the sovereign grace of God in Christ Jesus to save him. Christ Jesus is able to save the devil's castaways. There are people in the world that some persons would not touch with a pair of tongs, but Jesus Christ will take them to his heart. There are sinners so black, and so deep down in the kennel of sin, that one would scarcely look at them, yet Jesus Christ will stretch forth his hand, and draw them up out of the horrible pit, and make them his children here and throughout eternity. Can any one of you say,—

'I'm a poor sinner, and nothing at all,
But Jesus Christ is my all in all'?

There is the whole gospel in those two lines; you must first feel that you are a poor sinner, and nothing at all, and then you must believe and take Jesus Christ as your all, and in all. May God give you grace that you may first feel your impotence, your helplessness, your nothingness, and may he then, by his Spirit, help you to lay hold on Christ Jesus, who is the Way, the Truth, and the Life! Believe on our Lord and Saviour Jesus Christ, who is the fulness of every empty sinner, and the life of every dead soul. He will for ever blot out all thy sins, and say unto thee, 'Go, and sin no more.' His name is called Jesus, for he is THE SAVIOUR, and he saves his people from their sins.

Note

* This was the last of four sermons preached in Belfast in the weekdays between Sundays 15 and 22 August 1858, a sermon on the latter date being identified in the account given in C.H. Spurgeon's *Autobiography,* volume 2, pp. 339–340 and *The Early Years,* pp. 511–513.

Lessons from Mount Nebo*

An unpublished sermon by C. H. Spurgeon, delivered at New Park Street Chapel, Southwark, on a Lord's-day evening in 1855

FORWARDED BY PASTOR T. W. MEDHURST, CARDIFF

'And the LORD spake unto Moses that selfsame day, saying, Get thee up into this mountain Abarim, unto mount Nebo, which is in the land of Moab, that is over against Jericho; and behold the land of Canaan, which I give unto the children of Israel for a possession: and die in the mount whither thou goest up, and be gathered unto thy people.'—Deuteronomy 32:48–50.

THERE is no spot in the Holy Land that is not full of marvellous interest. There walked the feet of our Divine Redeemer; there the great events which preceded and succeeded the declaration of the gospel had their arena. In Jewish history, methinks, Mount Nebo must have been one of the most notable spots. It stood just as a boundary mountain between the people in the wilderness and the people settled in Canaan. It was when the children of Israel reached this mountain, and when their leader had climbed to its summit, and there died, that the people were permitted to enter into that goodly land which Jehovah had sworn should be their inheritance for ever.

To the Christian, also, mount Nebo is full of interest. He looks on Old Testament history in the light of the New Testament; he sees in all the types and shadows of the old law prefigurings of the gospel dispensation. In the deeds of olden times, he sees the pictures and prophecies of the great deeds of the New Covenant. Let us go then unto mount Nebo, and learn there certain gospel lessons.

I. WE LEARN FROM MOUNT NEBO THE WEAKNESS OF THE LAW. Moses had to 'die in the mount.'

When we see mount Sinai, we see the law magnified; for Sinai is covered in smoke, and bounds are set round about the mountain of the Lord, and from the summit thereof he thunders in awful majesty. We go away with the loftiest notions concerning the law, and we are overwhelmed with terror at the thought that God has declared it with his own lips. We descend into the plains, and there we see Moses, the representative of the law, with a face so calm, and yet so stern and just, that we are almost ready to fall down before him, feeling that, with his shining countenance, the place whereon he stands is holy ground.

We follow him in all his movements during the forty years in the wilderness, and we perceive that he acts with such wisdom and such power, that we are ready to say, 'If this be the law, and if Moses be its representative, what more can we desire?' There we view the hosts of Israel marching through the desert, with steady tramp, every tribe in its ordained place. We do not see the tribe of Judah occupying the place of the tribe of Reuben, nor the tribe of Dan usurping the position which belongs to Simeon. When the trumpets blow, the people march; when the pillar of cloud stops, the people pitch their tents. There is never a dispute as to situation. Here is the spot where such a tribe must make its encampment, and there is the spot marked out for another. Everything is in order; and whether on the march or encamped, they are always prepared for the attacks of the enemy, should he fall upon them. These men were raw, undisciplined people, who came out of Egypt without having been trained as soldiers; and, as they had suffered under a despotism, they were all the more likely to rebel. How marvellous, then, that Moses should have been able to bring such a nation into a condition of order! Again we are ready to exclaim, 'What better leader do we want than Moses, who can thus transform a race of slaves into an orderly army of mighty warriors? What more do we want? Is not Moses sufficient, and more than sufficient? You tell us of the gospel; but what want we with that? Is not the law sufficient for all purposes? Does it not accomplish all that could be desired?'

So says *the Moralist,* 'See how orderly law and morality can make a people! Without law, they had become a race of wild beasts, without order, without system, beyond control; but give them law, teach them meekly to obey, and how orderly they act, with what strict propriety they live!' In like fashion talk *the Puseyite and the Ritualist,* 'See how regularly our people go to church; mark how attentive they are to all the rubrics! Don't they all contribute a piece of holly at Christmas, to decorate their church? See how ready they are to turn toward the East! Mark how they all bow at the name of Jesus! Do not the boys of the church school touch their hats to the squire and parson? Do not all the girls curtsey when they see the clergyman? What more do you want? Is not the law sufficient? *Preach morality;* teach the rules and ceremonies of *the church,* then the nation will become all you can desire!' The truth is, when we look at these things, we are apt to say, 'Yes, yes, certainly it all appears very well from your standpoint!' Just as, when we see Moses ordering the people, and leading them through the wilderness, we think, 'Ah! it is all so excellent.' *The Secularist* next comes up, and he says, 'Sir, it is all very well for you to tell your people not to steal, not to commit adultery, and not to swear; all these things are proper, and necessary for keeping them in order while they are here in this world; go on teaching the law, and you shall have our respect. We will give you an article in *The Reasoner,* and publish your portrait as being a first-rate secular minister, because you so eloquently preach the things which will benefit man while travelling through the wilderness. *We* do not care about the gospel, neither do we require it; we are in this world at present, and *we want something which suits us in this world.* We do not want to be told about the world to come; this world is enough for us.' So still, you see, it comes to this in the end, Moses is after all quite enough for many people. There is no need for Joshua, or for Jesus, in the view of the *moralist,* the *legalist,* the *ceremonialist,* and the *secularist.*

Now come with me unto mount Nebo, and there you will see that *the law is not sufficient.* Ah, Moses! thou couldst right well lead the children of Israel through the wilderness, thou couldst form this undisciplined host into a regular army, thou couldst control them, thou couldst do all this as a prophet of the Most High God; no one was equal to thee as a king in Jeshurun; but now, Moses, thou failest; thou has led the people to the brink of Jordan, but thou canst lead them no further. Moses, thou must 'die in the mount whither thou goest up, and be gathered unto thy people.'

Without a Joshua, what is now to be done to lead the people through the floods of Jordan to the inheritance on the further shore?

Thus we learn the doctrine that, while law and true morality may have a tendency to keep men in order, and to enable them to go through the wilderness, and, sometimes, with some degree of holiness and comfort to themselves, yet there is another land beyond the flood, and the law fails to lead men thither. On the ground of law alone, no man can see the face of God and live; no man can approach him who 'is a consuming fire.' Moses may lead Israel to the borders of the wilderness; the law may conduct us to the very verge of Jordan; yea, the law may bring us so near, by carnal security, that we may even dream of being admitted within the gates of Heaven. We may, confiding in our observance of the law, become so calm in our conscience, that we may imagine ourselves to be as pure as God's holy angels. An unconverted man may, even on his death-bed, look forward to eternal bliss; but, alas! he is looking forward in delusion, he is expecting that which can never be accomplished. Moses cannot, anyhow, conduct any sinner into Heaven; he cannot, by any means, lead the sinner into the Promised Land of Canaan above. Ye, who are seeking to obtain Heaven by your obedience, learn that your obedience will not serve you when you come to die. In the next world, it will not be our obedience, but the obedience of Christ Jesus, that will avail us; it will not be our doing, or our believing, our living, or our suffering; it will be Christ's living and Christ's suffering which must serve our turn in eternity. Our good works may go as far as the edge of Jordan, but on mount Nebo they must die; and there, our boasted morality will be but as the baseless fabric of a vision, which swiftly fades away. Rely, therefore, no longer on Moses; but seek Jesus. He will be your Leader into the Land of Promise.

II. ON MOUNT NEBO, A DEATH-BLOW WAS GIVEN TO SUPERSTITION. There Moses died, and the Lord buried him; 'but no man knoweth of his sepulchre unto this day.'

The Romanist, you know, tries to keep the bones of his 'saints.' He puts them in various places where they may prove attractive, and there he exhibits them for the admiration of the deluded and misled multitude, professing to believe that by these bones of the saints there can be wrought cures and miracles. On the spot where a reputed saint is buried, they set up a high altar, and perform masses, and to such places pilgrims resort. They say, 'Should not the place where this good man died be honoured? Should not his bones be held in reverence? May not good be done by such things? Did they not take unto the sick handkerchiefs or aprons from the body of Paul, and were not miracles wrought by them? (Acts 19:12.) And is it not likely that by the bones of the saints good may be done?'

The answer to this is, that on mount Nebo there died a man who had never an equal among the human race (See *Metropolitan Tabernacle Pulpit,* No. 1,966, 'The Death of Moses,' also *The Sword and the Trowel,* February, 1893, pages 50–54). Except the Lord Jesus, there was never a man of woman born equal in all respects to Moses. If there be a character which approximates very nearly to our idea of perfection, it is that of Moses. It is well-nigh impossible to detect any lack of virtue, or any deficiency in the character of Moses. He was remarkable for his meekness; but he was quite as remarkable for his justice, his humility, his self-denial, his desire to give up everything, 'esteeming the reproach of Christ greater riches than the treasures in Egypt' (Hebrews 11:26). There was never another mere man to whom Moses could be counted second; was it then not natural that, when he died, a costly tomb should be erected to his memory? Was it not natural that *his bones* should be preserved? 'Joseph, when he died, gave commandment concerning his bones' (Hebrews 11:22). Why not, then, preserve the bones of Moses? Why not carry them into the promised land? What potency there would have been in those bones to drive out the Canaanites! With the bones of Moses in the midst of the army, woe unto the Philistines! In seasons of drought, would not the bones of Moses have brought down rain from Heaven? Might not his bones have restored hearing to the deaf, and sight to the blind? But the Lord did not leave such a temptation in the way of a superstitious and fickle race like Israel of old. He did not permit them to reverence the dead body of Moses, he did not even allow them to know where Moses was buried. They could not worship his body, for the Lord God himself buried him in a secret sepulchre in a valley in the land of Moab.

This was a death-blow to superstition. Israel of old were a superstitious people. The brazen serpent, which Moses lifted up in the wilderness, that the serpent-bitten might look upon it, and be healed, was, in the days of

Hezekiah, used for the purposes of superstitious worship. 'The children of Israel did burn incense to it;' therefore Hezekiah, in righteous indignation, called it 'Nehushtan'—a piece of brass, and brake it in pieces, in his zeal for the Jehovah of hosts (2 Kings 18:4). Thus this 'precious relic' was destroyed, because by means of it the children of Israel lapsed into idolatry. If the Spirit of Truth were ever to enter into the Church of Rome, what a bonfire would be made of all her relics! The 'old cast clouts and old rotten rags' and broken bones would all be brought out, and burned in the streets, as the Ephesians 'brought their books together, and burned them before all men' (Acts 19:19). Happy for Rome, and happy for the world at large, the dawning of the day when her superstitions—worse than the superstitions of Greece and Egypt,—shall be destroyed, and she shall turn unto the Lord, if ever that day shall dawn! We fear such a day will not dawn; and if it come not, we know that assuredly God has threatened Rome that he will cast her into the flood of his wrath, and sink her and all her allies like a millstone, to rise no more for ever. Let the summit of mount Nebo, therefore, teach us this truth, that our God will not have us pay superstitious reverence to departed men. He himself buried Moses, and placed his dead body out of the reach of those who would seek it to do it reverence.

III. From mount Nebo learn another important lesson. Moses had led the children of Israel through the wilderness; and, though he himself was not to dwell in the promised land, it was his privilege to see it from the mountain of Nebo, from the top of Pisgah, and to rejoice in it, though he himself had to die without entering therein. Our lesson, then, shall be this: WE, WHO SERVE THE LORD, ARE HELPING IN OUR HUMBLE MEASURE TO LEAD THE PEOPLE OF GOD THROUGH THE WILDERNESS.

There is a promised land, there is a better age, and it is drawing nigh. A thousand promises are bringing it upon their wings. Bright with glory, the promises are all ready for their fulfilment; even now, the sun that is to lighten every land has begun to tinge the horizon with its grey dawn, and you and I have been hoping, and are hoping still, that we may live to see the dawn of the millennium, when Jesus shall stand in the latter days upon the earth, in the midst of his waiting people. It is sometimes our fond hope that our ears may hear—

Chapter 14

'The song of Jubilee,
      Loud as mighty thunders roar,
Or the fulness of the sea,
      When it breaks upon the shore.'

We have perhaps flattered ourselves that, ere these eyes are sealed in the darkness of the tomb, they shall see the King in his glory, our Redeemer in person standing upon this earth. This has sometimes been our day-dream. We have thought this, and more than this; we have thought that, before our hairs are whitened with age, before our frame has lost its strength, before it yields itself to death, we shall see the happy halcyon days wherein the gospel shall prevail, wherein the sound of war shall be silenced, wherein the outpouring of floods of blood shall be stayed; when every idol shall be cast down from its throne, and Rome shall be hurled from her seven hills, and Mahomet's crescent shall no more cast its baleful light across the nations. Beloved, we may never see these glorious times; on our tombs the epitaph may be written, '*These all, having obtained a good report through faith, received not the promise. These all died in faith, not having received the promises.*' Well, if we may not live to enter into that land of promise, if we must die before the Lord comes to reign triumphantly from the river to the ends of the earth, let it be our consolation that we can—

'Climb where Moses stood,
And view the landscape o'er.'

Even now, I stand by faith a preacher of the Word in troublous times, when sin and wickedness overflow the land; and, by faith, I look through the centuries which may roll away before those happy days shall arrive, yet I see in vision the days when the Son of man shall reign upon this earth, when the helmet shall hang idly in the hall, and the spear shall no longer be used for the purposes of destruction. I see the earth ploughed with the sword with which man once slew his fellow-man, and the vine pruned with the lance which was once imbrued with blood. I see the whole earth become one glorious temple of the living God, and upon the very bells of the horses is written, 'Holiness unto the Lord.' I see all nations, like kindred drops, melting into the one common sea of humanity. I see monarchs and their thrones dashed to pieces as a potter's vessel. I see the stone, 'cut out without hands,' become a great mountain, filling the whole earth with joy and happiness, such as no time has ever seen, except that happy time before man disobeyed his Maker. I see a new Heaven and a new earth wherein dwelleth righteousness. Hark! I hear the universal anthem. The dwellers in the rocks and the inhabitants of the vales shout to each other in joyous songs. I hear every kindred and every tribe unite, and there breathes not a human being who does not use his lips for song, there beats not a heart that is not full of gratitude, there gleams not an eye that is not brightened with joy because the Lord God Omnipotent reigneth. 'Hallelujah!' Let the word echo round the earth and the main. Children of God, often think of these glorious times. Chant the lay of the future; do not always lament the past, or denounce the present. Sometimes anoint your eyes with eye-salve, and look into the future, and anticipate its triumphs; and, meanwhile, buckle on your harness, grasp your sword with a tighter grip than ever, and afresh go forth to do battle with sin and with iniquity, remembering that the battle is the Lord's, and that the issue of the fight will be eternal victory for the great Captain of our salvation.

IV. From mount Nebo learn yet another lesson. IF WE ARE THE CHILDREN OF GOD, WE MAY EXPECT, EVEN WHILE ON EARTH, TO HAVE VIEWS OF HEAVEN.

Moses, ere he died in the mount whither he had gone up, beheld the land of Canaan, which Jehovah had promised to 'give unto the children of Israel for a possession.' So, even here, we sometimes have views of Heaven; but specially may we have such views when we are hard by the narrow stream of death. Dying Christians, when the solemn hour approaches, frequently have, on a sudden, a great stillness come over them, like the quiet of the Sabbath eve in some far-off dell where the hum of cities can never reach. You look at the dying saint, and you mark something about him that is unearthly, and you eagerly listen, for he begins to talk in a different style from that in which he has ever spoken before. 'Hark!' he exclaims, 'did you not hear that?' 'No,' you answer, 'I heard nothing; what was it?' The dying Christian says, 'I thought I heard music, sweeter than any I had ever listened to before; what can it be?' And then he exclaims, 'Oh, yes; yonder they are, there! There! There they are!' You ask, 'What are they?' He replies, 'I know not; they seem as though they were the angels of God come to convoy me to Heaven.' Does the departing believer really see those bright beings? Or, is he dreaming, is he delirious, is his mind wandering? No, he is still in his clear and natural senses, and in their full possession, too. Hearken again, for he speaks once more, 'Yes, I see it! Oh, glory, how bright thou art; how sweet thou art! I am dying! I feel that I am dying; yet it seems not like dying, I am just beginning to live. Heaven is coming down to me. I am going up to Heaven.' I might repeat many more of the sayings that have been thus uttered by God's children; they are something more than uninspired. I feel quite certain that many of those who die in the Lord have seen Heaven before they have reached its golden gates. They have heard Heaven's melodies. They have almost, even while here, joined in the Heavenly worship. It seems as if the Lord does sometimes take away the veil which hides from us the unseen. Just as the spirit stands on the verge of eternity, sunlight has streamed into the eyes of the dying saints; they have climbed to the top of mount Nebo, and they have seen the Heavenly landscape spread out before them.

Let us at times go, and take a view of the Promised Land. Come, Christian brother, you and I must die; there is the stream of Jordan, and we must pass through it; what have we to hope for on the other side of the flood? When we were singing just now, I took notice of one of our brethren in the Lord, a member of this church, whom I know to be very poor; and he was singing,—

'On Jordan's stormy banks I stand,
    And cast a wistful eye
To Canaan's fair and happy land,
    Where my possessions lie.'

I was thinking to myself, how very strange it seems and yet how marvellously true, from that poor man's lips! He is singing about his 'possessions', though he never had a rood of ground in his life that he could call his own; and at this moment he has not a solitary piece of gold belonging to him; his purse is empty, yet he sings of his possessions,—

'Canaan's fair and happy land,
  Where my possessions lie.'

Yet it was no rhapsody; it was concerning a great truth our poor brother sang. If we are believers on the Lord Jesus Christ, beyond the narrow stream of death there lie our possessions. Mark their length and breadth; canst thou tell the length and breadth of that Heaven which consists in the Saviour manifesting himself to thee without a veil between? Canst thou dream of the bliss of that land, the blessedness of which consists in communion with the Father, with the Son, and with the Holy Spirit? Canst thou conceive of the innumerable company of angels thou wilt see welcoming thee, when thou sittest in the general assembly and Church of the first-born, whose names are written in Heaven? It only needs that one dying gasp to put thee with the noble army of martyrs, with the glorious band of conquerors. Look on the other side of the narrow stream of death, and see thy Saviour throned in light. There, by his side, is an empty throne *waiting for thee*. There is the crown already fashioned ready to fit *thy* head. There is the white robe made ready to array *thee*. See you not some there who will be glad to welcome you to that blessed land? Mothers, there are your departed children; widows, there are your lamented husbands, waiting to again clasp your hand; children, there are your venerable parents who have gone before you. Oh! what happy meetings with those who have gone before us, when we shall thus see them again, and they will receive us into their arms with an eternal embrace! Yes, we shall see them, for they are not lost, but only gone before us a little while. On Nebo's mount, even now we seem to be within hail of them; even now we can imagine them replying to our signals.

'E'en now by faith we join our hands
  With those who went before;
And greet the blood-besprinkled bands
  On the eternal shore.'

But it is not only your friends and relations whom you will see in Heaven; there are others, those great ones who were so much admired when here on earth. You have read the marvellous story of *The Pilgrim's Progress;* there, you shall see the glorious dreamer himself, dear John Bunyan. There, you shall see Milton, who on earth praised his God in soul-transporting periods. There, you shall see those great ones who carried light into the darkness,—the grand Reformers of a wicked age. Martin Luther, John Calvin, Philip Melancthon, and Ulrich Zwingli, shall greet you on that eternal shore. Soon we shall meet with those we have loved, with those who founded our church, with those who preached in our pulpits, with those who knelt by our bedsides in the hour of sickness, and who have themselves ascended to our Father and their Father, to our God and their God.

If, by faith, you can go one step further, you will remember that, if you stand on mount Nebo's summit, the sweetest view you will have will be *to see yourself there!* There is a way of giving one's self a double life. I know that I am here; but it is easy for me, even now, to transport myself to Heaven in imagination,—nay, not merely in imagination; but, as it were, to foretaste its enjoyments in the conception that I am there. Christian, can you see yourself in Heaven? Can you see yourself made rich beyond all dreams of wealth? Canst thou conceive upon thy head a crown which doth outshine the stars, a golden harp in thy hand, sandals of light on thy feet, and a body which glistens like the sun,—not poor flesh and blood like this,—but akin to cherubim and seraphim, and such mighty spirits as surround the throne of Immanuel? Canst thou not even now see thyself in the bosom of thy Saviour? Canst thou not hear thyself saluted by his glad welcome, 'Enter thou into the joy of thy Lord'? Canst thou not see thyself sitting down with angels, and feasting with the spirits of just men made perfect? If thou canst, thou hast such a heart's ease that thou mayest return to thy house, and to thy business; and losses, and crosses, and sorrows, and griefs innumerable may befall thee, but these shall all appear lighter than feathers: for now thou canst say, as thou couldst never have said before thou hadst this glorious vision, 'I have a building of God, a house not made with hands, eternal in the heavens. I know that, when this earthly house of my tabernacle shall be dissolved, I shall dwell with God in a city which hath foundations, whose Builder and Maker is God.'

Now may the Lord be pleased to give repentance to all those that fear him not! Such a sermon as this seems as if it would not be of much use to sinners; but I think the old Puritan was not far from being right when he said, 'When you talk about such sweet things, they set poor sinners' mouths watering after them.' May it be so with you just at this moment! I close with that passage of sacred Scripture which the Holy Spirit has so often employed as a glorious key to unlock the doubts of seeking souls: 'This is a faithful saying, and worthy of all acceptation, that Christ Jesus came into the world to save sinners.' If now you desire to escape from hell, to be saved from your sins, and to go to Heaven, 'Believe on the Lord Jesus Christ, and thou shalt be saved.' The Lord help thee to believe on Jesus by his Holy Spirit! Believe, and be saved. Amen.

Note

* 'Is it not most appropriate that this sermon by Mr Spurgeon should appear in "his own Magazine" for the first time, and that without any human plan or design, on the anniversary of the month in which *he* also ascended into the mount Nebo? The beatific vision he so graphically described in the year 1855, may he not really have been seeing it during the ever-memorable month of January, 1892,—the month at the close of which he was privileged to enter into the Promised Land, and to join in the anthem sung by the heavenly choristers, "Blessing, and honour, and glory, and power, be unto him that sitteth upon the throne, and unto the Lamb for ever and ever"? When, dear reader, shall *we* be among them?—T. W. M.' Published in *The Sword and the Trowel*, January 1896.

An eternal distinction*

An unpublished sermon by C. H. Spurgeon, delivered 40 years ago [early 1856?], at New Park Street Chapel, Southwark

FORWARDED BY PASTOR T. W. MEDHURST, CARDIFF

'And these shall go away into everlasting punishment: but the righteous into life eternal.'—Matthew 25:46.

THESE solemn words I read as an introduction to my subject, which is, the eternal distinction between the righteous and unrighteous. From the beginning, there has been the seed of the woman and the seed of the serpent; and here at the end, we have the sheep and the goats, the blessed of the Father and the cursed; those who 'go away into everlasting punishment,' and those who 'go away into life eternal.'

Men who study the human race with regard to the physical conformation of the body, divide mankind into several distinct classes. Though they can clearly perceive that all men have sprung from one parentage, yet they divide them into various families, according to differences in the colour of their skin, in the conformation of their head, and of other members of the body. Spiritual men divide the human race into *only two classes*. Though they know that all have sprung from one pair, yet they hold and teach that there are now on the face of the earth two families as distinct and separate from one another as night from day. Not only do they say there are two such families now, but they affirm that it is a doctrine of Holy Scripture that these two families have always existed ever since Adam sinned and was driven forth from the garden of Eden. There are two streams, the one black and filthy, and the other clear as crystal, which flowed side by side from the beginning of time. You find an Abel offering an acceptable sacrifice, and in the same field with him a fierce and murderous Cain. You hear of Enoch, who 'walked with God,' and of

Lamech, who gave himself over to wickedness. You read of the population of the earth being reduced to eight persons, who were saved in the ark, and in that ark there was not only a holy Noah, but his impious son, Ham. As the world increased, there was Abraham in his tent worshipping God, and commanding his household to walk in the fear of the Most High, while Sodom and the cities of the plain revelled in the most filthy lusts. In the days of Moses, Israel, the people of God, were enslaved in Egypt, and there were the Egyptians worshipping their gods of wood and of stone, bowing down to the works of their own hands. Israel marched forth into the wilderness, and was there the Assembly of Jehovah. There were those who brought an evil report of the land, there were multitudes who believed not and who died in the wilderness; there were also Moses and Aaron, Joshua and Caleb, who, selected from the rest of the people, represented the Lord's specially chosen ones. When Israel settled in the Promised Land, there were those who walked after the lusts of their own eyes, and there were a few found faithful to their God. Passing on in history, you find a Saul and a David, a Solomon and a Jeroboam, a Hezekiah and an Omri. So, right on, we see two distinct classes. In the midst of abounding iniquity in Babylon, there are Daniel, Shadrach, Meshach, and Abed-nego. You have also Mordecai sitting in the gate of the king, and the wicked Haman plotting against his life. The people of God ever stand out distinct from those who indulge in worldliness and rebellion against the Lord. It was so in the time of Christ, it has been so ever since, and it will be so until the Son of man shall come in his glory.

No period of the world's history has been so black as to be destitute of one or two stars; and no period has been so bright as to be wholly without clouds. The two have always stood together, the ebony representatives of the dominion of sin, and the snow-white sons of Zion, made white, because washed in the blood of the Lamb. Turn to any country you choose into which Christian truth has penetrated, and you will find these two families never mixing together, always distinct, as if made by two different persons; as distinct as if one was the offspring of hell, and the other the offspring of God,—the righteous and the unrighteous. It is so today; it is so with the people who are at this present moment gathered together in this building. If our lives could be written, and our stories could be told, it would be sufficiently manifest that, though there may be little distinction between us as to our dress, manners, customs, and country, yet our hearts and desires are wide as the poles asunder, even though we are gathered together here to worship God. There are two men and two women sitting together in the same pew, and one of each shall be taken, and the others left. You look the same, sing the same, and attend the same, yet the two families are as unmixed now as they were when the sons of men first met to praise the Lord, and the sons of hell first assembled to dance in lasciviousness. Universal history shows that God has made a broad distinction between them that fear him and them that fear him not.

Yet, if you ask me, '*Has God made a uniform distinction between the righteous and the wicked in the outward dealings of his providence?*' or, 'Has God always shielded his people from all ill of every kind?' or, 'Has God always followed the wicked with the streams of his wrath?'—to these questions I must answer, '*Certainly not!*' If pestilence stalks through the land, it lays low the reverent head of the hoary saint as well as the head of the veteran rebel. If battle rages, the city noted for prayer may as easily fall a prey to fire and sword as the city which has become filthy as the cities of the plain. If an earthquake comes, it makes no distinction between the houses of saints and sinners. When a flood deluges the land, it covers the broad acres of the children of God as well as those of their ungodly neighbours. Not only so, but it seems sometimes as though God acted more favourably towards the wicked than towards the righteous. It was David who said, 'I have seen the wicked in great power, and spreading himself like a green bay tree.' 'I saw the prosperity of the wicked. For there are no bands in their death: but their strength is firm. They are not in trouble as other men; neither are they plagued like other men; … their eyes stand out with fatness: they have more than heart could wish.' 'But as for me, my feet were almost gone; my steps had well nigh slipped. For I was envious at the foolish, when I saw the prosperity of the wicked.' The righteous appear sometimes like the heath of the desert, or like a tree cut down, and seemingly dead, while the wicked man towers aloft, like the soaring poplar, and glories in the pomp of his wealth, and in the grandeur of his power. This has caused many a good man to murmur, 'Verily I have cleansed my heart in vain, and washed my hands in innocency. For all the day long have I been plagued, and chastened every morning.' The Christian, in the bitterness of his soul, says, 'Surely this cannot be just, for God is causing the wicked to prosper while he has cast his own people down to the earth! Lazarus has his sores licked by the dogs, though his prayers have been heard in Heaven; while the rich man is clothed in purple and fine linen, and fares sumptuously every day, though the wrath of God has gone out against him, and the bread which is in his mouth is cursed by the Almighty!'

God does not usually make any distinction between the righteous and the unrighteous in the arrangements of his providence in this world. A man's health or wealth is no indication of the favour of God, and a man's poverty or sickness is no sign of God's displeasure. He may be extremely poor, yet very godly; or he may be very rich, yet extremely wicked. Our outward circumstances are but little affected by, or indicative of, the state of our hearts toward God. In the providence of God there is no difference: 'for he maketh his sun to rise on the evil and on the good, and sendeth rain on the just and on the unjust.' The dew distilled alike on Mount Zion and on Mount Gilboa. In these respects, God has made no distinctions; but has put the righteous with the wicked, and the wicked with the righteous.

In other solemn and vital respects, *God has made an eternal distinction between the righteous and the wicked.* My text declares that this distinction will be eternal in its continuance: 'And these shall go away into everlasting punishment: but the righteous into life eternal.' The punishment of the unrighteous, and the life of the righteous, will be both alike eternal; so says the Lord Jesus Christ himself.

First, *God has made an eternal distinction between the righteous and the wicked from before the foundation of the world.* Men may deride eternal things, they may imagine they would be well content if they could share this world's good, and pawn any great advantage which might accrue to them from any difference made in eternity. They are like the profane Esau, who preferred a mess of pottage to the birthright. They know not that eternal things are the gold, and that earthly things are but the dross. God often gives the most of the dross to the wicked, because they are not his children; but he gives to his children 'durable riches and righteousness.' He says, 'I lead in the way of righteousness, in the midst of the paths of judgment: that I may cause those that love me to inherit substance; and I will fill their treasures.' He gives his children the Bread of Heaven, and the Water of Life; these are the choice gifts which he denies to others.

God has made an eternal distinction between the righteous and the wicked in his Book of Life. There, the name of every saint stands recorded. Appended to each name is the solemn covenant, the certain and unconditional promise: 'To this man will I look, even to him that is poor and of a contrite spirit, and trembleth at my Word.' 'And they shall be mine, saith the Lord of hosts, in that day when I make up my jewels.' As for the ungodly, in the Book of Life their names have no place. God has passed them over in his election. They live and die without faith, they pass out of the world without repentance. It is thus that the wicked give a sure proof that, when the Lord chose his own people, he left them, and passed them by, suffering them to go on in their own evil ways; and, at the last, they will bring on their own heads, by their own sins and transgressions, the merited eternal punishment which will be their portion. O sinners, you may despise the Christian; but he knows that he possesses an eternal treasure that is worth more than a thousand mines of your perishing gold! The believer's name is 'written in the Lamb's Book of Life;' he was chosen of God before the foundation of the world; his name from eternity was engraved on the breastplate of Jesus. The wicked may laugh now at the righteous, but the righteous know that the day will surely come when it will be their turn to pity the wicked, because they have chosen the dross and dung of this passing world, while the righteous, being graciously directed by the sovereign love of God, have chosen the things which will last throughout eternity.

Next, *God has made a marked distinction between believers and unbelievers in the two ordinances of his Church.* There are but two ordinances,—sometimes falsely called 'sacraments'—and these two ordinances are BAPTISM AND THE LORD'S SUPPER. Neither of them has been made for unbelievers; but the Lord has made both of them for his people, and for his people only. The ordinance of Baptism is for believers, and believers only: '*He that believeth and is baptized shall be saved.*' As for the Lord's Supper, he has spread his table for his own children, and for his own children only. He has fenced and guarded it with solemn threatenings, warning anyone from going to that table who cannot truly and reverently eat of the body and drink of the blood of Christ; not in a literal and carnal manner, but in a spiritual sense. Listen to this terrible Scripture: 'Whosoever shall eat this bread, and drink this cup of the Lord, unworthily, shall be guilty of the body and blood of the Lord. But let a man examine himself, and so let him eat of that bread, and drink of that cup. For he that eateth and drinketh unworthily, eateth and drinketh damnation' (or 'condemnation') 'to himself, not discerning the Lord's body.' Come, either to what ye call 'Holy baptism' or to Christ's communion table, ye who know him not, and angels are there with their swords drawn to defend the sacred stream, and to guard the holy table from such intruders. But come, thou trembling child of God, and none shall say thee, 'Nay.' 'Come in, thou blessed of the Lord; wherefore standest thou without?' 'See, here is water; what doth hinder' *thee* 'to be baptized?' 'If thou believest with all thine heart, thou mayest.' Canst thou say, 'I believe with the heart that Jesus Christ is the Son of God, and I rely upon him alone for salvation'? If thou canst, there is nothing on earth or in heaven to hinder thee from being baptized, and coming to his table. Jesus says to all his people, 'Eat, O friends; drink, yea, drink abundantly, O beloved.' But, O ye that believe not in Jesus Christ, and fear not God, cherubic wings are spread against you, and the solemn ban of God is on you, if you dare draw near to the ordinance of Baptism, or touch the sacred elements on the Lord's table. If you belong to Christ, you may draw nigh; you may come, and eat, drink, and be satisfied; for the Saviour gives you hearty welcome to his Church. He himself invites you, and bids you come. Thus has God, in his ordinances, made a difference by threatening those who touch holy things with unholy hands, while he opens wide the gates of entrance to his own people whom he has bidden to observe them.

Then, *God has made a distinction in favour of his children in respect of the precious privileges which he has laid up for them.* The very fact that God has admitted them into his family by adoption, and has made them his children, fills them with wonder and admiration. God calls us his children, and makes us his heirs. 'If children, then heirs; heirs of God, and joint-heirs with Christ.' If the sinner, living in his sins, pretends to be a child of God, the destroying angel will unsheath his sword, and thunder forth threatenings against him; but when the believer prays, 'Our Father, which art in Heaven,' he is not going beyond his right, for all believers can say, 'Thou, O God, art our Father, though Abraham be ignorant of us, and though Sarah acknowledge us not. We know we have been adopted into thy family, for the Holy Spirit himself beareth witness with our spirits that we have been born from above, and he breathes into our souls a sense of God's paternal love.' God saves his people from all their sins. He has removed far from them all their guilt, and has clothed them with the righteousness of Christ. Being justified by faith, they have peace with God through the Lord Jesus Christ. This is not the portion of the wicked; God says that they have no peace. Conscience is at peace with the righteous, because conscience has been pacified with the blood of Christ; and, instead of threatening him, conscience now smiles upon him. Christ's blood has been applied to him, and his sin has been cleansed away. Conscience says, 'It is well!' and so the believer has peace,—a peace which passes all understanding, a peace to which the wicked cannot attain. The heir of Heaven may lay his hand on all the precious things of the eternal covenant; he may claim personal election, effectual calling, redemption, justification, sanctification, as his very own. He can turn over the pages of the Book of Grace, and say, 'All things written herein are mine; the gifts of God, the purchase of my Saviour's blood.' But if the wicked man shall do this, the flaming sword of divine justice will turn every way against him, to protect the Tree of Life from his unholy touch.

Further, *God has made a distinction between the righteous and the wicked in respect of the dealings of his providence.* 'Now,' says Mr Critic, 'he is going to contradict himself.' Ah! I dare say. I should not be very sorry to do that if it were only to set *you* talking; for it is a fine thing sometimes to see how fast your tongue runs. Now then, sharpen your pencil, and write it all down, for you will then see that I am not contradicting myself. God does make a difference in his providence, not in its outward manifestation, but secretly and really. Outwardly, the saint and the sinner may be just alike; but they are not so inwardly. When the Christian's house is burned down, there is a blessing with it; but when the sinner's house is burned down, there is a curse with it. When ungodly men suffer pain, to them it is a part of the curse; but when the righteous suffer, to them there is no curse, for

Christ has borne away all their curse. The sorrows of the worldling are like the wasp, which can only sting, while the sufferings of the Christian are like the bee, which gathers honey everywhere, and sometimes from apparently the most unlikely flowers. There is nothing of the curse in the calamities which fall upon the righteous. He can say with Habakkuk, 'Although the fig tree shall not blossom, neither shall fruit be in the vines; the labour of the olive shall fail, and the fields shall yield no meat; the flock shall be cut off from the fold, and there shall be no herd in the stalls; yet I will rejoice in the Lord, I will joy in the God of my salvation. The Lord God is my strength.' If the harvest fail, if the cattle are diseased, if business be stagnant, if the ships rot in the docks, the song of the believer is still, 'I know that my Redeemer liveth!' If Christ has redeemed us from the curse of the law, if he has been made a curse for us, then there can be no curse in our trials and afflictions. But, to the wicked, their troubles are punishments for their sins; they come upon them, not from the hand of the Father, but from the hand of the Judge. Sinner, when God smites you now, he smites you with the back of his sword, not yet with its edge; but *you shall feel that in hell,* unless you repent! When God smites the believer, it is with the rod with which he chastiseth his children, whom he tenderly loves even while he smites. Then, a thousand afflictions may come upon the righteous, but there is no curse with them; the godly taste not one drop of the gall and wormwood of Jehovah's wrath. The afflictions of the wicked are different; they have an edge, a sharpness, about which the suffering believer knows nothing: 'The curse of the Lord is in the house of the wicked: but he blesseth the habitation of the just.' Hence, worldly men despair when they lose anything; they are sometimes ready to curse God and die if they are bereaved of their children. The believer is enabled by grace to bow his head, and exclaim, 'The Lord gave, and the Lord hath taken away: blessed be the name of the Lord.' The righteous man feels that there is no anger in bereavement; he does not turn against his God as though he were dealing harshly with him; but he kisses the rod even as it falls upon him. So that thus, in the dealings of his providence, God makes a distinction between the righteous and the wicked.

These distinctions are, however, small as compared with the distinctions which shall be made. *The great distinction between the righteous and the wicked is yet to come.* There will be a distinction in the last hour, when we come to die. At times, as the wicked man dies, his eyes are half opened; and as he looks across the black stream of death, he sees nothing to invite him on the other side. He starts back! He fears to die! There have been cases in which wicked men have seemed as though they saw frightful sights, and heard horrible sounds, before they actually departed from the body. The death-beds of some wicked men have been so frightful that even their nurses have been terrified. Many infidel death-beds have been marked by fearful scenes. Simpson, in his *Plea for Religion,* has collected accounts of a number of such scenes. We cannot read of the deaths of such men as Tom Paine, of D'Alembert, of Voltaire, and of many others, without seeing how fearful it has been for such men to come before the Maker whose existence they have denied. The wail of sorrow has been unapproachable and unparalleled. As for the pains of a woman in travail, they are as nothing compared with the pangs of the wicked in the grip of death. How different with the righteous! Said good Mr Haliburton, when on his death-bed, 'Here I lie, racked with pain,—weak, but yet strong. In a few moments I shall know more of the glories of God than any of you. Farewell!' 'Oh!' said godly John Hyatt, 'I am resting on the Rock; and if I had a thousand souls, I could commit them into the hand of Christ.' Someone told John Rees of the reward awaiting him after death. He said, 'My reward? I'll tell you what I'll do with it; I'll lay it at the Redeemer's feet,—

"And crown him Lord of all."'

John Owen just finished the last sheets of his book on *The Glory of Christ,* and said, 'Ah! put them away; I shall write no more. I am now about to see the glory of Christ for myself!'

But this is only the threshold of the eternal world. It is not always so that the righteous die rejoicing, and that the wicked die in agony. We have heard of the Roman emperor who died dressed up, as if he should say, 'Have I not played my part well?' Ordinary sinners have died peacefully, and hypocrites have departed with a text of Scripture in their mouth, and a hymn upon their tongue; while many a child of God has fallen asleep in the dark without any sign of joy. The real distinction will be, 'When the Son of man shall come in his glory, and all the holy angels with him, then shall he sit upon the throne of his glory: and before him shall be gathered all nations: and he shall separate them one from another.' Then shall the righteous be welcomed into the kingdom prepared for them from the foundation of the world; and then shall the wicked hear the dreadful sentence, 'Depart from me, ye cursed, into everlasting fire, prepared for the devil and his angels.' Now hearken to my text again: '*And these shall go away into everlasting punishment: but the righteous into life eternal.*'

Oh, that these lips had language to describe THE ETERNAL DISTINCTION BETWEEN THE RIGHTEOUS AND THE WICKED! See, they are gathered together, they are standing in the vast plain, the great white throne is set, and on it is seated the Judge! The righteous and the wicked stand together, they have started from their common graves, from the same rock-hewn tombs, from the same cemeteries, from the same battlefields, from the same oceans. They stand together before the throne of God; and now the books are opened, now the eternal distinction is declared. Israel, despised and rejected of men, followers of the meek and lowly Jesus, the man of sorrows; believers who have been men of sorrows themselves, persecuted, afflicted, tormented, men and women of whom the world was not worthy,—now, Zion, has come thy bridal day! Now, Jerusalem, unto thee has come the day wherein thou shalt put on thy glorious apparel, and shalt stand forth confessed a queen; no more degraded, and despised, and smitten, as thou wast by them that kept the vineyards when thou camest forth seeking for fruit for him who was thy Lord. Now, indeed, O Church, O bride of Christ, thou shalt be known! There is silence in Heaven. The pulse of Time is still. The very light which shoots so dimly from the sun seems as if its wings were more downy than before. And now the trumpet waxes loud and long, and every heart that is not ready for the great reward quails with terror.

Now the dividing-time has come, and the King says to those on his right hand, 'Come, ye blessed of my Father.' Now see how the vast multitude is divided. The father is on the right hand, and his family is on the left. The godly daughter is separated from her terror-stricken mother. Those who despised the Saviour of their parents are now exposed to the anger of the

God whom they rejected. The righteous have all ascended to God, and have taken their seats around the throne, and now, instead of one Judge, there are ten thousand times ten thousand sitting by his side, judging with him as co-apparitors with the King of kings. Now the book is opened,— *the book of the condemned,*—the book on which blood was never sprinkled; and oh! what tongue shall describe the weeping, and wailing, and gnashing of teeth? If the cries of St Bartholomew, the shrieks of St Cecilia, and the vespers on the dreadful battle-field, could mingle in one doleful *miserere,* yet it could never reach such an awful depth of horrible wailing as then shall issue from the lips of the lost! It must have been a fearful shriek that pierced the sky when the watery walls gave way, and overwhelmed both Pharoah and his host in the Red Sea: but not such a shriek as shall be heard when the walls of the universe give way, and fall upon all those who have despised their Creator, and rejected the Saviour who shall then be their Judge! I know not how to picture the dreadful scene, to portray the fearful terror, or to describe that terrible shriek. Then shall be heard the great cry throughout the hosts of the wicked, such as there has been none like it, nor shall be like it any more for ever.

And now, my hearers, where will you be in that dread day? Will you sing with the righteous, or shriek with the wicked? Shall the perpetual song of the redeemed, or the howlings of the damned be yours? Alas! many of you well know,—for your conscience tells you it is so,—that if, tonight, your souls were required of you, your account would be doleful. Ah, young man, thou hast begun to swear! Ah, old man, thou hast been a blasphemer these many years! Young woman, thou hast heard the gospel scores of times, but all to no profit! Many of you are as far from God as ever, after many faithful warnings and honest rebukes. Remember the wrath to come! the wrath to come! the wrath to come! Oh, my God, when I think of what eternity is; when I turn over in my mind that dreadful fact, that some among us, that perhaps many of us, yea, that all who die without repentance and faith, must be eternally accursed, I shudder! It is enough to make one's blood like ice within the veins. For ever, for ever, for ever lost! Launched on a sea of fire, without knowing where to steer, and drifting on in one undeviating track for ever and for ever! Doomed to climb, perpetually, the topless steeps of a mountain which has no summit, and that mountain, a mountain of woe and misery. You poor, impenitent sinner, will have to climb that mountain for ever, and for ever, and for ever! Suppose a great mountain, and suppose a little bird should come to that mountain once every million of millions of years, and take away one grain of earth at a time, till the whole were removed; after all these millions of millions of years, eternity would be no more finished than when the process had just begun. Go on till thought and imagination fail, and conception is at a loss, on, and on, and on; but the goal is just as distant, the end is not one whit nearer than when you started.

Oh! believe on the Lord Jesus Christ, all ye who know yourselves to be lost without him. Cast yourselves upon him, for he has said, '*Him that cometh to me, I will in no wise cast out.*' 'Seek ye the Lord while he may be found, call ye upon him while he is near. Let the wicked forsake his way, and the unrighteous man his thoughts: and let him return unto the Lord, and he will have mercy upon him; and to our God, for he will abundantly pardon.'

'Ye sinners, seek his grace,
    Whose wrath ye cannot bear;
Fly to the shelter of his cross,
    And find salvation there.

'So shall that curse remove,
    By which the Saviour bled;
And the last awful day shall pour
    His blessings on your head.'

May God, in his infinite mercy, grant it, for Christ's sake! Amen.

Note

* Published in *The Sword and the Trowel,* March 1896

Chapter 16

Jesus Christ—'The Breaker'

A sermon by C. H. Spurgeon, delivered at Queen's Square Chapel, Brighton, on Wednesday evening, 23 April 1856

FORWARDED BY PASTOR T. W. MEDHURST, CARDIFF

'The Breaker is come up before them: they have broken up, and have passed through the gate, and are gone out by it: and their king shall pass before them, and the LORD on the head of them.'— Micah 2:13.

GOD'S people have wandered hither and thither, some on the mountains of pride, some into the deep glens of despair, some into the green and poisonous pastures of self-righteousness, others to the arid and burning sands of licentiousness and dissipation. One of the most difficult things in the world for man to do would be to collect the scattered sheep of God into one fold; indeed, it would be altogether impossible for mortal might to accomplish so wondrous a miracle; but God has promised that he will gather all his people together, wheresoever they may have strayed. The verse immediately preceding our text has this sure and comforting promise: 'I will surely assemble, O Jacob, all of thee; I will surely gather the remnant of Israel; I will put them together as the sheep of Bozrah, as the flock in the midst of their fold: they shall make great noise by reason of the multitude of men.' No matter how far they may have wandered, how extensive may have been their ramblings, how great may have been their errors, they shall, nevertheless, by sovereign grace be reclaimed. 'For the Son of man is come to seek and to save that which is lost,' and he will 'leave the ninety and nine in the wilderness, and go after that which is lost, until he find it.' There is not one of the Lord's wandering sheep, however far it may have strayed, but shall ultimately be carried upon the shoulders of the Good Shepherd right into glory,—

'While Heaven's resounding mansions ring
    With shouts of sovereign grace,'

because Christ has rescued it from the lion and the bear that threatened to devour it.

But, if one thing be even more difficult than gathering the sheep together, it is leading them all the way from their pastures here, to their glorious fold in Heaven. When we consider what obstacles there are in the way of the Lord's flock,—a constant, persevering, indefatigable enemy ever striving to destroy them, that roaring lion that 'goeth about, seeking whom he may devour,' mountains piled upon mountains, and rivers that are not to be forded, but must be crossed, ere the sheep can enter within the promised rest,—we may indeed exclaim with wonder, 'Who is sufficient for these things? Who shall lead the ransomed flock of God into the blessed fold of Heaven? Who shall be the Great Shepherd who shall conduct the Lord's sheep into the dwelling-place of the redeemed?'

The answer to our questions is seen in our text. There may be obstacles, there *are* obstacles; but here, flock of God, is your solace and comfort: 'The Breaker is come up before them: they have broken up, and have passed through the gate, and are gone out by it: and their king shall pass before them, and the Lord on the head of them.' He marches in front of his sheep, the Good Shepherd clearing the way; the Pioneer of the heavenly army; the Breaker, breaking through every difficulty; the king, overcoming all foes.

If the Lord shall enable us, this evening, we shall discourse a little, first, on *the title of our Saviour as 'the Breaker'*: '*The Breaker is come up before them.*' Then, after we have done that, we shall put the enquiry to ourselves, *Are we among the number who 'have broken up, and have passed through the gate, and are gone out by it'? Has our King gone before us? Is the Lord at the head of us?*

I. We will first consider THE TITLE OF JESUS CHRIST—'THE BREAKER.' He who hath many crowns, hath many titles. Jesus, the King of kings, hath many names, each of them fraught with meaning, and full of sweetness. Perhaps the title which we least seldom notice is that which occurs in our text. We have dwelt full frequently upon Christ the LAMB; we have noticed, oftentimes, Christ the PRIEST; we have referred again and again to Christ the PROPHET, and to Christ the KING; but seldom have we spoken of Christ the BREAKER. So come now, dear friends, and let me speak to you of the title of our Lord and Saviour Jesus Christ which is mentioned in our text, that is, the Breaker.

First, Christ is the Breaker, for *he broke the power of Satan*. In years long gone by, the arch-enemy of God rebelled, and thenceforward became the arch-enemy of man. He coiled himself, like a huge serpent, around this world, intent to crush it; he held the entire human race beneath his sway, and there seemed to be no hope of deliverance. By-and-by, a promise shone out like a new star in the dark firmament, gleaming with this cheering message: 'I will put enmity between thee and the woman, and between thy seed and her seed; it shall bruise thy head, and thou shalt bruise his heel' (Gen. 3:15). Centuries rolled away, and then that Seed of the woman appeared, an infant of a span long; and it was not long before he commenced his combat with the enemy. He had two great battles, at the beginning and the end of an awful struggle which was protracted through his entire life.

In the wilderness, Christ fought the arch-enemy; foot to foot they stood, and long and hard they wrestled. Thrice did the foeman try to throw the Saviour to the ground; but thrice he repulsed him, crying, 'It is written;'—'It is written again;'—'For it is written.' It was a stern fight; but, at last, the Almighty Breaker became the Victor: 'then the devil leaveth him, and, behold, angels came and ministered unto him.'

Oh, what a conflict was that which our Saviour had with Satan in the garden, and on the cross! What a wrestling it was amongst the olive-trees of Gethsemane! There, the Lion of the tribe of Judah and the lion of the bottomless pit fought for their lives. There, the seed of the serpent and the Seed of the woman struggled together. There, Satan grasped the Saviour, and so tightly did he press him, that his body was covered with a sweat that 'was as it were great drops of blood falling down to the ground.' Ah, certainly, that was a desperate tug! Christ then felt full well, even through his armour of proof, the pressure of his adversary's grasp. Satan held him until, almost overcome, he cried, 'O my Father, if it be possible, let this cup pass from me: nevertheless, not as I will, but as thou wilt.' Satan thus bruised the heel of Christ; and then, later, he smote him yet again and again; on his head, for a crown of thorns was there; he smote him on his cheeks, shame and sorrow gushed adown them; on his shoulders, for the cruel lash of tyrants scourged him; and at last Satan yelled, 'Aha! aha! Thou Prince of life and glory, I have thee now; my Foeman, thou art nailed to the cross! Where now is the vaunted power of him who was to crush to powder the iron limbs of death? Where is the strength of him who was to overcome his foes? I have thee now, O Christ, I have achieved the victory over thee!'

Just then, the Saviour bowed his head, and with a loud voice cried, 'IT IS FINISHED!' He sprang from the cross, and, though the astonished fiend sought to find shelter in the pit, Christ, the Omnipotent Breaker, pursued the arch-fiend down to hell, shouting, 'Traitor to God and man, this my bolt shall find and pierce thee through; though thou descendest to the remotest caverns of hell, my shaft shall reach and slay thee there!' The Sovereign Breaker sought and found Satan, lashed him to his chariot wheels, dragged him near the gates of Heaven; the angels gathered on the battlements to behold the wondrous sight of him who had led captivity captive, and to listen to him as he cried, 'Come, angelic hosts, stand round and see how I have triumphed over my mighty foe.' Then, seizing the old dragon, he exposed him to their view, and hurled him down to the pit,— defeated, crestfallen, with all his hopes crushed, there to lie, weltering in fell despair for ever! Christ broke the power of Satan in that glorious day when he entered Paradise in triumph, and received gifts for men.

What, then? My brethren, we are often vexed by the power of the enemy, and at times we are exceedingly afraid lest we should fall by his hands. O believer, fear not, thine enemy is a broken enemy, a conquered foe!

'Though hell and sin obstruct thy course,
Yet hell and sin are vanquished foes;
Thy Saviour nailed them to his cross,
And sang the triumph when he rose.'

Satan! why should I fear him? He may have a sword, but the edge of it is blunted; he may shoot his arrows, but the points of his barbed shafts have been taken from them by the Saviour; he cannot hurt us, he may worry, but he cannot devour. Pilgrim, art thou afraid to come by the den of lions? Fear thou not, their power is broken. Art thou fearful of the den of leopards? Fear thou not, their teeth are drawn. Tremble not, O Christian! thou shalt overcome because thy Saviour overcame; the day shall yet dawn wherein thou shalt put thy foot upon the neck of Satan, trample on him, and tread him beneath thy feet, and thou shalt be made more than conqueror through him that loved thee. The Mighty Breaker is gone up before thee, so thou hast only to fight against a foe who is already overcome.

In the second place, *Christ is the Breaker of hearts*. What hard things hearts are! They are compared to the nether-millstone, which is the harder of the two, because it is subject to the greater pressure. Such is the heart of man; how often have we tried to charm it into softness! But, alas, how unavailing have been our endeavours! The minister has preached the thunderings of the law, he has launched the lightning of Jehovah from the pulpit! The sinner has trembled for a moment, and has wept; but, oh! wonder of wonders, he has wiped the tears away ere even he has left the sacred edifice, and he has not trembled to rush into fresh sins within an hour after he has rejoined his companions. Law and terrors did but harden him, for they were working all alone.

Another time, the preacher selected for his theme that which was gentle, and soft, and affecting, for he said, 'Surely, the story of a Saviour's woe will melt them; surely, the proclamation of free grace must win their souls.' He preached, till his eyes were filled with tears, and his heart was moved with tenderness; he talked of a bleeding Saviour, and pointed to that Saviour's wounds; he preached of the love of Jesus to Mary Magdalene and Saul of Tarsus; and lo, the sinner wept again even as he had wept before! It was wonderful how much he wept, but it was far more wonderful how soon his tears were dried up; like the morning cloud and the early dew, they quickly vanished.

Dost thou not remember, my brother, how oft thy friends tried to break thy hard heart? There was thy loving mother shedding tears over thee as she talked of the Saviour's grace; thy father's warnings came to thee, but thou wast unmoved. Thou didst put away all the tears of thy mother, and all the entreaties of thy father. Ministers pleaded with thee, yet thy heart would not yield; but oh! canst thou remember, brother, that sweet hour when Jesus came to thee, and said,—

'Say, poor sinner, lov'st thou me?'

Canst thou remember when thou couldst not help answering, and saying, 'Nay, Lord, I feel I do not love thee'? Dost thou not remember when Jesus said, 'Sinner, thou art in awful peril,' when he made thee feel that thou wast in dire danger, and when he caused the scalding tears of repentance to flow down, like a river, from both thy streaming eyes? Dost thou remember, brother, how he showed thee his hands and his feet, how he bared his side, and said, 'See here; I opened this my side, I opened this my heart to pour forth a fountain of precious blood to wash away all thy sin'? Ah! it was not hard for thee to weep then; the Breaker of hearts had come. He had only to touch our souls, and they melted; then our rocky hearts dissolved, as snow upon the lower mountains when the sun shineth upon them; our hearts began to melt when Jesus did his love display.

How often since that glad hour, when our hearts have again become hardened, when Christ has come once more, have we set him in the midst, and said, 'Lord Jesus, we will be thine; thou shalt be ours; we give ourselves to thee!' Oh! sweet thought, minister of the gospel, thou dost not have to break hearts, for 'the Breaker is come up before them.' I love to come into the pulpit with a full and certain faith that this is the case. There are some, in every congregation we address, to whom the Word will come with power. Many may laugh at the preacher, and scorn God's truth; but of some, at least, it shall be said, 'The Breaker is come up before them.' When we speak in our Master's name, the seed falls on good, broken soil. When we utter his message, each word tells, each syllable has its power, because the Breaker is gone up before us. It is not for us to go first; we want the Breaker to go *before us,* then all our work in breaking hearts shall be easy work.

I have often compared a congregation to a heap of ashes piled up; somewhere in the heap there are hidden some steel filings. We bring the magnet, it attracts the steel filings, but it leaves the ashes. So, there are some in the midst of this congregation who are being attracted out of the ungodly mass; they are drawn, and then they run after Christ. But who is it that makes the heart ready to hear the Word? It is 'the Breaker.' Sweet name, and it becomes him well. My hearer, hast thou ever felt Christ to be a Breaker to thy soul? Has he ever melted thy spirit? Didst thou ever feel broken in heart? Oh, bow down before the Lord! Let me tell thee, if thou art never broken in heart, thou shalt never enter Heaven. Thine heart must be ground small before thou wilt be received there. God pounds our hearts in the mortar of contrition, he grinds us in the mill of conviction, till we are broken all to pieces; hast thou been so broken? Canst thou bless thine Almighty Breaker that, though man could never break thine heart, though thou couldst not do it thyself, yet that Jesus alone, thy blessed Saviour, has proved himself the Breaker of thine heart?

In the third place, *Christ is the Breaker of the chains of Justice.* There sits within this audience a man in chains. He knows it not, he thinks himself to be free; but he is a prisoner, his hands, his feet, his entire being is in chains. Though he thinks he walks freely on the earth, he hath but the freedom of a condemned convict, who can only walk round and round his cell, and look through the solitary slit in the wall, by which the sunlight enters. So, some sit here 'condemned already,' not believing in Christ. Some of you are wearing invisible fetters; they are none the less mighty on that account. You are carrying manacles and chains about with you, and when you die, those fetters shall be riveted for ever, and ye yourselves shall be dragged to execution, like chained culprits forced to the gallows, to die, to be lost, to be punished with the just terrors of the justice of God. Some of us felt ourselves in slavery once, we had chains upon us like the rest of mankind; but, glory to sovereign mercy, now we are free, and we love Christ, the Breaker of our bonds!

Perhaps there is a friend here who was once bound hand and foot, and who tried to free himself from the chains that bound him; but the more he tried to do so, the more firmly did those chains hold him, and the more completely did he manacle himself by his own exertions. He went to that blacksmith, Mr Morality, and asked his leave to put his chains upon his anvil, that he might thus try to break them; but when he came away from making the trial, he found that he was more firmly fettered than before. Can you remember when you seemed to be chained all over, waiting only for the executioner to strike the last blow? Some passed by you, and laughed at your miserable condition, while your chains rattled in your ears their horrible mockery. Your friends tauntingly exclaimed, 'It is very easy to break off such little fetters as these;' but you knew those fetters were made of sterner stuff than to be broken by mortal might. In despair, you cried, 'I am chained; I am lost; I am condemned; I am going to perdition; that is my certain destiny.' But, oh, you will never forget that happy moment when Christ, the Breaker, passed by, and said to you, 'Poor sinner, thou art in chains.' Thou saidst, 'Lord, I know it.' 'Poor sinner, thou canst never get rid of those chains.' 'Lord, I know it.' '*Sinner, canst thou trust me?*' 'Lord, who art thou?' 'I am the Great Saviour, the Deliverer of captives: if thou wilt trust in me, I will break off thy chains for thee.' 'Lord, thou art very kind, but I have no faith.' 'I will give thee faith. *Sinner, wilt thou trust me?*' 'Ay, Lord, even to the world's end.' 'Well, then, I will take thy fetters from thee.' He touched thee; and, oh! in a moment, it was wondrously true; thy manacles fell to the earth, thy chains dropped on the ground, thou wert free, and thou didst leap for joy, and cried, 'I am free, free, free! I am forgiven! I am a miracle of mercy! I am a sinner saved by grace!'

Never did emancipated slave leap from his slavery with more ardour than we did when our Glorious Breaker set us free. Never did poor refugee tread with greater joy the free shore of England than did we when we found ourselves thus delivered from our sins. Never did poor galley-slave, released from his weary tugging at the oar, rejoice so much as we, when we saw our fetters broken, cast into the furnace, and we leaped up God's freed men. We could have sung all the day long; our heart was like a city lighted up for an illumination; our eyes overflowed with joyful tears; our feet, like roes, did leap the hills; our soul was the very concentration of song, while we rejoiced that Christ, the Heavenly Breaker, had given us glorious, perfect, entire, eternal liberty.

Bondslaves! BOND SLAVES! BOND SLAVES! Christ has bidden us sound the trump of jubilee, and proclaim the year of release. Art thou fettered by sin? There is One who can break thy fetters. Hast thou the iron chains of guilt upon thee? He, the Heavenly Breaker, like another Prometheus, has volunteered to remove thy guilt. He comes, he comes, the Breaker of chains! Look to him, and he shall free thee. Cast thine eyes up towards him, and he shall give thee freedom, he shall give thee liberty; though thou wast dead, yet shalt thou live; though thou art loaded with twice ten thousand chains, a prayer, a look, shall release thee from thy load.

'He is able,
He is willing: doubt no more.'

Oh, that my message might reach the ears of some poor convicted sinner! How I should rejoice that another was added to the list of Christ's freed men, and another struck off the list of Satan's bond slaves! Mighty Breaker! break the chains off this congregation; make, O make this people free!

In the fourth place, *Jesus Christ is the Breaker of all obstacles which impede us on our road to Heaven.* The first traveller through the pathless desert hath a rough road; those who follow him will find a smoother path. Christ was the Pioneer on the road to Heaven; he found it a wilderness, but the track is well-trodden now. 'The Breaker is come up before them.' If you have to pass over the bleak mountains, look closely, and you will find a footprint; look closer still, it is the footprint of a man; look again intently, lo! it is the print of a pierced foot, for your Saviour has passed that way before you.

'Why should I complain of want or distress,
Temptation or pain? He told me no less;
The heirs of salvation, I know from his Word,
Through much tribulation must *follow their Lord*.'

They could not 'follow their Lord' if he had not gone before them. What foolish people even many Christians are! There is an old proverb which says, 'Never cross a bridge before you come to it.' How many Christians are filled with sorrow on account of imaginary troubles! Many timid Christians have a trouble manufactory in their own houses; they sit from morning to night endeavouring to make trouble for themselves. We have quite enough real trials to bear; and if we make any more of our own, we have no promise that God will give us grace to bear our self-made sorrows.

How unwise are those people who crowd a whole year's troubles into a single day! The brave Spartan ranged his little troop in a narrow pass, Thermopylæ, and slew his enemies as they came up one or two at a time. If he had been foolish enough to have ventured into the plain to fight that mighty host of Persians all at once, he would soon have been overcome. Believer, stand in the narrow path of today; as thy troubles come, by divine grace slay them one by one; but, I beseech thee, never go into the broad plain of tomorrow, lest thou be overwhelmed by the vast hosts. Troubles usually come one or two at a time, and when they do come, it is for us to have at them, strong in the strength of Jehovah, and so to destroy them. If thou puttest together the troubles of a year, and seekest to bear them in a day, how canst thou expect to have grace sufficient? Thou didst ask this morning, 'Give us this day our daily bread;' dost thou want all at once a month's supply? Thou hast the promise: 'Thy shoes shall be iron and brass; and as thy days so shall thy strength be.' Dost thou expect a year's strength in a single day? Believe me, my fellow-Christian, thy cup of sorrow will be quite full enough without thine additions. Let this cheer thee wheresoever thou art going: 'The Breaker is come up before them: they have broken up, and have passed through the gate, and are gone out by it: and their king shall pass before them, and the Lord on the head of them.' Oh, methinks it is sweet to go anywhere where Christ has gone before! Pilgrims in the Holy Land delight in spots where they can find traces of the Saviour. Christians may find a Holy Land in all their experiences of sorrow, for their Saviour was 'a man of sorrows, and acquainted with grief.' Sorrowing Christian, in all those gloomy Gethsemanes of thine, thou dost hold fellowship with Jesus Christ thy Lord and Saviour! Cheer up, Christian! Take heart, man! Courage, O believer! 'The Breaker is come up before them,' 'and the Lord on the head of them.' Sing, then,—

'Through floods and flames, if Jesus lead,
    I'll follow where he goes;
"Hinder me not," shall be my cry,
    Though earth and hell oppose.'

In the fifth place, *Christ Jesus is the great Breaker of death*. When Jesus died, he was laid in the tomb. His enemies 'went, and made the sepulchre sure, sealing the stone, and setting a watch.' Outside Joseph's own new tomb, the Roman soldiers watched while the body of Jesus lay buried therein. Then the hope of immortality seemed to be crushed for ever. The Saviour is dead and buried, and the scorner, death, points with his finger to the empty cross whereon the Saviour died, and cries aloud, 'There is no hope of immortality now, for he who was to bring it is dead.' There lay the Saviour, sleeping the sleep of death. Sleep on, O Almighty Conqueror, for thou wilt yet arise to fight thine own battles! Behold, there is a great earthquake; the angel of the Lord descends from Heaven, he rolls back the sealed stone from the mouth of the sepulchre, out springs the Saviour, death's Victor, clothed in light, radiant with resurrection glory,—

'Death of deaths, and hell's destruction.'

Christ gained the victory over sin and Satan, he broke the power of death and the grave. 'Death is swallowed up in victory. O death, where is thy sting? O grave, where is thy victory?'

Now, beloved, what have we to do when we die? Nothing, but to meet the shadow. Death is vanquished. Christ slew death. He broke death's power. Christian, be not afraid of death, it is but a shadow; the shadow of a dog cannot bite, the shadow of a lion cannot rend in pieces, then fear not '*the shadow of death*.' I thought, some time since, if death be a shadow, there must be a light somewhere. Death is nothing but the shadow of the bright light of Heaven. We have but to go through the gloomy 'valley of the shadow of death'; on the other side there is a brilliancy which excelleth all the light we have ever imagined. We who believe in Jesus need not fear to die, for death is conquered. Christ Jesus has come up from the Jordan before all his redeemed ones. Methinks I see the Christian die. Christ comes to his side, and says, 'Come on, beloved, I will go with thee.' The believer puts his foot into the cold waters; he hears a second foot splash in the stream, and a voice saying, 'When thou passest through the waters, I will be with thee; and through the rivers, they shall not overflow thee.' 'What, Lord, art thou about to cross the stream with me?' 'Yes, my friend, did I not so promise? Fear not: for I have redeemed thee.' The believer takes another step, and another, and another, and he hears the Saviour still accompanying him through the waters; and as the billows dash upon him, still he hears his Lord's voice saying, 'Fear thou not, thou art mine, I am thy Saviour.' When the cold dark stream threatens to overwhelm him, he feels the arms of Jesus round his loins strengthening him, and lifting him up, and so he sings, 'My flesh and my heart faileth: but God is the strength of my heart, and my portion for ever.' He seems about to sink, but the Saviour bears him up, and whispers, 'Hold on, beloved!' Another step, another groan, another sigh, and then the spirit has gone;—gone! but not unattended, for Christ is still with him, and bears him up; and with attendant angels on each side, he flies upwards to Heaven, and the Saviour presents the ransomed spirit to his Father. *Blessed death!* once a curse, but now a blessing, for Christ, the glorious Breaker, hath broken the power of death.

In the sixth place, *Christ has broken down every obstacle that opposes his reign on earth.* 'He breaketh the bow, and cutteth the spear in sunder; he burneth the chariot in the fire.' Christ, the Breaker, is coming soon. I look for my Master's advent; I know not when he will come, but I should not be surprised to see the Lord Jesus Christ tonight or tomorrow morning. 'In such an hour as ye think not, the Son of man cometh.' To the world of the ungodly, like a thief in the night, unseen, the coming of the Lord stealeth through the earth's dark shade. Monarchs must then give up their sceptres, and kings resign their crowns, which shall be trampled in the dust, to make way for the coronation of the King of kings, and Lord of lords. Old Popery of the seven hills, we thank our God thy days are numbered; the Almighty Breaker is coming up against thee. Vain thy mitre and crosier, proud bishop, then! Thy lordly pretensions shall then be dashed in pieces; the Sovereign Breaker is coming up against thee. Thou false prophet, Mohammed, when he comes, thy crescent shall wane, and all the sabres shall be snatched from earth's mighty ones. Ye may arise, ye kings of the earth, and mighty rulers, and 'take counsel together against the Lord, and against his anointed;' but it shall be all in vain. He 'will overturn, overturn, overturn, until he come whose right it is,' and he will burn all the chariots in the fire. 'The Breaker is come up before them.' We shall not much longer preach without our Master; we shall not long have to mourn an absent Saviour; the clouds shall soon vanish, and reveal the golden wings of the descending Christ. All the earth shall see him come; even now the sound of his chariot-wheels may be heard in the distance. And when he comes, what a victory it will be! His troops will not march on to an uncertain fight, but to conquer, and to win the day. Now we wrestle hard, and fight a fearful conflict; but when he comes, there shall be heard the shout, 'Alleluia! Alleluia! Alleluia! Alleluia! for the Lord God Omnipotent reigneth.' But a little while, and he shall come. We are no prophets to foretell days or years; the Lord Jehovah hath said that it is not for us 'to know the times or the seasons.' But he cometh! He cometh! He cometh! Vain the pomp, the pageantry of war; vain the pride, the power of man; vain everything that sets itself against the King of kings; it shall fall as Jericho fell. No great mountain can stand before our Almighty Zerubbabel. He comes! He comes! 'The Breaker is come up before them: they have broken up and have passed through the gate, and are gone out by it: and their king shall pass before them, and the Lord on the head of them.'

'The Breaker broke the powers of hell,
    Did all its hosts o'erthrow,
Death, hell, and sin, the monster train,
    He openly did show.

'He dragged them to the judgment seat,
    Then cast them down to hell;
The power of his almighty arm
    His hellish foes did quell.

'The Breaker broke the barrier down,
    Which law and sin had made;
He did fulfil all righteousness,
    And full redemption paid.

'Through death he did destroy the grave,
    And made an end of sin;
Gave honour to the holy law,
    And righteousness brought in.

'We'll sing the Breaker's power to save,
  And triumph in his name;
Let all the powers within us join,
  To spread his matchless fame.'

II. Now briefly let us ask, ARE WE AMONG THE NUMBER WHO 'HAVE BROKEN UP, AND HAVE PASSED THROUGH THE GATE, AND ARE GONE OUT BY IT'? HAS OUR KING GONE BEFORE US? IS THE LORD AT THE HEAD OF US?

I wonder, dear friends, how many of us know anything about Jesus Christ, the Breaker? Has Christ ever broken your heart? One says, 'Pshaw! I do not want a broken heart.' It may be very well for you to say so while you are in life, but it will be another matter when you come to die. I have read a story to this effect. A traveller once lost his way in the woods, and seeing in the distance a light, he said, 'That is a cottage; I will go and rest there this evening.' Approaching nearer, he perceived a number of lights, and heard voices. 'Ah!' said he, 'perhaps that is a meeting of Christians, I will go and join them.' It was a solemn sight, and, in some degree, a singular one. They had cut down the trees in the forest, and laid them across for seats. The scene was illumined by several pine torches, which threw a lurid glare over some faces, but left others in darkness. He listened to the speaker; to his consternation, it was an atheist cursing his Maker, and daring him to do his worst against him. The good man was shocked, astonished, and thought he must stand forth to vindicate the honour of his Lord; but he trembled lest he should not prevail, and a good cause should suffer through the feebleness of its advocate. He need not have trembled; from one corner of the meeting there rose up a middle-aged man, strong and stalwart. Leaning on his staff, he said, 'Gentlemen,—I wish to say a word about the mighty orator who has just sat down. A few days ago, I walked by the side of a river, and saw a boat with one man in it. He did not understand the art of rowing, and his boat was being carried down to the rapids. I saw that man kneeling in his boat, and heard him cry, "O God, save me!" I heard him confess that he had once blasphemed God, and doubted his being; but now he cried, "O God, save my soul, if not my body!" I stood on the shore, and heard the shrieks of that poor wretch. I plunged into the waters; these strong arms rescued him, and brought him to the shore. ... The man who just now cursed his Maker is the self-same man who prayed to him in the boat. Judge ye what I say.' You may imagine the consternation of the listeners; they raised a shout of execration against the man who could pray to God one day, and blaspheme his name the next. Sinner, it is just so with thee. Thou mayest despise religion now; but when sick, a few nights ago, a shrill shriek of agony escaped thee; and if thou turnest not from the evil of thy ways, thou shalt ere long know that there is a God, and feel it, too. Thou shalt surely know that 'Tophet is ordained of old; yea, for the king it is prepared; he hath made it deep and large: the pile thereof is fire and much wood; the breath of the Lord, like a stream of brimstone, doth kindle it' (Isaiah 30:33). I trust there are none present who will ever know the meaning of these solemn words. May you, who are unconverted, now turn, and repent, and be saved! I trust there are many poor convinced sinners here who know themselves to be sinners, who feel they need a Saviour, and who are seeking him. Let them not fear that the Saviour will not accept them. If thou dost know thyself to be a sinner, there is no reason in the world why thou shouldst not know thyself to be a saint. All that is necessary is to feel thyself unholy and unclean, and, just as thou art, to trust in Jesus to save thee. We have seen men write on the flag-stones in London, '*I am destitute.*' We can never pass by such without in some degree relieving their necessities, although *we* may be unwise in doing so, having been so frequently imposed upon. But, sinner, if thou art *really* destitute, and art sitting by the wayside, begging that Jesus, the Son of David, may have mercy upon thee, as surely as thou art a living sinner today, thou shalt be a living saint soon. I care not what thy sins may be, the blood of Jesus Christ, God's Son, can cleanse thee from all sin. Faith in the atoning sacrifice of Jesus will save thee.

'Venture on him, venture wholly,
　　Let no other trust intrude;
　　　　None but Jesus
　　Can do helpless sinners good.'

If a helpless sinner wants to come to Christ, and asks, 'What must I do to be saved? What is it to believe?' here is the answer, 'Simply take Jesus

Christ at his word, and he has said, "Him that cometh unto me, I will in no wise cast out."'

Allow me to finish with an illustration. There is, in our National Gallery in London, a picture by Raphael of Moses lifting up the serpent in the wilderness. When you look at that picture, you fancy you hear Moses crying, 'Look, look, look!' In that picture there is one stout brawny man trying with all his might to pull off the serpents. They twist around him, coil on coil; with all his endeavours he cannot prevent their deadly poison from being instilled into his blood. He must die; his lips blacken, his eyes are sunken in their sockets. Another is seen, the serpents are twisting around him, and one eye is already swollen; but the other, in agony, is turned upward toward the brazen serpent; see, there is life coming back to him; for he has looked, and therefore he lives. One thing pleased me more than any other, a mother holding up her little child in her arms, and around that little child the serpents are twisting; for children are sinners, and need the Saviour as well as grown-up people. The child is so small it cannot itself turn to the serpent of brass, so its mother is holding up the little one, that it may look and live. This is the holiest office of a mother, to hold her child up so that it may look to Jesus. Sunday-school teachers should do the same; get their scholars to look to Jesus. In addressing sinners, tonight, I would that I could take them up in my arms, and, pointing them to Jesus Christ, cry, 'Poor sinner, look, look, look!' There is nothing to be *done* in salvation. 'It is finished.' 'Salvation is of the Lord.' It is only,—Look and live,—*looking* and *living,* because Jesus Christ has had all the *doing* and the *dying.* There are no great miracles to be performed, no wondrous impossibilities to be done. 'The Breaker is come up before them.' The act of the sinner is simply this, to look to the wonderful Breaker; and even that look of faith the Holy Spirit enables the sinner to take. Sinner, art thou bitten? Dost thou know that thou art a sinner? Look away from thyself, and look to Jesus.

'High on the cross the Saviour hung,
High in the heavens he reigns;
Here sinners, by the old serpent stung,
Look, and forget their pains.'

I shall never cease exhorting sinners to '*look*' for that word, '*look,*' was the means of my own salvation as I sat in a pew in a little obscure chapel, whither, driven by stress of weather, I listened to a minister whom I have never seen nor heard since. I know not what else besides he said, I was sad and weary on account of sin, but these words he uttered: 'Sinner, dying sinner, young man, *look*, LOOK, LOOK.' I looked; I cannot tell my joy, and I shall not try; but next to that joy will now be mine if some poor soul will 'look' to Christ tonight. Works will drive you from the Saviour, but the look of faith brings you to him. It does not matter how black you are, if from head to foot you are covered with serpent-bites, if you are as black as Satan himself, if you look to Christ, he will save you. If you are, in your own feelings, one of the cast-offs of hell, too bad for the devil; if even Satan himself has cast you away, you may yet look to Christ, and, looking, you shall surely be saved. Come, O come, now come to Jesus, sinner, come! God help you to come, poor sinner! He will, if you are such as he has called. May he add his blessing, for Jesus Christ's sake! Amen, and amen.

The death of Moses*

A short sermon, by C. H. Spurgeon, written more than 40 years ago [1857 or earlier]

'So Moses the servant of the LORD died there in the land of Moab, according to the word of the LORD.'—Deuteronomy 34:5.

O NE of the most fitting subjects for the contemplation of a living man is 'Death.' There is no subject more calculated to moderate our desires, or put our judgments in order, than the dread subject of *mortality*. But, alas! how seldom does it dwell upon our mind! How constantly do we shun the mere mention of it! The same feeling which prompts us to say, 'Bury the dead out of our sight,' leads us to lay the finger on the mouth of Death, and bid him be silent. How very few are our visits to the grave! The iron gates of the tomb grate too horribly upon their hinges to be pleasant to us; we seldom look within, save when they open wide, and some one of our friends is dragged within. Even then, we glance but briefly, and turn speedily to the things of time and sense.

Wherefore this unwillingness to meditate on death? Do we hope to escape, like the foolish ostrich, by shutting our eyes and covering our heads? Is it not wise to talk with Death, to walk with him in his gloomy gardens, to visit the secret places where the weary cease from troubles, and the great and small sleep on the same couch? Such a course would familiarize us with the skeleton monarch; and, as the well-trained war-horse fears not the fire, the smoke, or the rattling of the musketry, so should we, 'fearless of hell and ghastly death,' calmly await our doom.

With Christian men, aversion to the thought of death is most inconsistent with that hope of immortality which is our glory and our crown. We will now follow Moses to his grave; and I trust, however we may have feared death, we may exclaim, in a better sense than the poet Virgil intended, '*Facilis descensus Averni*' 'The way to death is easy; yea, made smooth by the comforts of the Saviour's grace.' 'Let us also go, that we may die with him,' said Thomas, when our Lord was going to his death; and so I say, 'Let us go and visit the leader of the tribes in the wilderness.' Let us consider,—

    I.   THE VETERAN.
    II.   THE ASCENT.
   III.   THE PROSPECT.
   IV.   THE DEATH.
   V.   THE BURIAL.
   VI.   THE ALLEGORY IN IT ALL.

I. Let us go to the camp of Israel, and see THE VETERAN LAW-GIVER.

It is a day of solemn assembly, the people are gathered, by their companies, listening to someone who, standing apart, is pouring out a strain of song. Who is he who speaks so eloquently? It is Moses,—once the stammerer,—who, like the swan, is singing his death-song. What a sight to have seen Moses at that moment! He was 120 years old, and what an eventful life his had been! Forty years he had spent in the palaces of the Pharaohs, and had learned all the secrets and wisdom of Egypt; forty years he had led a retired pastoral life amid the vast plains of Northern Arabia; and forty more he, by faith, had been treading the pathless wilderness.

Oh, what a history that man could unfold! He once lay a weeping infant in the ark of bulrushes, next he stood in regal halls, then as a persecuted man he fled to Midian. Providence conducts him to a well, where he has an interview with the daughters of Jethro, one of whom becomes his wife, and he himself becomes a shepherd. God secludes him, that he may ruminate on knowledge already acquired; but a change passes over the scene. The burning bush marks the boundary of his pastoral life, and now we find him back in the old palaces of Egypt, once his home. Here he works wonders, and afflicts the field of Zoan; his purpose is accomplished, but the curtain falls not. In that drama of a life there are other scenes; we see him, in the might of God, dividing with his rod the sea, and drowning therein the court and chivalry of Egypt. We see him prostrate in prayer, or braving the terrors of Sinai, or fasting forty days while, as one greatly-beloved, he talks with God.

A life more eventful cannot be conceived; and now there he stands, uttering the peroration of his life-long sermon, putting the seal to his finished testimony. Is he not venerable; is there not something to be revered in him? We cannot hope to live to the age of Moses, or to do all that he did; but his life says to us who are young, 'O youth, wouldest thou in thy latter days be honoured? Then, walk as Moses did, who chose the reproach of Christ rather than the treasures in Egypt.' And you, ye grave and venerable seniors, happy are ye if ye can look at Moses without a blush, or if, like him, ye can welcome death with song.

What is most remarkable in Moses is, that his eye did not wax dim, neither did his natural force abate. His eye, when he looked for the last time on the tents of Jacob, flashed with the same fire as when he saw the people dancing before the calf. His arm was as strong as when he smote the Egyptian, his foot as firm as when he put off his shoe at Horeb, and his mind as unimpaired as when he studied in the palaces of Memphis. The exposure in the wilderness, the cares of a nation, the murmurs of rebels, had not worn him out. He was an iron man, like the law which he promulgated, and his strength was equal to his day. We cannot hope thus to endure as to our bodies. Time will bleach our locks, care will plough its furrows on our brow, the grinding must sound faintly, and the lookers-out at these windows must be darkened. But, in another sense, we may hope to be like Moses. Our strength shall be renewed like the eagle's. Waiting on the Lord, we shall not faint, nor grow weary; and, even in age, we shall have in our hearts the greenness and vigour of youth.

We might say more upon this veteran, but we will not, save just this one thought. How few are spared to old age! Death mows the tender plants, and seldom allows them to ripen, far less to go into the sere and yellow leaf. O ye fathers, ye are the vanguard of our army! May God long spare you, but may he ever remind you of the deep responsibility which rests upon your spared heads!

II. THE ASCENT.
Moses now leaves the throng, and climbs the mountains of Abarim, up the sides of Nebo, on to its very peak, called Pisgah. He goes up there, and he goes there to die! He had climbed the quaking rocks of Sinai, to enter within the cloud-covered circle, and hear the voice of God. Now he climbs

for another purpose. The Lycurgus of Israel retires to die. We talk of going *down* to the grave; this man went *up* to his. And truly, if we judged rightly, we should not say a Christian goes down into the grave, but goes *up* to his tomb. Sweet thought! We shall ascend above the dusky world, and get into a clearer atmosphere ere we die. The house where a Christian dies is usually, as it were, built on a hill. He sees others weeping; but he cries, 'Weep not for me.' He sings, he claps his hands. The air is purer and balmier up yonder where he lies. His lowly bed is really a lofty divan where, like an honoured monarch, he reclines in peace. Perhaps Moses looked back with sorrow at leaving his people; but when he looked up to the top of the hill, he went on with joy, saying, like Abraham, 'Abide ye here, while I go and worship God yonder.'

We remark that Moses ascended this mountain alone. Aaron could climb Sinai with him, Joshua could ascend Horeb with him; but neither Aaron nor Joshua could climb Pisgah with him. Aaron and Hur held up the hands of Moses on the hill when Joshua fought with Amalek in the valley; but against the last enemy there is no mortal helper to stand with Moses. The old mountain-ranger leans on no human arm, he is alone. And, beloved, you and I must die alone. None can enter the gates of the grave with us. Death is a turnstile that admits but one at a time.

But then, Moses needed no one. He was a strong man; he could climb the steep rock, he could follow the track of the wild goat, or if necessary, like the chamois hunter, could leap from crag to crag. Had it not been so, the everlasting arms would have carried him up, or have cut steps in the hard granite that he might rise with ease to the appointed summit. O brethren, here is a precious word for you, when dying time is come! The message will not be, 'Go down into the vaults of death,' but, '*Get thee up into the top of Pisgah.*'

III. THE PROSPECT.

We know why Moses must die aloft, it is that he may have a vision of Canaan. All is still on the mountain top: he is too high to hear the din of the multitude below. He reclines upon a massive overhanging rock, and looks around. Not far off runs the stream of Jordan, and he sees the fields and hills beyond it; but the human eye cannot of itself see clearly things remote, and therefore his eyes are touched with Heavenly eyesalve, and now how wide the prospect! Nothing is obscure now. In the distance, he sees the mountains of Lebanon, not as an unformed and cloudy mass, but he can see the very cedars waving upon the mountain's side. Carmel, and the Great Sea at its foot, are present to him. Tabor, and Hermon, and Zion, and Bashan, he sees clearly. There are the vales of Eshcol, and there the softly-flowing waters of Siloa. From palm-treed Jericho to Naphtali, from Dan to Beersheba, all is visible to his eye.

Oh, how delighted must he be at the vision of the rivers of milk and honey! There is the consummation of his hopes,—the promised land of Canaan. Moses never had such a view before; and beloved, let me tell you that you too shall have the same view as Moses had. Death is the Christian's minaret, which he climbs at the fixed hour. Death is the Christian's observatory, whence he looks, with the glass of faith, far beyond Saturn's ringed orb, or the belted star of Jove, up to the boundless realms of light where his possessions lie. To enlarge on the scene were useless; where an angel might fail, let a mortal be silent. Eye hath not seen, nor ear heard as yet, the glories which on the mount of death shall be revealed to us.

IV. The Death.

But the prospect must fade away. Like every other scene on earth, even this is but a dissolving-view, and it must sweetly melt away into another. The green field must become a shining pavement, the Jordan must give place to the river of the water of life, and over all must rise the jasper light of the sapphire city. Moses dies, as the best must do. He dies;—none saw him, so that we cannot describe the scene. Did he with his last breath pray for Israel? We cannot answer. Did he mention the name of the Crucified when his quivering lip gave forth its last utterance? 'Tis all unknown. Ask the old rocks of Nebo, ask the wild winds which swept the mountain side, and chanted his funeral dirge. We know not, and we seek not to know; all we are told is that Moses died there 'according to the Word of the Lord.' And surely this is enough; or if not, we can know no more.

However, let us improve his death; let us preach a short funeral sermon upon him, though his body is, like the drowned mariner, unfound, a secret treasure hidden in the great unknown.

Moses' death, was, in part, *a chastisement. He* had sinned at Meribah. He called the people rebels; he spoke to them instead of to the rock, and smote the rock instead of speaking to it. He failed once, and he dies. He might have entered the promised land, or been carried to Heaven in a chariot of fire, but that one blot prevented. God had been dishonoured; and although the sin had been forgiven, chastisement must be inflicted. God never lays any penal vengeance at our door if we are his; but his paternal hand must strike for correction. Oh, the doubly-awful nature of sin! It kept the meekest man out of Canaan; let us therefore fear lest, through sin, we go halting all our days.

But we must notice *the mercy* mingled with it all. If Moses must die, he shall die sweetly. Some physicians coat their pills with silver, and God doth gild the bitter morsel of death with the glory to be revealed. The Jewish Rabbis affirm that the text teaches that God kissed away the soul of Moses; and, as nearly all the eminent commentators have thought this worthy of mention, I mention it as a very delightful idea.

Die he must, even though the marrow is moist in his bones, though his knees totter not, neither are his joints loosed. So must we die, even if we be as great as Cæsar, as rich as Crœsus, as wise as Solomon, as strong as Samson, or as meek as Moses. The oak of a thousand years' growth must, if it be not felled earlier, at last become a hollow mansion for owls, and in the end fall down to the earth a rotten ruin. And he who, like the patriarch Moses, has his eye undimmed, must one day sleep in death. But, Christian, God will make it as easy as possible to thee, as sweet as bitter can be, and as soft as nature changed by grace will allow.

V. The Burial.

Now the last struggle is over, the hallowed clay is forsaken by its once-active tenant. It remains to be buried; and, in order that the Jews might never worship the relics of Moses, God buried him. Whether he cleft the rock, and laid him in a natural sarcophagus; whether the flowers bloom over his head, or thunders date their birth from his place of emtombment, we know not, for he is hidden till the day shall declare it. Michael guards his dust from the demon who would unveil his secret. It may not be known.

What learn we here? We learn the vanity of the pomp and display which often accompany a funeral. It may be well that Nelson and Wellington should have their bodies drawn in gorgeous cars with all the wealthy of the nation as mourners; but 'vanity of vanities, all is vanity.' How much more solemn to be buried by the Almighty in secret and silence, than to be lowered into the vault with the Dead March in *Saul* and volleys from noisy guns! Christian, it is right to desire a burial and a tomb; but if thou hast none, dread it not. Thou wilt need no 'storied urn, or animated bust.' Thy God will find thee as well if thou shalt lie in the caves of ocean as if thou didst rest in an abbey. The neglected, overgrown corner of a churchyard will be as near the throne as the poets' corner or the monarch's mausoleum. Thou mayest love to think of a tombstone, and of the few sweet flowers which shall be on thy grave; but if thine humble resting-place be all unknown, then fear not, but trusting thy soul to thy Lord, have confidence that the several atoms of thy body shall be precious in his sight, and shall arise at his summons.

VI. We close our discourse with AN ALLEGORY.

Moses is the law, with eye undimmed by age, and unimpaired by years, able to see sin, and strong to punish it in the sinner.

Moses led the people to the edge of the wilderness, but not into Canaan; nor can the law ever land one poor sinner in Paradise.

Moses died, so is the law dead to every Christian. He died not of old age, but by the Word of God; so did the law die to us by the Word of Jehovah when he justified us. And, as Moses' body is buried, and cannot be found, even so is the damnatory power of the law buried by Christ, 'and if we search to find our sins, our sins can ne'er be found.'

Oh, that, like Moses, we may go Heavenward when we die; like him, enjoy a beatific vision; and, like him, close our eyes on earth to open them in the New Jerusalem for which our spirits pant!

O Lord, help *me!* Amen.

Note

* Published in *The Sword and the Trowel,* February 1897.

'Come, ye children'*

A sermon to Sunday-school teachers, delivered by C. H. Spurgeon, at the Temple, St Mary Cray, Kent, on Wednesday afternoon, 20 February 1856

FORWARDED BY PASTOR T. W. MEDHURST, CARDIFF

'Come, ye children, hearken unto me: I will teach you the fear of the LORD.'—Psalm 34:11.

IT is a singular thing that good men frequently discover their duty when they are placed in most humiliating positions. Never in David's life was he in a worse plight than that which suggested this Psalm. It is headed, 'A Psalm of David, when he changed his behaviour before Abimelech; who drove him away, and he departed.' This poem was intended to commemorate that event, and was suggested by it. David was carried before King Achish, the Abimelech of Philistia, and, in order to make his escape, he pretended to be mad, accompanying that profession of madness with certain very degrading actions which might well seem to betoken his insanity. He was driven from the palace, and, as usual, when such men are in the street, it is probable that a number of children assembled around him. You have the sad story told in 1 Samuel 21:10–15. In after days, when David sang songs of praise to Jehovah, recollecting how he had become the laughing-stock of little children, he seemed to say, 'Ah! by my folly before the children in the streets, I have lowered myself in the estimation of generations that shall live after me; now I will endeavour to undo the mischief,—"Come, ye children, hearken unto me: I will teach you the fear of the Lord."'

Very possibly, if David had never been in such a position, he would never have thought of this duty; for I do not discover that he ever said in any other Psalm, 'Come, *ye* children, hearken unto me.' He had the cares of his cities, his provinces, and his nation pressing upon him, and he may have been at other times but little attentive to the education of youth; but here, being brought into the meanest position which man could possibly occupy, having become as one bereft of reason, he recollects his duty. The exalted or prosperous Christian is not always mindful of 'the lambs.' That duty generally devolves on Peters, whose pride and confidence have been crushed, and who rejoice thus practically to answer their Lord's question, as the apostle did when Jesus said to him, 'Lovest thou me?'

Departing, however, from this thought, let me address myself to the text: 'Come, ye children, hearken unto me: I will teach you the fear of the Lord.' First, I shall give you *One Doctrine;* secondly, I shall give you *Two Encouragements;* thirdly, I shall give you *Three Admonitions;* fourthly, I shall give you *Four Instructions;* and fifthly, I shall give you *Five Subjects for Children,* all taken from the text and context.

I. First, I will give you ONE DOCTRINE. 'Come, ye children, hearken unto me: I will teach you the fear of the Lord.' The doctrine is, that *children are capable of being taught the fear of the Lord.*

Men are generally wisest after they have been most foolish. David had been extremely foolish, and now he became truly wise; and being so, it was not likely he would utter foolish sentiments, or give directions such as would be dictated by a weak mind. We have heard it said by some that children cannot understand the great mysteries of religion. We even know some Sunday-school teachers who cautiously avoid mentioning the great doctrines of the gospel, because they think the children are not prepared to receive them. Alas! the same mistake has crept into the pulpit; for it is currently believed, among a certain class of preachers, that many of the doctrines of the Word of God, although true, are not fit to be taught to the people, since they would pervert them to their own destruction. Away with such priestcraft! Whatever God has revealed ought to be preached. Whatever he has revealed, if I am not capable of understanding it, I will still believe and preach it. I do hold that there is no doctrine of the Word of God which a child, if he be capable of salvation, is not capable of receiving. I would have children taught all the great doctrines of truth without a solitary exception, that they may in their after days hold fast by them.

I can bear witness that children *can* understand the Scriptures; for I am sure that, when but a child, I could have discussed many a knotty point of controversial theology, having heard both sides of the question freely stated among my father's circle of friends. In fact, children are capable of understanding some things in early life, which we hardly understand afterwards. Children have eminently a simplicity of faith, and simplicity of faith is akin to the highest knowledge; indeed, we know not that there is much distinction between the simplicity of a child and the genius of the profoundest mind. He who receives things simply, as a child, will often have ideas which the man who is prone to make a syllogism of everything will never attain unto. If you wish to know whether children can be taught, I point you to many in our churches, and in pious families,—not prodigies, but such as we frequently see,—Timothys and Samuels, and little girls, too, who have early come to know a Saviour's love. As soon as a child is capable of being lost, it is capable of being saved. As soon as a child can sin, that child can, if God's grace assist it, believe and receive the Word of God. As soon as children can learn evil, be assured that they are competent, under the teaching of the Holy Spirit, to learn good. Never go to your class with the thought that the children cannot comprehend you; for if you do not make them understand, it is possibly because you do not yourselves understand; if you do not teach children what you wish them to learn, it may be because you are not fit for the task; you should find out simpler words, more fitted for their capacity, and then you would discover that it was not the fault of the child, but the fault of the teacher, if he did not learn. I hold that children are capable of salvation. He who, in Divine sovereignty, reclaimed the grey-haired sinner from the error of his ways, can turn a little child from his youthful follies. He who, in the eleventh hour, findeth some standing idle in the market-place, and sendeth them into the vineyard, can and does call men at the dawning of the day to labour for him. He who can change the course of a river when it has rolled onward, and become a mighty flood, can control a new-born rivulet leaping from its cradle-fountain, and make it run into the channel he desireth. He can do all things; he can work upon children's hearts as he pleases, for all are under his control.

I will not stay to establish the doctrine, because I do not consider that any of you are so foolish as to doubt it. But, although you believe it, I fear many of you do not expect to hear of children being saved. Throughout the churches, I have noticed a kind of abhorrence of anything like child piety. We are frightened at the idea of a little boy loving Christ; and if we hear of a little girl following the Saviour, we say it is a youthful fancy, an early impression that will die away. My dear friends, I beseech you, never treat child piety with suspicion. It is a tender plant; do not brush it too hard. I heard a tale, some time ago, which I believe to be perfectly authentic. A dear little girl, some five or six years old, a true lover of Jesus, requested of her mother that she might join the church. The mother told her she was too young, and the poor little thing was exceedingly grieved. After a while, the mother, who saw that piety was in her child's heart, spoke to the minister on the subject. The minister talked to the child, and said to the mother, 'I am thoroughly convinced of her piety, but I cannot take her into the church, she is too young.' When the child heard that, a strange gloom passed over her face; and the next morning, when the mother went to her little bed, she lay with a pearly tear on each eye, dead for very grief; her heart was broken, because she could not follow her Saviour, and do as he had bidden her. I would not have murdered that child for a world! Take care how you treat young piety. Be very tender in dealing with it. Believe that children can be saved just as much as yourselves. I do not believe in infant baptism, because the New Testament does not teach it; but I do most firmly believe in the salvation of children, and when the child believes in Jesus, I at once cheerfully baptize that child, and receive him into the full fellowship of the church. When you see the young heart brought to the Saviour, do not stand by and speak harshly, mistrusting everything. It is better sometimes to be deceived than to be the means of offending one of these little ones who believe in Jesus. God send to his people a firm belief that little buds of grace are worthy of all tender care!

II. Now, secondly, I will give you TWO ENCOURAGEMENTS, both of which you will find in the text.

The first encouragement is that of *pious example*. David said, 'Come, ye children, hearken unto me: I will teach you the fear of the Lord.' You are not ashamed to tread in the footsteps of David, are you? You will not object to follow the example of one who was first eminently holy, and then eminently great. Shall the shepherd boy, the giant-slayer, the sweet psalmist of Israel, and the mighty monarch, leave footprints in which you are too proud to tread? Ah, no! you will be happy, I am sure, to be as David was. If you want, however, a higher example even than that of David, hear the Son of David while from his lips flow the sweet words, 'Suffer the little children to come unto me, and forbid them not, for of such is the Kingdom of Heaven.' I am sure it would encourage you if you always thought of these examples. You who are teaching children, are not dishonoured by that occupation; some may say, 'You are only a Sunday-school teacher,' but you are a noble personage, holding an honourable office, and having illustrious predecessors. We love to see persons of some standing in society take an interest in Sabbath-schools. One great fault in many of our churches is that the children are left for the young people to take care of; the older members, who have more wisdom, taking but very little notice of them; and, very often, the wealthier members of the church stand aside as if the teaching of the poor were not (as indeed it is) the special business of the rich. I hope for the day when the mighty men of Israel shall be found helping in this great warfare against the enemy. In the United States we have heard of presidents, of judges, members of Congress, and persons in the highest positions, not condescending, for I scorn to use such a term, but honouring themselves by teaching little children in Sabbath-schools. He who teaches a class in a Sabbath-school has earned a good degree. I had rather receive the title of S.S.T. than M.A., B.A., or any other honour that ever was conferred by men. Let me beg you, then, to take heart, because your duties are so honourable. Let the royal example of David, let the Godlike example of Jesus Christ inspire you with fresh diligence and increasing ardour, with confident and enduring perseverance, still to go on in your blessed work, saying as David did, 'Come, ye children, hearken unto me: I will teach you the fear of the Lord.'

The second encouragement I will give you is, *the encouragement of great success*. David said, 'Come, ye children, hearken unto me:' he did not add, 'perhaps I will teach you the fear of the Lord,' but, 'I *will* teach you.' He had success; or, if he had not, others have. The success of Sabbath-schools! If I begin to talk of that, I shall have an endless theme; therefore, I will not commence. Many volumes might be written on it, and then when all were written, we might say, 'I suppose that even the world itself could not contain all that might be written.' Up yonder, where the starry hosts perpetually sing God's high praises, up where the white-robed throng cast their crowns before his feet, we shall behold the success of Sabbath-schools. There, too, where infant millions assemble Sabbath after Sabbath, to sing,—

'Gentle Jesus, meek and mild,'

we see with joy the success of Sabbath-schools. And up here, in almost every pulpit of our land, and there in the pews where the deacons sit, and godly members join in worship, there is seen the success of Sabbath-schools. And far away across yonder broad ocean, in the islets of the South, in lands where those dwell who bow before blocks of wood and stone, there are the missionaries who were saved in Sabbath-schools, and the thousands, blessed by their labours, contribute to swell the mighty stream of the incalculable, I had almost said infinite, success of Sabbath-school instruction. Go on, dear friends, go on with your holy service; much has been done already, but more shall yet be done. Let all your past victories inflame you with fresh ardour, let the remembrance of your triumphs in previous campaigns, and all trophies won for your Saviour on the battle-fields of the past, be your encouragement to press on with the duty of the present and the future.

III. Now, thirdly, I will give you THREE ADMONITIONS. The first is, *recollect whom you are teaching:* 'Come, ye children.' I think we ought always to have respect to our audience; I do not mean that we need care if we are preaching to Mr So-and-so, Sir William this, or my Lord that,— because in God's sight such titles are the merest trifles; but we are to remember that we are preaching to men and women who have souls, so that we ought not to occupy their time by things that are not worth their hearing. But when you teach in Sabbath-schools, you are, if it be possible, in a more responsible situation even than a minister occupies. He preaches to grown-up people, to men of judgment, who, if they do not like what he preaches, can go somewhere else; but you teach children who have no option of going elsewhere. If you teach the child wrongly, he believes you; if you teach him heresies, he will receive them; what you teach him now, he will never forget. You are not sowing, as some say, on virgin soil, for it has long been occupied by the devil; but you are sowing on a soil more fertile now than it ever will be again,—soil that will produce fruit now, far better than it will do in after days; you are sowing on a young heart, and what you sow will be pretty sure to abide there, especially if you teach evil, for that will never be forgotten. You are beginning with the child; take care what you do with him. Do not spoil him. Many a child has been treated like the Indian children who have copper plates put upon their foreheads, so that they may never grow. There are many who are simpletons now, just because those who had the care of them when young gave them no opportunities of getting knowledge, so that, when they became old, they cared nothing about it. Have a care what you are after; you are teaching children, mind what you teach them. Put poison in the spring, and it will pollute the whole stream. Take care what you are after, sir! You are twisting the sapling, and the old oak will be bent thereby. Have a care, it is a child's soul you are tampering with, if you are tampering at all; it is a child's soul you are preparing for eternity, if God is with you. I give you a solemn admonition on every child's behalf. Surely, if it be murder to administer poison to the dying, it must be far more criminal to give poison to the young life. If it be evil to mislead grey-headed age, it must be far more so to turn aside the feet of the young into the road of error, in which they may for ever walk.

The second admonition is, *recollect that you are teaching for God*. 'Come, ye children, hearken unto me; I will teach you the fear of the Lord.' If you, as teachers, were only assembled to teach geography, it might not injure them eternally if you were to tell the children that the North Pole was close to the Equator; or if you were to say that the extremity of South America was hard by the coast of Europe; or if you assured them that England was in the middle of Africa. But you are not teaching geography, or astronomy, nor are you training the children for a business life in this world; but you are, to the best of your ability, teaching them for God. You say to them, 'Children, you come here to be taught the Word of God; you come here, if it be possible, that we may be the means of the salvation of your souls.' Have a care what you are after when you pretend to be teaching them for God. Wound the child's hand if you will; but, for God's sake, do not wound his heart. Say what you like about temporal things; but, I beseech you, in spiritual matters, take care how you lead him. Be careful that it is the truth which you inculcate, and only that. With such a responsibility, how solemn your work becomes! He who is doing a work for himself, may do it as he likes; but he who is labouring for another, must take care to please his master; he who is employed by a monarch must beware how he performs his duty; but he who labours for God must tremble lest he doth his work ill. Remember that you are labouring for God, if you are what you profess to be. Alas! many, I fear, even among you, are far from having this serious view of the work of a Sunday-school teacher.

The third admonition is, *remember that your children need teaching*. The text implies that when it says, 'Come, ye children, hearken unto me: I will teach you the fear of the Lord.' That makes your work all the more solemn. If children did not need teaching, I would not be so extremely anxious that you should teach them aright. Works of supererogation, works that are not necessary, men may do as they please; but this work is absolutely necessary. Your child needs teaching. He was born in iniquity; in sin did his mother conceive him. He has an evil heart; he knows not God, and he never will know the Lord unless he is taught. He is not like some ground of which we have heard, that hath good seed lying hidden in its very bowels; but, instead thereof, he hath evil seed within his heart. God can place good seed there. You profess to be his instruments to scatter seed upon that child's heart; remember, if that seed be not sown, he will be lost for ever, his life will be a life of alienation from God; and at his death everlasting punishment must be his portion. Be careful, then, how you teach, remembering the urgent necessity of the case. This is not a house on fire, needing your assistance at the engine; nor is it a wreck at sea, demanding your oar in the lifeboat; but it is a deathless spirit calling aloud to you, 'Come and help me.' Therefore, I beseech you, teach the fear of the Lord, and that only; be very anxious to say, and to say truly, 'I will teach you the fear of the Lord.'

IV. That brings me, in the fourth place, to FOUR INSTRUCTIONS, and they are all in the text.

The first is,—*Get the children to come to your school:* 'Come, ye children.' The great complaint with some teachers is, that they cannot obtain scholars. In London, we are having a canvass of the children; that is a good idea, and you ought to have a canvass of every country village, and of every market-town, and get into the Sunday-school every child you can. My advice to you is, get the children to come by all fair and right means. Do not bribe them; that is a plan to which we strongly object, and it is only adopted in schools of the lowest order, schools of so mean a class that even the fathers and mothers of the children have too much sense to send them there. 'But, then, Farmer Brown won't employ them, or the squire will turn them out of their situations; or, if the children don't go to the school on Sundays, they shall not go on week-days.' Oh, that beggarly trick of bribing! I wish there were an end of it; it only shows the weakness, and degradation, and abomination of a sect that cannot succeed without using so mean a system. But with the exception of that method, do not be very particular how you get the children to school. Why, if I could not get people to come to my chapel by preaching in a black coat, I would have regimentals tomorrow, I would have a congregation somehow. Better do strange things than have an empty chapel, or an empty schoolroom. When I was in Scotland, we sent a bellman round a village to secure an audience, and the plan was eminently successful. Spare no right means, but do get the children in. I have known ministers who have gone out into the streets on the Lord's-day afternoon, and talked to the children who were playing about, and so induced them to come to the school. This is what an earnest teacher will do; he will say, 'John, come into our school; you cannot think what a nice place it is.' Then he gets the children in, and in his kind, winning manner he tells them stories and anecdotes about girls and boys who loved the Saviour, and in this way the school is filled. Go and catch the children. There is no law against it; all is fair in war against the devil. So my first instruction is, get the children, and get them anyhow that you can.

The next is, *get the children to love you, if you can.* That also is in the text, 'Come, ye children, hearken unto me.' You know how we used to be taught in the dame's school, how we stood up with our hands behind us to repeat our lessons. That was not David's plan. 'Come, ye children,—come here, and sit on my knee.' 'Oh!' thinks the child, 'how nice to have such a teacher, a teacher who will let me come near him, a teacher who does not say, "Go," but "Come!"' The fault of many teachers is that they do not get their children near them; but endeavour to foster in their scholars a kind of awful respect. Before you can teach children, you must get the silver key of kindness to unlock their hearts, and so secure their attention. Say, 'Come, ye children.' We have known some good men who were objects of abhorrence to children. You remember the story of two little boys who were one day asked if they would like to go to Heaven, and who, much to their teacher's astonishment, said that they really should not. When they were asked, 'Why not?' one of them said, 'I should not like to go to Heaven because grandpa would be there, and he would be sure to say, "Get along, boys; be off with you!" I should not like to be in Heaven with grandpa.' So, if a boy has a teacher who talks to him about Jesus, but who always wears a sour look, what does the boy think? 'I wonder whether Jesus is like you; if so, I shouldn't like him.' Then there is another teacher, who, if he is provoked ever so little, boxes the child's ears; and, at the same time, teaches him that he should forgive others, and be kind to them. 'Well,' thinks the lad, 'that is very pretty, no doubt, but my teacher doesn't show me how to do it.' If you drive a boy from you, your power over him is gone, for you will not be able to teach him anything. It is of no avail to attempt teaching those who do not love you; so, try and make them love you, and then they will learn anything from you.

The next instruction is, *get the children's attention.* That is in the text, 'Come, ye children, hearken unto me.' If they do not *hearken,* you may talk, but you will speak to no purpose whatever. If they do not listen, you go through your labour as an unmeaning drudgery to yourselves and to your scholars, too. You can do nothing without securing their attention. 'That is just what I cannot do,' says one. Well, that depends upon yourself; if you give them something worth attending to, they will be sure to attend. Give them something worth hearing, and they will certainly hearken. This rule may not be universal, but it is very nearly so. Don't forget to give them a few anecdotes. Anecdotes are very much objected to by critics of sermons, who say they ought not to be used in the pulpit; but some of us know better than that, we know what will wake a congregation up; we can testify, from experience, that a few anecdotes here and there are first-rate things to get the attention of persons who will not listen to dry doctrine. Do try and gather as many good illustrations in the week as you possibly can; wherever you go, if you are really a wise teacher, you can always find something to make into a tale to tell your children. Then, when your scholars get dull, and you are losing their attention, say to them, 'Do you know the "Five Bells"?' If there is such a place in the village, they all open their eyes directly; or you ask, 'Do you know the turning against the "Red Lion"?' Then tell them something you have read or heard which will secure their attention to the lesson. A dear child once said, 'Father, I like to hear Mr So-and-so preach, because he puts so many "likes" into his sermon;— "like this, and like that."' Yes, children always love those '*likes.*' Make parables, pictures, figures, for them, and you will always get on. I am sure, if I were a boy listening to some of you, unless you told me a tale now and then, you would as often see the back of my head as my face; and I do not know, if I sat in a hot schoolroom, but that my head would nod, and I should go to sleep, or be playing with Tom on my left, and do as many strange things as the rest, if you did not strive to interest me. Remember, then, to make your scholars 'hearken.'

The fourth admonition is, *have a care what you teach the children:* 'Come, ye children, hearken unto me: I will teach you the fear of the Lord.' I have spoken upon that theme already, so, not to weary you, I only hint at it, and pass on.

V. In the fifth place, I will give you FIVE SUNDAY-SCHOOL LESSONS, five subjects to teach your children; and these you will find in the verses following the text.

The first thing to teach is, *morality:* 'What man is he that desireth life, and loveth many days, that he may see good? Keep thy tongue from evil, and thy lips from speaking guile. Depart from evil, and do good; seek peace, and pursue it.'

The second is, *godliness, and a constant belief in God's oversight:* 'The eyes of the Lord are upon the righteous, and his ears are open unto their cry.'

The third thing is, *the evil of sin:* 'The face of the Lord is against them that do evil, to cut off the remembrance of them from the earth. The righteous cry, and the Lord heareth, and delivereth them out of all their troubles.'

The fourth thing is, *the necessity of a broken heart;* 'The Lord is nigh unto them that are of a broken heart; and saveth such as be of a contrite spirit.'

The fifth thing is, *the inestimable blessedness of being a child of God:* 'Many are the afflictions of the righteous: but the Lord delivereth him out of them all. He keepeth all his bones: not one of them is broken. ... The Lord redeemeth the soul of his servants: and none of them that trust in him shall be desolate.'

I have given you these five sub-divisions, now let me refer to them one by one. Here, then, is a model lesson for you: 'Come, ye children, hearken unto me: I will teach you the fear of the Lord.' David commences with an interrogative, 'What man is he that desireth life, and loveth many days?' The children like that thought; they would all wish to live to be old.

With this preface, he commences to teach them *morality:* 'Keep thy tongue from evil, and thy lips from speaking guile. Depart from evil, and do good; seek peace, and pursue it.' Now, we never teach morality as the way of salvation. God forbid that we should ever mix up man's works in any way with the redemption which is in Christ Jesus! 'By grace are ye saved through faith, and that not of yourselves, it is the gift of God.' Yet we teach morality while we teach spirituality; and I have always found that the gospel produces the best morality in all the world. I would have a Sunday-school teacher watchful over the morals of the boys and girls under his care, speaking to them very particularly of those sins which are most common to youth. He may honestly and conveniently say many things to his children which no one else can say, especially when reminding them of the sin of lying, so common with children, or the sin of petty thefts, or of disobedience to parents, or of breaking the Sabbath-day. I would have the teacher be very particular in mentioning these evils one by one; for it is of little avail talking to them about sins in the mass, you must take them one by one, just as David did. First look after *the tongue:* 'Keep thy tongue from evil, and thy lips from speaking guile.' Then look after *the whole conduct:*

'Depart from evil, and do good; seek peace, and pursue it.' If the child's soul is not saved by other parts of the teaching, this part may have a beneficial effect upon his life, and so far so good. Morality, however, by itself is comparatively a small thing. The best part of what you teach is *godliness*. I said not, '*religion*,' but *godliness*. Many people are *religious* after a fashion, without being godly. Many have all the externals of godliness, all the outside of piety; such men we call 'religious,' but they have no right thought about God. They think about their place of worship, their Sunday, their books, but nothing about God. He who does not respect God, pray to God, love God, is an ungodly man, whatever his external religion may be. Labour to teach the child always to have an eye to God; write on his memory these words, 'Thou God seest me.' Bid him remember that his every act and thought are under the eye of God. No Sunday-school teacher discharges his duty unless he constantly lays stress upon the fact that there is a God who notices everything that happens. Oh, that we were more godly ourselves, that we talked more of godliness, and that we loved godliness better!

The third lesson is, *the evil of sin*. If the child does not learn *that*, he will never learn the way to Heaven. None of us ever knew what a Saviour Christ was till we knew what an evil thing sin was. If the Holy Ghost does not teach us the exceeding sinfulness of sin, we shall never know the blessedness of salvation. Let us seek his grace, then, when we teach, that we may always be able to lay stress upon the abominable nature of sin. 'The face of the Lord is against them that do evil, to cut off the remembrance of them from the earth.' Do not spare your child; let him know what sin leads to. Do not, like some people, be afraid of speaking plainly and broadly concerning the consequences of sin. I have heard of a father, one of whose sons, a very ungodly young man, was taken off in a very sudden manner. The father did not, as some would have done, say to his family 'We hope your brother has gone to Heaven.' No; but overcoming his natural feelings, he was enabled, by Divine grace, to assemble his children together, and to say to them, 'My sons and daughters, your brother is dead; I fear he is in hell. You knew his life and conduct, you saw how he behaved; and now God has snatched him away in his sins.' Then he solemnly told them of the place of woe to which he believed, yea, almost knew he was gone, begging them to shun it, and to flee from the wrath to come. Thus he was the means of bringing his children to serious thought; but had he acted, as some would have done, with tenderness of heart, but not with honesty of purpose, and said he hoped his son had gone to Heaven, what would the other children have said? 'If he is gone to Heaven, there is no need for us to fear; we may live as we like.' No, no; I hold that it is not unchristian to say of some men that they are gone to hell, when we have seen that their lives have been hellish lives. But it is asked, 'Can you judge your fellow-creatures?' No, but I can *know* them by their fruits. I do not judge them, or condemn them; they judge themselves. I have seen their sins go beforehand to judgment, and I do not doubt that they shall follow after. 'But may they not be saved at the eleventh hour?' *I* have heard of *one* who was, but I do not know that there ever was another, and I cannot tell that there ever will be. Be honest, then, with your children, and teach them, by the help of God, that 'evil shall slay the wicked.'

But you will not have done half enough unless you teach carefully the fourth lesson,—*the absolute necessity of a change of heart.* 'The Lord is nigh unto them that are of a broken heart; and saveth such as be of a contrite spirit.' Oh! may God enable us to keep this constantly before the minds of the taught, that there must be a broken heart and a contrite spirit, that good works will be of no avail unless there be a new nature, that the most arduous duties and the most earnest prayers will all be as nothing, unless there be a true and thorough repentance for sin, and an entire forsaking of sin through the grace and mercy of God! Be sure, whatever you leave out, that you teach the children the three R's,—Ruin, Redemption, and Regeneration. Tell the children they are *ruined* by the Fall, and that there is salvation for them only by being *redeemed* by the blood of Jesus Christ, and *regenerated* by the Holy Spirit. Keep constantly before them these vital truths, and then you will have the pleasing task of telling them the sweet subject of the closing lesson.

In the fifth place, tell the children of *the joy and blessedness of being Christians.* 'The Lord redeemeth the soul of his servants: and none of them that trust in him shall be desolate.' I need not tell you how to talk about that theme; for if you know what it is to be a Christian, you will never be short of matter. Ah, beloved! when we get on this subject, our mind cares not to speak; it would rather revel in its bliss. Truly was it said, 'Blessed is he whose transgression is forgiven, whose sin is covered.' 'Blessed is that man that maketh the Lord his trust.' Yea, verily, blessed is the man, the woman, the child that trusteth in the Lord Jesus Christ, and whose hope is in him. Always lay a stress upon this point,—that the righteous are a blessed people, that the chosen family of God, redeemed by blood and saved by power, are a blessed people while here below, and that they will be a blessed people for ever in Heaven above. Let your children see that you belong to that blessed company. If they know you are in trouble, if it be possible, come to your class with a smiling face, so that your scholars may be able to say: 'Teacher is a blessed man, although he is bowed down by his troubles.' Always seek to keep a joyous face, that your boys and girls may know that your religion is a blessed reality. Let this be one main point of your teaching, that though 'many are the afflictions of the righteous,' yet 'the Lord delivereth him out of them all. He keepeth all his bones: not one of them is broken. ... The Lord redeemeth the soul of his servants: and none of them that trust in him shall be desolate.'

Thus have I given you these five lessons; and now, in conclusion, let me solemnly say that, with all the instruction you may give to your children, you must all of you be deeply conscious that you are not capable of doing anything in the securing of the child's salvation, but that it is God himself who, from the first to the last, must effect it all. You are simply a pen; God can write with you, but you cannot write anything of yourself. You are a sword; God can with you slay the child's sin, but you cannot slay it of yourself. Be ye, therefore, always mindful of this, that you must be first taught of God yourself, and then you must ask God to use you to teach; for unless a higher Teacher than you work with you, and instruct the child, the child must perish. It is not your instruction that can save the souls of your children; it is the blessing of God the Holy Spirit accompanying your labours. May God bless and crown your efforts with abundant success! He will surely do so if you are instant in prayer, constant in supplication. Never yet did the earnest teacher or preacher 'labour in vain in the Lord,' and often has it been seen that bread cast upon the waters has been found after many days. So may it be with all of you, dear friends, for our Lord Jesus Christ's sake! Amen.

Note

* This sermon was was later rearranged to form a few of the chapters in Spurgeon's book *Come ye Children*.

Chapter 19

'Seest thou this woman?'*

A sermon, delivered at St Martin's Hall, Long Acre, on
Wednesday evening, 3 September 1856, by C. H. Spurgeon

FORWARDED BY T. W. MEDHURST, CARDIFF

'Seest thou this woman?'—Luke 7:44.

O
UR Lord was no great favourite with the Pharisees; he was too
honest for them; he too often reproved their self-righteousness,
and warned them of the impossibility of their being saved by their
own good works; therefore, they always disdained his company, and
despised him. But, on this occasion, we find him in the house of a Pharisee.
If I read aright, this man, whose name was Simon, had been a leper, and he
was one of the many whom our Saviour had restored, therefore he felt
some degree of affection for the Saviour's person, out of gratitude for the
marvellous cure which Jesus had wrought upon him; and he therefore
invited Jesus Christ to his house, but not, as Matthew the publican did, to a
feast which he had made especially in honour of him. Our Saviour went to
the Pharisee's house on this ground, that there was something hopeful in
Simon's case. He was at least grateful for the temporal mercy he had
received; and though our Saviour would, perhaps, rather have sat down
with the publican, he chose not to refuse the invitation of the Pharisee;
teaching us that, although we ought to visit the good for our own profit, yet
we ought also to visit the hopeful for their profit, and in hope that God may
bless the visit to their salvation. However, so ill was the welcome which
Jesus received, that Simon even forgot to bring him the much-needed basin
and ewer, from which he might refresh with water his weary feet; he forgot
to give also to his cheek the usual kiss of hospitality, betokening his
welcome. In fact, Simon treated Jesus most disrespectfully,—in any way
but that which the Lord deserved at his hand. But our blessed Master kept

his seat at the Pharisee's table; he was not offended, as some of us might have been; teaching us that we ought to be careless of the mere punctilios of life, and that we ought not always to insist on every point of courtesy, and every iota of that which is called '*politeness*.' If we can do good thereby, we should not mind rude things, but put up with them, bear with them, and say nothing about them; but by holding our peace, hope that our great end, the end of doing good, will be subserved.

However, what Simon forgot to do, or what he omitted intentionally, was done by a woman. There was one outside the door, who had more love to Jesus in her heart than there could have been in a thousand hearts such as Simon's. 'Seest thou this woman?' She passed by the door, and looked within; she thought she saw her blessed Saviour reclining with his feet towards the door. She looked, and looked again; and when she perceived that it was he and no other, she sped home as quickly as she could, and reached down from the place where she kept it, a choice 'alabaster box of ointment of spikenard very precious,' which had never been opened. Her love dictated to her the thought that she would 'break the box,' and pour the precious ointment upon him, and that she would 'wash his feet with tears,' and 'wipe them with the hairs of her head.' She came running back. Yes, it was, most assuredly, her blessed Lord, and there were his dear feet! But the Pharisee saw 'this woman', and he scowled upon her; she scarcely dared come within the portal of the Pharisee's house; but, at last, she made a bold venture, and approached her Lord; and, oh! when she saw the feet of that man whom she loved so much, her tears began to fall in torrents upon his feet; and seeing she was well washing them with her tears, she undid her glorious tresses (with which, no doubt, she had aforetime entrapped many a soul), and she made a towel of her hair; and she kissed his dear feet again and again, in a very rhapsody of love, scarcely knowing what she did, so lost was she in her affection for the dear Saviour who had been pleased to forgive her all her thousands of sins, and to make her one of his very own.

Simon 'saw' that woman; he thought it was an improper act for any woman to kiss the feet of Jesus, but more especially for such a woman to do so; and he thought within himself, 'What! that woman? I have known her; she has been one of the worst of all women; yet Jesus lets her kiss his feet. Ah! I would not endure that touch, not I; I would spurn her from mine house. She! she contaminates this room; she stains the very floor of my pure domicile!' He would fain have cried, 'Begone, woman, begone this very moment!' But he said within himself, 'This man, if he were a prophet, would have known who and what manner of woman this is that toucheth him: for she is a sinner.' But Jesus knew his thoughts, and turning to him, said, 'Simon, I have somewhat to say unto thee. And he saith, Master, say on. There was a certain creditor which had two debtors: the one owed five hundred pence, and the other fifty. And when they had nothing to pay, he frankly forgave them both. Tell me therefore, which of them will love him most?' Simon, not seeing the drift of the parable, 'answered and said, I suppose that he, to whom he forgave most.' 'And he said unto him, thou hast rightly judged. And he turned to the woman, and said unto Simon, Seest thou this woman? I entered into thine house, thou gavest me no water for my feet; but she hath washed my feet with tears, and wiped them with the hairs of her head. Thou gavest me no kiss; but this woman since the time I came in hath not ceased to kiss my feet. My head with oil thou didst not anoint; but this woman hath anointed my feet with ointment. Wherefore I say unto thee, Her sins, which are many, are forgiven; for she loved, much: but to whom little is forgiven, the same loveth little. And he said unto her, thy sins are forgiven. And they that sat at meat with him began to say within themselves, Who is this that forgiveth sins also? And he said to the woman, thy faith hath saved thee; go in peace.' The woman, who doubtless had stood motionless to catch every word her Saviour said, and with tears still coursing down her cheeks, went away blessed.

We are about to do what Jesus exhorted Simon to do, to look at this woman; and as we look at her, we shall see four things in her. First, *Seest thou this woman's sin?* Secondly, seest thou *abounding grace?* Thirdly, seest thou *fervent love produced by abounding grace?* And, fourthly, seest thou *pious works the fruit of fervent love?* And then further, seest thou abounding sin, more abounding grace, fervent love and good works, all backed up with the remarkable statement, 'Verily I say unto you, wheresoever this gospel shall be preached in the whole world, there shall also this, that this woman hath done, be told for a memorial of her'? (Matthew 26:13.)

I. First, then, we have before us tonight, THIS WOMAN'S SIN: 'Seest thou this woman?'

She was a woman whom the Pharisee would have left on the other side of the street; and as he passed her, he would have cursed her in his heart, and called her, by way of compliment, 'Dog,' or, if he had been very hard-hearted, something worse than that. He would have wished that the wind from her side of the way should never blow on him, but that he might always be on that side, from which, perhaps, some holy wind might sweep a little blessed piety from him, and haply blow it upon her. When she walked along the street, good men seemed abashed, and looked, and went their way. She had often been reproved, she had often been warned, doubtless; but still she kept on in the paths of sin and infamy. I cannot tell you whether she had broken her mother's heart, or whether she had brought her father's grey hairs prematurely to the grave. I cannot tell you how many hundreds she had deluded, how many she had snared, and how far she herself had plunged in wickedness. It is enough to say that she was one who merited above many, because of her open sin, that term, 'a sinner.' Yet our Saviour said to Simon, 'Look at this woman! Look at her! Do not be ashamed, she will not hurt you; look at her!' It is not at all times well to look at sin; but, dear friends, I bid you also to look at this woman; for here, 'where sin abounded, grace doth much more abound,' so that the sting of sin is taken away. Look at her, look at her! nay, turn not away, turn thine eye here: 'Seest thou this woman?' Come, fix thy gaze upon her for one moment, as she was in all her sin and iniquity; come, look at her! 'But why,' sayest thou, 'why must I look at her, and see her great sin?'

I answer, first, *look at her that you may pity her*. It does us good, sometimes, to see great sin, that we may learn to pity those who have been so far led astray as to indulge in it. Nowadays, we have a lot of mawkish modesty in our churches; ministers must not think of telling the people about the sins that exist all around them. According to common thought, we must not call a man 'adulterer' or 'fornicator' now; such words are not polite! I say,—Out on such modesty; it is devil's modesty. If men sin, let us tell them plainly of their deeds; and if they be sinners, let us talk to them plainly of their sins. Many in the present day are so gentlemanly that they think, for them to go after a poor drunkard, and pick him up in the streets, would entail inevitable disgrace upon them. To go out at midnight, and gather the outcasts off the streets, and bring them into the Dormitory, that they may be reclaimed;—oh, we are too great, we are too good for that sort of work! We have such fine ideas of ourselves that we cannot stoop to pick up men, though our Saviour stooped all the way from Heaven to save our souls. I admire what I heard Mr Gough say once, 'We shall never do much good till we go down into the kennel of sin, and run our arms right down into the filth, in order to pull men and women out.' I am persuaded that it is not the ordinary style of gentlemanly preaching, nor the ordinary style of gentlemanly acting, that is required; we must go down into the dens and kennels, into the alleys and courts. We must climb the creaking stairs, and enter the dismal garret; we must go after the loathsome, the wicked, and the corrupt. The good need not our sympathies, but the evil demand them. Therefore should we seek the evil most, and go after them, if haply we may be made the means of the salvation of their souls.

I say to thee, dear friend, 'Seest thou this woman?' As she flits by thee in the street, pray for her. If thou canst not say anything *to her*, put up a prayer to God *for her*. Despise her not in thy heart, but pity her; for fallen though she be, she is a woman yet. Ah! she is such a woman still that, in spite of all her sin, she may one day sing in Paradise, as loudly as John himself, if God shall have mercy on her soul. Therefore, pass her not by with thy lip curled, and with thine eye averted; but pity her, pity her still. Look down on her, not with contempt, but with the eye of compassion. Seek to do what thou canst to raise her, remembering that in the self-same image in which thou wast created, she was created, and, fallen though she be, she is still one of God's creatures, as thou art; therefore thou oughtest to love and seek to save her. There are many persons, whom you would keep clear of on earth, whom you will find in Heaven; and, mayhap, sirs,—God grant it may not be so!—those you despise may be there, and you yourselves cast out; for many a time has it been proved to be true, that the publicans and the harlots enter into the Kingdom of Heaven before the self-righteous, who think themselves so much their superiors. 'Seest thou this woman?' Sinner though she be, look on her, that thou mayest pity her.

There is another reason why thou shouldst see 'this woman' in all her sin, and not be ashamed to look at her. *Look at her that thou mayest humble thyself before God.* Remember that all that 'this woman' is, thou mightest have been. 'Nay,' sayest thou, 'I never could sin as she did; I could never go astray as she has done.' What! art thou so proud as to think thine heart good, when the Scripture tells thee that, 'The heart is deceitful above all things, and desperately wicked: who can know it?' I tell thee, man, if thou hadst been in the same circumstances as hers, and had the same temptations, thou mightest have fallen sooner than she did, and have gone yet further astray, though haply still thou mightest have been called 'respectable', while thou wert the greater sinner of the two. You say, 'I never would have sinned like that!' God help you, if that is how you talk! You may have sinned just so ere many days have gone. 'Indeed,' say you, 'I never should sin and go astray as she has done.' Beware! 'Pride goeth before destruction, and a haughty spirit before a fall.' Consider thyself, 'lest thou also be tempted.' Even good men and good women have not always kept clear of great sins, take heed that thou boast not thyself too much lest some sad fall bring thee also down. Oh, sometimes, when I see some of the worst characters in the street, I feel as if I could break my heart with tears of gratitude that God has never let me act as they have done! I have thought, if God had let me alone, and had not touched me by his grace, what a great sinner I should have been! I should have run to the utmost lengths of sin, dived into the very depths of evil, nor should I have stopped at any vice or folly, if God had not stopped me. I feel, if you do not, that I should have been a very king of sinners, if God had let me alone. And, believe me, so would you, if grace had not restrained you, or circumstances had not kept you from open sin. If you had not been guarded by parents, fettered by the bond of grace, as I trust many of you are, you too might have been there, as well as 'this woman' on whom you look with scorn. Therefore, I beseech you, humble yourselves before God, and look up, and bless his holy name that he has made you to differ. Remember John Bradford's exclamation; when he looked out of the window, and saw a murderer on the road to Tyburn, he used to say, 'There goes John Bradford, but for the grace of God!' And none know what black crimes we might commit, even in the next twenty-four hours, if sovereign mercy did not stop us, or at least if circumstances did not prevent us. Then, 'seest thou this woman?' It is a sight of great and aggravated guilt; but look at her carefully; and, looking thus, imitate her not, save in her penitence; but, I beseech thee, humble thyself, and pity her.

II. Secondly, 'Seest thou this woman?' SHE IS A TROPHY OF ABOUNDING GRACE.

Though this woman was once the worst of sinners, see, she now stands there weeping! Why? Because Jesus Christ has blotted out, as a thick cloud, her transgressions, and, as a cloud, her sins, and now she is one of the trophies of sovereign grace. Of old, when Roman conquerors came home from the wars, they rode in a chariot drawn by milk-white chargers, and had the captive monarchs led in chains before them, while banners taken from the foe, and riches they had obtained from every city they had ransacked, were carried along in triumph. The Romans crowded their house-tops to see the pageant go through the street, and showered down roses on the conquerors as they rode along. Oh! I can tell you of a triumph soon to come, when Christ shall ride through the streets of Heaven, with the spoils of hell's dominion, with sinners whom he has ransomed; with spoils of garments washed in blood, made whiter than driven snow; not with men who are made slaves, but with men emancipated; and among these trophies, in that great day, will be found 'this woman' to whom Christ forgave so much. She will be led along Heaven's golden streets as a special wonder of God's grace, while angels clap their wings, and glorified saints shout 'Hallelujah!' because so great a sinner has been snatched from hell, and made an heir of Heaven. Come, then, and look at 'this woman,' upon whom angels shall one day gaze with wonder and amazement, seeing in her so astounding an instance of sovereign grace and mercy!

See the sovereignty of grace. Why was '*this woman*' chosen? There doubtless were many harlots in Jerusalem at that time; but, so far as we know, unto none of them was Jesus sent, save unto one of the worst of them, 'this woman.' Many there were who were good and amiable, but unto none of them did mercy come, but unto 'this woman … who was a sinner.' Why was that? Echo answers, 'Why?' God only knows why; it was his sovereignty. He gives where he pleases, even to the most undeserving, that it may be seen that it is not of debt or of works, but wholly and entirely of his own rich sovereign grace.

Let me tell you a parable. The angel of mercy one day descended from

Heaven, and when he alighted on earth, he walked along the streets. He saw the Pharisee bind on himself his phylactery, and make broad the border of his garments, and the angel hastened by saying, 'I have no blessing for him, for he thinks he has no need of mercy.' He went a little further, and there was the Rabbi turning over the books, and pondering their pages. He was wise, ay, very wise, for he had the key of knowledge; but he himself would neither enter the Kingdom of Heaven, nor suffer others so to do; and the angel of mercy clapped his wings, and said, 'I have not been sent to you, for you know no need of mercy.' He went a little further. There was the devotee at his penance, trying to work out a righteousness of his own by torturing his own flesh; and the angel said, 'I am not sent to you; for you, it seems, can pardon your own sins by penance, and blot out your own guilt by your own sufferings.' Then, as the angel went along, he heard the voice of one who said, 'I the chief of sinners am, and I need the mercy of God.' He listened; it was in a lonely room upstairs where the pleading voice was heard. There could be no doubt as to the awful trade that woman had carried on; but there she was, kneeling by her bedside; the tears were rolling down her cheeks, and her heart was ready to burst within her. The angel stopped, and listened, and he heard her tell a tale of infamy that almost made his holy mind shudder. He marked her, as she repeated all her grievous offences, and wept before God, and asked for pardon; and the angel paused just for a moment, and looked at her, wondering that God should send him down to her. He thought within himself, 'Is this the woman?' and he turned to the roll on which her name was written, and found she was indeed the very one, and he whispered in her ears sweet words of comfort. He, by the Holy Spirit, applied to her some precious promises of the Word, and she rose from her knees, and cried, 'I am forgiven! I am forgiven! I'm a miracle of grace!' Stop, angel, stop, ere thou goest, answer me this question, 'Why didst thou fly thither? Why didst thou not enter into the palaces of kings, or into the houses of courtiers? Why not stop at full many a merchant's house in that busy street?' The angel answers, 'I had no errand there; I was sent to the chief of sinners, for there was I most required. Those others believed that they did not need mercy, therefore I went not to them; but "this woman" knew she was a sinner, and sought forgiveness from the Lord, so I came to bring a pardon for her from her Saviour.' Beloved, admire the sovereignty of God's grace, that he gives his pardon just where he pleases, entirely irrespective of men. 'Have I not a right to do what I will with mine own?' is the question God always seems to ask. He is ever saying, 'I will have mercy on whom I will have mercy, and I will have compassion on whom I will have compassion.'

See next, *the vast extent of the atonement,* which could wash such a sinner 'whiter than snow.' She was very sinful, very sinful indeed, yet all her sins were washed out by the Saviour's blood. *We* need the Saviour's blood to wash *our* sins away; and 'this woman' did not need any more than that. That which will just suffice for us, sufficed for her, too. Let me picture a scene. There is the 'fountain opened for sin and for uncleanness.' The invitation is given, 'O ye sinners, come and wash!' Here comes a man who has, by Divine grace, been led to see his lost estate, but who has been preserved from open immorality; he comes to the fountain,—a pure, spotless character, in the eye of the world; black, however, in his own esteem. He washes, and as he comes out of the fountain, whiter than driven snow, he sings a song of grateful praise, and blesses God. But, lo, here comes another! see, he is blacker than the one who went before; he has committed sins that men have seen. Will the fountain suffice for him, too? See, he plunges in, and comes out as white as the first one. See, there comes another, and he is black from head to foot; he is deeply stained with sin; he is all unholy, unclean, nothing else but sin. Will that blood cleanse *him?* Will that bath suffice for him? Surely it may wash away a part of his guilt, but it cannot wash away all his blackness. Mark, be attentive! Look down, ye angels! That black sinner steps into the bath, he is buried in its flood; he comes up, and oh, I see him! Who is this that cometh up from the washing fair and clean? Who is this that riseth up from the fountain, washed throughly from his iniquity, and cleansed from his sin? See, again, there comes 'this woman!' She also plunges into the fountain, and she is washed, and made clean. Black she was, yea, black as hell when she went down; but white she is, yea, white as Heaven now she has come up from the cleansing flood. Admire, then, the mighty power of the atoning blood. Instead of disputing about whether the atonement be general or particular, enquire whether it has been applied to *you.* Instead of asking the extent of the atonement, ask whether it has extended to your soul, whether it has washed you, whether you have been baptized into its cleansing stream, and have been made pure. If you have not been cleansed in the fountain of atoning blood, however great that atonement, it avails nothing for you. You are lost, lost, lost, unless the blood of Jesus Christ cleanses you from all sin.

See, once more, 'this woman' as an instance of abundant grace, and regard her as *a trophy of the Holy Spirit's power* as well as of the power of redemption. This poor woman was excessively vile, and she, by the Holy Spirit's influence, was made penitent. If there could step upon this platform some wondrous man, who should tell you that he could work miracles, who should bring before you a piece of adamant, and say, 'Adamant, dissolve!' and the adamant should immediately run away in drops, what would you say of that man? If, next, he should present to you a piece of ebony, and by simply saying to it, 'Be white!' the ebony should immediately turn to snowy whiteness, what would you say of that man? Would you not say that he possessed powers, mighty and marvellous, beyond those of any other mortal man? Such was the power of the Holy Spirit in this woman's heart. She had doubtless heard of Jesus, yes, and probably she had laughed at him many a time. What! she turn religionist? What! she wash the feet of Jesus? Ah, no! she scorned any such idea as that. The Pharisee passed by, and sneered at her; was she going to turn penitent to be such a hypocrite as she believed him to be? The Saviour approached, and perhaps she thought he had nothing for her, so she went on her way. I have often wondered how it was that this poor woman came to be converted. George Whitefield has a very curious passage on this subject in one of his sermons, I must refer to it because it is a very singular thought of his. He says that, one day, Jesus was preaching in the Temple, and *he supposes* this woman to have been Mary the sister of Martha. For once, the good man was mistaken, as the name of 'this woman' is, for good, and wise, and kind reasons, not known, but Whitefield says: One day, Jesus was preaching in the Temple, and Martha came to hear him;—a very good, staid sort of woman she was;—and, hearing Jesus, she thought within herself, 'If I could get my poor sister Mary to come to hear this preacher, I should not wonder if she would be converted.' So Martha went home, and said, 'Mary, a man is preaching a sermon in the Temple, do come and listen to him.' 'Oh, no!' answered Mary, 'I would not go to hear a sermon.' Then Martha began to use such winning arts, Whitefield tells you of them, but I dare not. 'Ay, do come,' she said, 'He has such a voice, there is such mellowness in it; never man spake like this man. There is so much grandeur and nobility about him; do come and see him.' So poor Mary went off to see and hear this wonderful man, and she tried to get a glimpse of him over the heads of the crowd. Presently, this man fixed his eyes on her, and looked at her specially apart from all the rest of the people, he stretched out his hands, and said, 'Come unto me, all ye that labour and are heavy laden, and I will give you rest.' Mary started, for she thought, 'He knows I am labouring and heavy-laden, too.' Then the Preacher went on to tell a story about a prodigal son, who had gone far astray, and wasted his living with harlots. 'Ah!' thought Mary, 'that is my case; have not I gone far astray?' He told of the loving father receiving and forgiving that prodigal son; and Mary stood, and, as she listened, she wept. So she went to Jesus, and he said that her sins might yet be forgiven, for he was the Son of man who had power on earth to forgive sins; and Mary believed on Jesus, and he sent her on her way rejoicing. This may have been the way 'this woman' was converted. That, however, we cannot tell; but certainly it was by the power of the Holy Spirit, and we cannot but admire and adore that mighty power which can break or dissolve hearts of adamant, and convert the worst of men, and the worst of women, so that they become the very best and brightest of saints.

Just one other remark, and then I will not detain you longer upon this head. It is this: as 'this woman' was an instance of sovereign grace, so, *if we are saved, we must all be saved by the same grace that saved her*. If you go to Heaven, you must elbow pick-pockets, and walk side by side with thieves and drunkards; I mean, with persons who were once such; but they are washed, but they are sanctified, but they are justified, in the name of the Lord Jesus, and by the Spirit of our God. There is only one road to Heaven for the chimney sweep and for Queen Victoria. There is only one path to glory for the poor and for the rich, for the moral and the immoral. There is but one gate to Paradise, and we must all be saved in the same fashion. 'What!' says one, 'am I to say the same prayer as this woman? Am I to go down on my knees as humbly as she?' Yes; there is not a girl in your Dormitory, there is not a woman in a Penitentiary, but if she come to God, she must come on the same footing as the best of us; and if we come to Christ, we must come just as she does. She comes with nothing at all, for she has nothing to bring; and we must come with nothing at all, too; we must all alike plead for God's mercy, all alike rely simply on God's grace. If we are not willing to come that way, we must take the consequences; for there is no other way. If we will not have that, we must take the direful alternative of being lost.

III. Now, thirdly, 'Seest thou this woman's' FERVENT LOVE?

Come, lukewarm souls, I have something to show you; I have something to make you marvel! You do not love your Saviour much. You say you do, you make a profession of it; but you do not love him much. Come, now, I am going to show you a specimen of fervent love. Shall I tell you how 'this woman' came to Jesus? She would never have wept for all the scoldings that could have been given to her. Her's was fervent love; but she would never have loved Christ for all the exhortations that might have been bestowed upon her. Her's was fervent love; but she would never have loved Jesus Christ for all the lectures of the most learned Pharisees, or the most intellectual Rabbis. What was it broke this woman's heart, and made her weep in penitence? It was nothing but *love;* and in that word there is a mighty power. There are very few who know how to spell that word so as to use it aright. Some think that, to reform the world, chains and fetters are fine things. Ay, sirs, ye shall use all the iron in the world before ye shall reform it in that manner. Some think that gibbets are noble things to exalt the character of our nation. Ay, they may hang us all, and yet they shall not have bettered us; and they may sweep away one half of this our race, but the other half shall murder just as much for all that. There is little good wrought by harsh means; and if you think you are going to reclaim people by looking surlily at them, you think altogether wrong. I would advise you to try to light a fire with a pail of water, and when you have done that, you are likely to convert a poor wanderer by frowning at her. I have often admired the manner in which some of our divines go to work to convert heretics; it reminds me of the story of a Quaker, who went to Rome with the firm intention of converting the Pope. When he arrived there, and got audience of his Unholiness, he said to him, 'Friend Pope, I have come here to convert thee; and in order to begin aright, I will tell thee thou art sure to be damned, for thy church is Babylon, and thou wilt be lost.' The Pope is said to have replied, 'Friend, I am much obliged to thee; and I have also to say to thee that, if thou art not out of my dominions in four-and-twenty hours, I will roast thee alive!' That was about the end of the poor Quaker's mission, because he began at the wrong end. He might have had very little success if he had begun at any other end; but he destroyed all hope by beginning as he did. So, no doubt, some of you think you could reclaim some of the worst of characters; do you not? Yet, perhaps, you would make them ten times worse than they are now, and make confusion worse confounded. But our Saviour was loving and kind to this woman, and that broke her heart. One soft word will often break bones more swiftly than a hard blow. He who would stand against a sabre cut, falls before the blow of one word of kindness. Kindness hath the arm of a giant; love is mightier than the sword; ay, more forcible than cannon, or all the armaments of war, are the words of Christian affection and love of humanity. This woman loved because she had been loved; so, I doubt not, we love Jesus Christ, because he first loved us.

Note, further, this woman's love had one particular about it that I wish every one of us had; *it made her very penitent.* I have sometimes heard persons talk so flippantly of loving Christ that I have been disgusted. I do not object, as some do, to those lines beginning, 'Dear Jesus,' because I read in the Bible of God's dear Son; but I have heard some people say, 'dear' 'precious' 'sweet Lord,' in their ordinary conversation, larding all their speech with pious utterances about Jesus which they do not mean, until I have been heartily sick of it all, and I have thought it would be better for them to cry now and then. To weep, instead of talking so much, would be a far better sign and proof of their love. This woman, while she loved her Lord, loved him with tears, not with words. She did not come canting and whining, and saying 'I love thee, my dear Lord.' No, she 'stood at his feet behind him weeping, and began to wash his feet with tears.' That is the true way of loving Christ. We should always remember that, however familiar our alliance is with him, there is a very great distinction between a man and Christ; that, however closely we are to approach him, we are only creatures yet, and it does not become us, as some do, to make ourselves as familiar with Christ as if he were nothing better than we are. If we love him, our love should be accompanied with penitence, and also with becoming reverence.

Mark, once more, *this woman's love was a very bold love*. She 'kissed his feet.' It was a bold stroke, after all, to come and kiss Christ's feet before that company. I have no doubt she flitted round about the door for some time, just like some poor robin tapping at the window in winter-time, and then, if you open it, it will fly away, afraid to come into the house. 'This woman' saw the Saviour, and oh, how she wanted to come to him! Oh, if she might but come behind him and weep! But it was a bold, bold deed to come in at all; for it was Simon's house, and Simon had no doubt often sneered at her. It was the Pharisee's house, and most likely he would put her out. Besides, kind as Jesus was, she might think that perhaps he would not bear such company as hers, and would bid her at once begone. Still, she boldly comes. Ah, ye timid Christians, this woman shames you! There is not half the difficulty in your way that there was in this woman's; yet how often you are ashamed of your Saviour! You do not come out and confess him; you have not joined the church yet. O sirs, let this woman teach you a lesson! See her; she is not ashamed of Jesus. I beseech you, be not ye ashamed of your Lord; yet be not impudent, for she was not; she 'stood at his feet behind him weeping;' not before him, but behind him. While we own our Lord, let us come behind him, weeping; showing boldness, but yet evidencing our humility. May we have such love as this!

IV. Fourthly, 'Seest thou this woman's' GOOD WORKS?

Wherever grace comes, it brings good works after it, if it be true grace. God's love in our hearts will be sure to beget holy works toward Jesus. This woman did *deeds of affection;* but I will not dwell on that, as I have hinted at it before. But she also did *deeds of humility.* Some, if they joined our churches, would not be content to kiss Christ's feet. No; they would want to fill the highest offices; we must make them ministers or deacons, they must be great amongst us. But 'this woman' loved her Lord so much that she thought it a great honour to kiss his feet. I have heard of a young man who said that he wanted to serve Christ, but when he went to the Sunday-school, and they gave him a class of very young children, he said, 'Oh, I am not going to teach such a class as that!' So he went off. He was not at all like 'this woman.' It was a very menial employment to wash the feet of Jesus; but she thought herself honoured when she did that. I have read of some good minister, who once said that all good deeds done for Christ were alike in honour. Said he, 'If there were two angels in Heaven, and God should send them down to earth, and tell one of them to sweep a street-crossing, and the other to rule an empire, the two would have no choice which to do, so long as they knew they could honour God in whatever they did.' So, if you love your Master, you will never be ashamed to do anything for him. I do not know that you would even scorn the Midnight Mission; you would not even loathe that, though, methinks, that must be the hardest work of all. Though I would not unduly honour man, yet I must honour that man who is not ashamed to pace the streets of London, night after night, to lay hold of the outcast and forlorn, and compel them to come in, to hear the voice of mercy, and be rescued from their sins. 'This woman' would not have blushed to do that work if it had been in her power, for she washed the Saviour's feet.

This woman's good works were also *very extravagant works*. She 'brought an alabaster box of ointment.' Mark says, 'an alabaster box of ointment of spikenard very precious; and she brake the box, and poured it on his head.' She did not wait to take the lid off, 'she brake the box.' Why did she not take the lid off? Because she wanted to give all to Christ; so 'she brake the box, and poured the ointment on his head.' It was extravagant to kiss his feet, and to wash them with her tears, and to 'wipe them with the hairs of her head.' But, mark you, there is no true love that is not a little extravagant. I never knew true love, even to our fellow-creatures, that was not a little extravagant sometimes; and certainly there can be no true love to God that is not extravagant. 'Oh!' says one, 'I never do an extravagant thing!' I never said you did, I never thought you did; I daresay you do not, for you have not much love to Jesus Christ. Many think that those are mad who try to serve their Master a little better than others. If we were all such Christians as we ought to be, we should be set down as insane directly; for we should perform such deeds of love to Christ, that even our fellow-members would say, 'Surely they must be mad to do such things as these.' It is a mercy so to act, sometimes, and let the men of the world think us mad if they like. It is my firm conviction that much of the so-called religion of this age is not worth having. I have seen this religion in some of those who, while they stand up to perform all kinds of offices in the sanctuary, who are even deacons or churchwardens, if they were asked to give to any institution, would look at you as if you were picking their pocket, and start you from their houses. I ask, 'How dwelleth the love of God in such men as these?' God's religion would make better men and better women of us all, and more earnest men and more earnest women; and, I trow, it would make us extravagant sometimes, and would make us do extraordinary deeds, which the world would say were nothing but sheer, downright madness. But we should not mind; we should know how to spell *wisdom* where the world would only read *folly*. 'This woman' did humble deeds, and she did extravagant ones into the bargain.

I must also say another thing: *this woman did a deed of self-denial*. I do not suppose she was a very rich woman, but she gave the best treasure she had. She gave the ointment which might have been sold for much; she gave to Christ the best thing she had in her house: 'an alabaster box of ointment of spikenard very precious.' Many boxes, no doubt, had she purchased for her own use in the days of her sin; but now she devotes all to her Lord; and she breaks the alabaster box that she may pour the precious ointment on his head. O dear friends, I do not believe that there is much religion in a man who does not sometimes make sacrifices for his Master, and deny himself! I often admire the self-denial of Mr John Wesley. When he was asked to send in an account of his plate that it might be taxed, and word was sent to him that a man so well known must have a considerable quantity to pay duty upon, he said he had only one spoon in London, and one in York, and until there should be no more poor left in the land, he did not suppose he should possess a third. That was self-denial in giving to the poor; but many like a cheap gospel and a cheap religion. I was reading in an American work, some time ago, an account of a man saying to one of his neighbours, 'You go a ruinous way to work with your religion; I always do it on the cheap; I don't suppose my religion costs me more than a dollar a year.' The other replied, 'The Lord have mercy on your stingy soul!' And I thought it was a very fitting response; but some people, if they were to make the comparison, would find that religion does not cost them so much as blacking their shoes. There are many people who pay quite as much for cleaning their door-knocker, and twice as much for cleaning their door-steps, as they expend in giving to the poor and the cause of God. Many spend more on a favourite lap-dog than they would on a poor child, if they met one destitute in the street. In fact, with many, the most trifling thing comes before Christ. If we were to measure your estimate of Jesus Christ by the amount of money you devote to his service, I am afraid some of you would look very badly. But it was not so with 'this woman.' She loved her Saviour so much that she would give him all. 'Ah!' says one, 'I am trying to get rich, and I intend leaving a very handsome sum to various societies when I die.' How kind that is, to leave your money when you cannot keep it any longer! Thank you for nothing, sir, for I can answer for one thing, if you could take it with you, we should have little enough of it. Leave some, if you can; but I should like to be my own executor. If I had any money that I wished to give to the Church of Christ, I would make him my Legatee, and give him my money; but I would give it with my own hands, and I would do it on the principle of economy, to save the probate and legacy duty.

Now, dear friends, I am going to plead for 'this woman.' Perhaps you have read in the newspapers, lately, the story of what Henry Ward Beecher did with that poor black woman who was about to be sold down South. He said to her, 'Sarah, come here,' and she stood up before the congregation. And then he told the people how this poor woman was about to be sold, and related all the horrors of her case. Up rose one gentleman, and said, 'I will pay the whole price for her freedom, if no one else will.' But when they made the collection, they found there was not only enough money to buy her from slavery, but her little boy also. A good sermon that, with a good practical conclusion. Now, I cannot show you 'this woman,' but I can picture her to you. Some of you have never seen her; I pray God you never may! Nothing grieves me more, when I return, often late at night, from distant journeys in the country, than to see here and there, the devil's nets spread wide, and poor souls waiting at the corners of the highways, like very spiders, to spring on every unguarded youth who comes that way. Oh! if I could fetch one of these poor creatures here, I would say to her, 'Poor fallen woman, wouldst thou renounce thy life?' She would say, 'Yes; but I have been to such-and-such an Institution, and they told me they could not take me in, because they had no funds. I went again, and desired to be reformed, but they could not receive me.' Say, men and women, shall this woman knock again, and be refused, or will you not tonight give something that will assist to throw wide open the doors? Shall she come and say, 'Let me lodge here; I am anxious to be reclaimed; I desire not thus to ruin my body and to destroy my soul, and to ruin and destroy the bodies and souls of more victims; I desire to walk henceforth in the ways of God, and to be saved;' and shall it have to be said again, 'We are grieved, we are sorry; there, take that trifle, it is all we can do for you; we have no room for you, we cannot receive you, because we have no funds'? No! I trust, in God's name, you will not commit such an act of cruelty, if you are able, in the least degree, to help the Institution for which I plead.

'Seest thou this woman?' Say not, 'She is an undeserving creature.' I warn you that it is a Pharisaic spirit that makes you think so. The more she sins, the more we should labour to reclaim her. Recollect, if you save one such as this woman, how many others you have saved. Consider how many she might have led astray. But once snatch her away from her evil career, and consider how many may be stayed at once from the downward course that surely leads to hell. There she is, poor sinful creature; she is left alone. Perhaps her sin is not so much her own as another's. Certainly, the profit, in ten thousand cases, is to her nothing, but it goes to worse people—oh, that God's earth should bear such wretches on it!—who gain their livelihood from the flesh and blood of such poor mortals as these. 'This woman' is willing to be reformed, willing to be reclaimed; ask my friend, the lieutenant, there, whether he has not met scores and hundreds who are willing to come into the Dormitory, but they cannot at all times find room for them, and do all they would for them. Therefore have I come here to plead with you; and if you think I have spoken somewhat too boldly, I ask no forgiveness; my subject demands plain speaking. I could speak in no other way to let you know what I meant. I ask again, have you no pity, no love, no sympathy for poor, lost outcasts? I beseech you, for their mother's sake, now in Heaven; for their father's sake, whose grey hairs are now hurrying to the grave; for the sake of your own sons, who may happen to be entrapped by her; ay! for your own sake, for your eyes are often offended by her; for Christ's sake, who has, I doubt not, bought many such as 'this woman' with his blood, and will yet lead them up to Heaven by his Holy Spirit; by what you yourselves owe to your Lord and Saviour Jesus Christ, and by what you have been forgiven yourselves, I beseech you, as much as lieth in you, now assist this Institution. I do not think I am wrong in pleading so hard. If any of you do not think the cause good, then, do not give your money. If you do not think the cause worth giving to, I would not thank you for a doit. But the cause is so good that, had I wealth, I would pour it out, that the work might be well maintained; and I plead from my own heart for this, perhaps more than I have done for many an institution for a long day past. With all my heart, I urge those of you who love their kind, and love the worst, as your Saviour did, now, as God shall enable you, to help these poor creatures; for our friends are helping them, and they want your assistance, and 'God loveth a cheerful giver.' Amen.

* * * *

* 'This Sermon was the means of two wanderers being received into the Dormitory. A young woman was passing by St Martin's Hall, in a very desponding state of mind, and in great physical distress; she saw the service announced, went in and listened with eager earnestness to the preacher; she was much impressed, stayed until the service was over, then made her sad case known, and she was admitted. Her case was a very painful one. One false step had plunged her into the wicked course which was hurrying her down to eternal destruction; but, through grace, she was arrested by this Sermon. The other wanderer was brought into the shelter of the Institution through the instrumentality of an aged Christian who was deeply impressed as she listened to the discourse of the earnest preacher. The text laid hold upon her mind, and she thought how many poor fallen ones she had passed by unheeded. A few days after, she saw a woman in a state of drunkenness; the text rushed into her memory, and she thought, "I do see this woman, and now, what is my duty towards her?" She conducted the wretched outcast woman home, visited her when she was sober, and reasoned with her on her terrible sin and its awful consequences. The aged believer was instrumental in bringing this woman into the safe shelter of the Home. This young woman had been cruelly deceived, and her hopes had been blighted under peculiarly painful circumstances.—T. W. M.' Published in *The Sword and the Trowel*, September 1897.

C. H. Spurgeon's most striking sermons, no. 9

BY T. W. MEDHURST, CARDIFF. PUBLISHED IN *THE SWORD AND THE TROWEL*, SEPTEMBER 1898

I AM happy to be able to furnish the readers of *The Sword and the Trowel* with the notes—hitherto unpublished—of a memorable discourse delivered by our beloved and glorified President nearly forty years ago. So far as can be ascertained, Mr Spurgeon's first sermons to a Welsh audience were delivered in the ancient village of Castleton, midway between Newport and Cardiff, on Wednesday, July 20, 1859. This visit is still greatly talked about by the aged people in the district; I have often been delighted to see their glistening eyes as they have related their recollections of this red-letter day in their past experience. Never in the annals of the village, either before or since, has there been anything at all approximating to the scene which was witnessed that day. For some time previously, it had been made known through Monmouthshire and Glamorganshire that the popular preacher, C. H. Spurgeon, would deliver two discourses in the open air at Castleton. The excitement among the people, and especially among the inhabitants of the hill-districts, in anticipation of the services, was immense. The question, 'Are you going to hear Spurgeon?' took the place of the usual remarks about the weather. The various railway companies ran excursion trains, and the result was an enormous gathering of people from all parts.

The first service began at eleven o'clock in the morning, in a field which was admirably adapted for the occasion, as it gradually sloped to a level at the bottom. The seats were arranged in a semi-circular form. Everyone had a full view of the preacher, and his powerful voice was distinctly heard by the nine or ten thousand persons assembled. Before announcing his text, Mr Spurgeon said:—

My dear friends, I most earnestly and humbly entreat your prayers that I may be enabled to preach the gospel with power this day. I do not know that at any time I ever felt my own weakness more than I do now. I recollect to what mighty men of God some of you have sometimes listened, ministers whose names ought to be held in reverence as long as any man's name endures on the face of the earth. I can scarcely hope to tread in the footsteps of many of those preachers whom you have heard. This, however, I can say to you,—you may have men in Wales who can preach the gospel *in a better manner* than I can hope to do, but you have no one who can preach A BETTER GOSPEL. It is the same gospel from first to last, and tells of the same Saviour, who is ready to receive the meanest, the feeblest, the most guilty, and the most vile, who come unto God by him. May the Holy Spirit graciously rest upon us now! I will read my text to you from the Gospel according to Matthew, the twenty-eighth chapter, and the fifth verse, and then Mr Davies, of Haverfordwest College, will read it to you in Welsh,—a feat which I cannot accomplish.

'And the angel answered and said unto the women, Fear not ye: for I know that ye seek Jesus, which was crucified.'—Matthew 28:5.

When the angel descended from Heaven, in all his brightness of glory he cast his lightning glance upon the keepers of Christ's tomb, and they, overcome with fright, 'did shake, and became as dead men;' there was no spirit left in them. Close by, stood two feeble women,—'Mary Magdalene and the other Mary,'—women with none of the strength possessed by those mighty soldiers, who had probably faced death in many a battle. Is it any wonder that these women also began to tremble? The angel, veiling his brightness, and putting away the lightning from his brow, turned to the women, and said, *'Fear not ye: for I know that ye seek Jesus, which was crucified.'*

Learn from this angelic message, dear friends, this truth,—bad men have always cause to fear, but good people never. The wicked may well tremble at the presence of the angel of the Lord; but the righteous may look old Satan in the face, and never fear. Come what may in this world, he who loveth not God has always fresh ground for alarm and dismay. O unsaved sinners, all Heaven is against you! Hell, with which you are leagued, is, notwithstanding, your enemy. You, who rebel against God, have nowhere a friend. Look up to the throne of God; there, stern, unyielding justice is against you. Look around the throne; there stand the peers of Heaven's high state, every one ready to punish sin, and to avenge the quarrel of God with sinful man. Look around you in the world, ye ungodly ones; everything is against you. Do you prosper? You are but fattening for your own destruction. Are you afflicted? Your afflictions are the first big drops of the hail of eternal wrath, if ye believe not in Jesus, and die in your sins. All things work together for ill to them that love not God, that despise his gospel, and that hate his Anointed. Be ye warned, O ye ungodly ones!

Ye who believe in Jesus, ye who are accepted in the Beloved, never have any cause to tremble, come what may. Let all the vials of wrath be poured out in the air, in the sea, and on the earth, yet let not your cheeks be blanched with fear. Let all the lightnings make the heavens to be in a blaze, and all the thunders be let loose, yet let those who love God never shake: for 'we know that all things work together for good to them that love God, to them who are the called according to his purpose.' Yea, the more earnestly and the more terribly 'all things work together,' the richer will be the blessings they will bring to the people of God. Suppose now that for three days the sun should not rise, and that the whole earth were wrapped in Egyptian darkness. Imagine the moon turned into a clot of blood, and that the stars, reeling to and fro like madmen, had left their places, and had fled away into infinite space. Conceive in the midst of the black darkness, uncheered by a single ray of light, that there should be a great earthquake, and that a voice should be heard as of a trumpet, even such a dreadful sound as was heard upon Mount Sinai. Think, next, that hell had opened its mouth, and that all the spirits of darkness had been let loose. Yet, even then, when the worst had come to the worst, the godly man might sing,—

'He that hath made his refuge God
    Shall find a most secure abode,

Shall walk all day beneath his shade,
  And there at night shall rest his head.'

Believers in the Lord Jesus Christ, let us never be afraid, but let us always rejoice. 'If God be for us, who can be against us?'

[The preacher next said that, in dependence upon God's grace, he would divide his discourse thus: in the first place, he would endeavour *to seek out the seekers,* those who were seeking Jesus; in the second place, he would endeavour *to meet the fears of those who were seeking Jesus;* he would try to bring the seekers' fears up to the great guns of the promises, blow them to pieces, and scatter them to the four winds of heaven; then he might possibly be able to say *a few closing words of application and exhortation.* Mr Spurgeon then continued:—]

I. First, dear friends, let us endeavour TO SEEK OUT THE SEEKERS,—those who, like Mary Magdalene and the other Mary, are *seeking Jesus with all their hearts.*

There are some people who seem to imagine they are to be carried to Heaven upon a feather bed; they think they have only to fold their arms, and go floating into Paradise. I wonder how such persons explain this text, 'From the days of John the Baptist until now, the kingdom of Heaven suffereth violence, and the violent take it by force.' The kingdom of Heaven is not to be taken by a sleeping soldier, neither are we to be carried to the skies 'on flowery beds of ease.' It is often no easy work to find the Saviour. The example of Mary Magdalene and the other Mary, in their overflowing love, in their unlimited confidence, in their earnest and passionate longing, must be followed and imitated. When I was seeking Christ, I worked harder than ever I did before, and underwent greater mental and bodily labour. Like the horse in the hunt, which, in the pursuit, requires neither whip, nor spur, nor bit, so must the conduct of the seeker be; and the true seeker will seek Jesus with all his heart, and mind, and soul, and strength.

The sincere seeker will industriously and continuously seek Jesus. It is not by prayer today and forgetfulness tomorrow that Jesus Christ is to be found. It is not the excitement of a sermon on the Sunday, and the still greater excitement of the whisky on the Monday, that will carry men to Heaven. We have known men and women under deep religious conviction, and have often noticed their earnestness in listening to the gospel; we have seen them crowd into the house of God, and stand during the whole service without any support to lean on; and they have not complained of weariness. Mere nominal, formal professors, seated in their comfortably-cushioned pews, will yawn and sleep, or complain of the service being too long, and grumble if the minister keeps them five minutes beyond the allotted time; but earnest seekers never complain of the length of the time they spend in the worship of the sanctuary. They will not object to walk twenty miles to the service, and the same distance back again, and think little of any sacrifices they have to make, being ready to go any distance to hear the gospel preached, if so be they can but find Jesus, who was crucified. Some people say they are *waiting* for the Lord; waiting for a special appeal, or manifestation. Waiting, are they? But waiting implies being ready. Suppose that I am staying at your house, and you say to me, 'Dear me, how late you are; I have been waiting tea for you for some time.' But the kettle is not boiling, and I see no preparation for the meal; and I say, 'I don't believe you have been waiting, or the tea would have been made, and you would have been prepared for my coming.' The soul that is really waiting for Christ, is the soul that is ready to receive Christ, the soul that is continually crying, 'Come, Lord Jesus, my heart is ready to welcome thee.'

The earnest seeker will not be particular as to where Christ is to be found, if so be that he can find him. When men have no living interest in religion, they are often most ready to fight for its every jot and tittle. The spiritually dead Churchman—and there are many such,—is ready to stand up for every door-nail belonging to Mother Church, and for every form and ceremony mentioned in the Prayer-book! The dead Baptist will fight and quarrel about the depth of the water, and the terms of communion. The dead Wesleyan will contend for the Conference, and Class Meeting, and the three years' system, and exclaim, 'I do not like those Reform fellows!' Until men are really anxious about Christ Jesus the Lord, they are the greatest bigots and sticklers for precedents that can be imagined; but when they are in downright earnest in their anxiety first to find and then to serve Jesus, then are they zealously affected for the spiritual welfare of others. There is a sinner dying of hunger, and he is crying for bread. The Churchman offers him the genuine square bread, baked in real Established tins; the Wesleyan comes with a nicely-baked cottage loaf; the Baptist presents the plain four-pound loaf, warranted full weight; the Congregationalist comes with his choice fancy bread; and the Primitive Methodist offers his crisp twist. 'Gentlemen,' says the starving man, 'I really do not care which bread it is, only give me *bread,* for I am starving. Give me of the Bread of Life now, and let us talk of other matters after my hunger is appeased.'

Once more, *the sincere seeker seeks Jesus early*. Satan keeps whispering, 'Tomorrow.' The true seeker knows that delays are dangerous, yea, that they may be damnable. True seekers seek the Saviour because they cannot help themselves; they are so hard pressed that they must seek Jesus, or perish. Some people ask when they are to pray. If a man is knocked down by a heavy blow, would you expect him to ask, 'When may I cry out? When may I get up?' The poor fellow would not be able to help crying out, and, naturally, he would get up as soon as possible. If it were arranged, in our hospitals, that the patients should groan at a certain hour in the morning, and then again at a certain hour in the evening, it might perhaps be better for the nurses and attendants; but the poor sufferers groan because they cannot help groaning. Nature must express its woes; it is just so with the sincere seeker, he has a spiritual necessity laid upon him, and he must seek, he must groan, he must cry out aloud, he cannot be silent. No sinner has ever yet gone to Christ who could stop away from him. I know a man who lets out horses. Someone went to him, and asked him how much he would charge for a horse for a day; he told him, and then the man went round to others, and tried to get one at a lower price. He did not succeed, and when he came back, the first man said, 'No, you have been round to other people in the town, and you shall not have my horse now.' Is it not a similar case with some seekers? They go to Moses, they ask him how much he will charge to take them to Heaven, and they find that his charges are very high. At last, when they go to the Lord Jesus Christ, it is from sheer necessity; but, blessed be his all-glorious name, the Saviour never turns any sincere seeking soul away. Jesus welcomes the seeker, and will in no wise cast him out, no matter to how many he has sought previously. Come to him now, come just as you are, and he will receive even *you*.

II. Now let us try TO SLAY THE SLAVISH FEARS THAT KEEP THE SEEKER FROM THE SAVIOUR. Would that we could bring up these fears, one by one, and pierce them through and through so that they should fall down dead!

One fear that agitates the seeking sinner is, lest he should not be one of God's elect. I had this fear firmly fixed in my soul when I was seeking Jesus. I went to one minister, who proved to be an unskilled physician; and he, pulling a long face, said, 'My young friend, you have nothing to do with the doctrine of election.' As I left him, I said to myself, 'I am not very grateful for what I have got out of him.' It is not wise to tell a distressed, seeking soul that he has nothing to do with the doctrine of election; he is not to be thus silenced. Yet the doctrine of election should never keep any sinner from coming to Christ, for he himself has said, 'Him that cometh to me, I will in no wise cast out.'

Here comes another, who says, '*I fear I have not come to Jesus Christ the right way.*' My friend, no one can come to Jesus Christ the wrong way. No man can come to Jesus, except the Father, which hath sent Jesus, draw him; and the Father will draw no sinner to Jesus the wrong way. Some people are troubled because they cannot tell the time of their conversion; but it is not necessary that anyone should know the time and place so long as he is sure about the fact of his conversion. Suppose, as I am walking through the streets of Castleton, I meet an old woman, and say to her, 'Well, mistress, how are you?' She answers, 'I am very well considering my age.' I ask, 'How old are you?' She replies, 'Nearly eighty; but I don't recollect exactly.' 'Well,' I say, 'but you know when and where you were born, do you not?' She says, 'No, I do not remember anything about that.' Suppose, then, I looked her full in the face, and said, 'My good woman, if you don't recollect *when* you were born, and don't know *where* you were born, depend upon it you are labouring under a delusion altogether, *you never were born, and you are not alive.*' I can almost imagine the old woman would answer, 'Get away with you, you insolent fellow, or I'll soon show you that I am alive.' My dear friends, let me suggest that you apply this illustration to your own case. If you are alive in Christ, you need not distress yourselves because you cannot tell *the time and place* when you were first quickened. If you can say with the man who had been blind from his birth, and whose eyes Jesus had opened, 'One thing I know, that, whereas I was blind, now I see,' you need not question the genuineness of your spiritual vision, because you cannot reply to the vain questionings of Satan.

Some believers have the strange fear that, perhaps, after all, they are not saved, *because they do not feel precisely as others feel;* their experience somewhat varies from that of other Christians. Remember, my dear friends, it is often the odd men that are saved. Christ's army is very much like David's ragged regiment; we read in the Book of Samuel (1 Samuel 22:2): 'And every one that was in distress, and every one that was in debt, and every one that was discontented, gathered themselves unto him; and he became a captain over them.' Your experience may not be on all fours with that of others; but have you come to Jesus Christ? Some have a terrible experience, others are like Lydia, 'whose heart the Lord opened;' but let not any distress themselves, or murmur, if they can say, 'I know whom I have believed.' 'Jesus is precious to me.' 'I am trusting in him.' The Holy Spirit has more ways than one of getting into the hearts of men. Sometimes he comes with a key, and places it in the well-oiled lock, and the door is gently opened. At another time he may come as with a huge sledge-hammer, and violently burst open the door. Never mind how the door is opened, if Jesus does but enter, bringing salvation with him.

Some are under the strange delusion that they may be the children of God one day, and the next day be the children of the devil. I cannot, for the life of me, imagine how I can be the child of JOHN SPURGEON today, and the child of TOM JONES, or of BEN LEWIS tomorrow. I cannot understand how a man can have two fathers, and especially two fathers who are fathers turn-and-turn-about. I know my earthly father, and while he lives, he must be my father; and if I am a child of God today, I shall be a child of God through all eternity.

'Once in Christ, in Christ for ever;
Nothing from his love can sever.'

You may belong to the awkward squad, but you have no need to fear, if you are seeking Jesus Christ, who was crucified. If you can truly say that you are on the side of Jesus, you have no cause for fear, for none can destroy you on earth or in hell.

* * * * *

The sermon was a most powerful discourse, delivered with impassioned earnestness and fire, never surpassed by the most eloquent of the Welsh preachers. The text in the evening was Revelation 14:1–3: 'And I looked, and, lo, a Lamb stood on the mount Sion, and with him an hundred forty and four thousand, having his Father's name written on their foreheads. And I heard a voice from heaven, as the voice of many waters, and as the voice of a great thunder: and I heard the voice of harpers harping with their harps: and they sung as it were a new song before the throne, and before the four beasts, and the elders: and no man could learn that song but the hundred and forty and four thousand, which were redeemed from the earth.' Every word of the preacher was plainly audible to the whole of the vast audiences at both the services; and at the close of the day it was remarked that his voice was as clear and as vigorous as at the commencement.—T.W.M.

A visit to Calvary

A sermon delivered by C. H. Spurgeon, at the Hanover Square Rooms, on 14 March 1856, on behalf of the Exeter Buildings' Ragged School

FORWARDED BY T. W. MEDHURST, CARDIFF

'And Pilate saith unto them, Behold the man!'—John 19:5

IT had been insinuated against Pilate that he was in league with Jesus Christ to set up a new monarchy in opposition to that of Cæsar. In order to refute that accusation, Pilate orders Jesus to be scourged. The soldiers put upon his head a crown of thorns; they spit upon him; they pluck his hair; they buffet him; and when all these cruelties and insults have been heaped upon his person, Pilate brings forth Jesus Christ from the Prætorium. Standing there, he addresses the people assembled in the street, tersely exclaiming, '*Ecce homo!*' '*Behold the man!*' 'This is the man with whom you charge me of conspiring against Cæsar. Is this how I would treat my accomplice? Would I in this way show my kindness and devotion to one whom I intended to set up as Cæsar's rival? Do you fancy that here you see marks of honour? Is that old purple coat the imperial robe which you say I wish to throw over his shoulders? Are these my kindnesses to my friend?' It must have been a very telling answer to their accusations; and they must have seen that a repetition of the charge would be a barefaced falsehood.

I think, also, that Pilate had another purpose to serve in bringing Jesus forward in this array of misery. I believe that he sincerely desired to deliver our Saviour from crucifixion, and he thought that, bloodthirsty as the people were, their vengeance would be satisfied at the sight of their victim in this extremity of suffering and sorrow, and that they would say, 'Let him go.' 'Surely,' he thought, 'this will satisfy them; though they had demons' hearts, this might content them; though, like fiends, they thirsted to show their cruelty, surely this would be enough.' But it was not so; like the tiger which has tasted blood, they were insatiable; and the very sight of his emaciated form, stained all over with the streaming gore, did but excite them the more loudly to cry, 'Crucify him! Crucify him!'

I believe that one of Pilate's purposes *was* answered; the people no longer suspected him of being an accomplice with our Saviour. But the other purpose, blessed be God, *was not* accomplished; for if it had been, we should have been unredeemed at this hour, and the sacrifice of Calvary would not have been offered for our redemption. Now I am going to leave Pilate, and I shall endeavour, by the help of God, to stand in his place, and with an entirely different motive, to say to each one of you,—

'BEHOLD THE MAN!'

May the Holy Spirit be with us, and, by his gracious power, reveal our Lord Jesus Christ visibly set forth crucified among you, so that, by the eye of faith, every one of you, whether you have seen him before or not, may now be enabled to look unto him who was crucified for our sins, who bore our griefs, and carried our sorrows! A view of Christ on Calvary is always beneficial to a Christian. We never hear a sermon concerning Christ crucified of which we disapprove, however inelegant its diction, if it be sound in doctrine. We never complain of our minister that he preaches too much concerning Jesus Christ. No; there can be no tautology where his name is mentioned; though a sermon should be little beyond the mere repetition of his Name, we would rejoice to hear it, and say,—

'Jesus, I love thy charming Name,
    'Tis music to mine ear.'

The French king said that 'he would rather hear the repetitions of Bourdaloue than the novelties of any other preacher.' So we can say of our Lord Jesus Christ, that we had rather hear the repetitions of Jesus than any novelty from any preacher whatsoever. Oh, how dissatisfied are our souls when we listen to a sermon that is destitute of Christ! There are some preachers who can manage to deliver a discourse and to leave Christ's name out of it altogether. Surely, the true believer, who is present on such an occasion, will say, with Mary Magdalene, 'They have taken away the Lord, and I know not where they have laid him.' Take away Christ from the sermon, and you have taken away its essence. The marrow of theology is Christ; the very bone and sinew of the gospel is preaching Christ. A Christless sermon is the merriment of hell; it is also a fearful waste of time, and it dyes with the blood of souls the skirts of the man who dares to preach it. But too much of Christ we cannot have. Give us Christ always, Christ ever. The monotony of Christ is sweet variety, and even the unity of Christ hath in it all the elements of harmony. Christ on his cross and on his throne, in the manger and in the tomb,—Christ everywhere is sweet to us. We love his name, we adore his Person, we delight to hear of his works and his words. Come, then, to Calvary awhile with me, that I may say to you, as Pilate said to the Jews outside his judgment hall, 'Behold the man!'

I would take you there with this object; first, *to instruct your intellect;* secondly, *to excite your emotions;* and, thirdly, *to amend your practice.* For we hold that religion consists of three things; sound doctrine, affecting the intellect; true experience, dealing with the emotions; and a holy life, fashioning the outward visible practice of every day. Our Lord Jesus Christ will benefit us in all these respects; and if, by faith, we are enabled to see him now, we shall go away edified in doctrine, blessed in experience, and sanctified in practice.

I. First, I beseech you to 'behold the man,' TO INSTRUCT YOUR INTELLECT.

The first lesson I would indicate to you,—for I shall not so much teach it as leave the Holy Spirit to teach it,—is concerning *the evil nature of sin.* See that man crucified, his hands extended upon the cruel tree. Mark the droppings of his precious blood. Do you see the thorny crown upon his head? Do you note the signs of suffering upon his whole frame? Do you observe his eyes sunk in their sockets? Do you behold the agony depicted on his countenance? Do you perceive the acute, unutterable anguish which he suffers? If thou dost see him aright, thou wilt see in him the evil of sin. In no other place wilt thou ever know how desperately vile is man's iniquity. This is the spot where guilt committed its direst crime. Sin is exceeding sinful when it is a *homicide;* but it is most sinful of all when it becomes a DEICIDE, and kills God. The vilest deed sin ever did was when it nailed the

Saviour to his cross, and there let him hang, the murdered victim of our sin. Would you really see sin? I might show you a thousand pictures of it. I might let you behold fair Eden blasted and withered, with all its fruits smitten, the moisture of its trees completely dried up, its fair walks covered with the leaves of decay. I might show you a heavenly pair banished, driven out to till the ground whence they were taken, with the swords of the cherubim flashing behind them; and when you saw that sight, you would execrate sin as a thing which drew the ploughshare over Paradise. I might make you hate sin, too, if I showed you, yonder, a drowned world, deluged by a flood. See where men, women, and children are sinking in the mighty waters, where the fountains above and the deeps below are clasping hands. Did you hear the shriek of the last strong swimmer, in his agony, ere he also was overcome by the boundless, shoreless sea? Behold the earth, waste and void, save where yon ark floats alone above the deluge! Do you enquire the cause of all this desolation? What loosed the bands of the great deep? What brought this awful destruction? SIN *did it*. What was that which devoured Sodom and Gomorrah, and rained fire and brimstone out of heaven upon them? What was that which swallowed up Korah, Dathan, and Abiram, and took them down alive into the pit? What hath peopled death's dominions? Whence those skeletons and bones? Whence yon hearse and funeral? And what has builded the gloomy chambers of Hades? What has made Gehennah hot with unquenchable fire? And what is that which hath given hell its everlasting torments, and furnished it with inhabitants beyond number, who live in eternal tortures and unutterable woe? Sin, *thou didst all this;* therefore do we execrate thee. Thou didst drown a world; thou didst dig the grave; thou didst pile the faggots of hell. We hate thee, sin; but yet, methinks, we might forgive thee if thou hadst not put Jesus Christ to death!

Christian, wilt thou not, henceforth, hate sin from this very fact, that the blood of thy Saviour is on it? Thou art tempted to do an act which thou knowest is wrong; it looks fair, and beautiful, and goodly, but examine it closely; it seems lovely and excellent, and thy heart goeth after it. Stop! Turn it round; do you see the blood mark upon it? That sin is stained with thy Saviour's blood. Wilt thou touch it now? Surely, nothing which has in the least contributed to his death can be loved by us. Will we not, henceforth, abjure, abhor, detest, and avoid everything that is sinful? What! do you call yourselves Christians, and yet live in sin? Do you nurse in your bosom the murderer of your Saviour? Do you hang upon your walls the dagger wherewith your best Friend was stabbed, and embroider on your clothes the image of his murderers? Will you still harbour sin, and love it, when sin slew your Lord? Nay, surely, your heart cries, 'I'll take vengeance against my sins, and slay the murderers, too.'

Another lesson I would give your understanding is this,—'Behold the man,' for then you will see *the inflexibility of divine justice.* Do we not all know that God's justice is inflexibly severe? If any man sin, the Law saith, 'Cursed is that man.' The law alters not in its thunder. 'Cursed! Cursed! Cursed!' is the sentence that continually sounds from Sinai. Have we not read that God 'will by no means spare the guilty'? And do we not know it to be a fact? Yet, beloved, there are some who preach an atonement which looks very much like the abrogation of divine justice. We have heard and read of divines whose theory of the atonement is something like this; although God hath solemnly declared himself to be angry at sin, and hath vowed to punish every sinner, yet Jesus Christ, in some way or other,—we know not how,—did something or other which allows God now to pass by our sins without punishing them at all. We have no faith in such an atonement as that; we believe that God is so just, that every sinner must be punished, and that every crime must inevitably receive its due penalty. We believe that all the punishment which God's people ought to have endured was laid upon the head of Christ; we look to his cross, and we there see God's justice satisfied only because all our guilt was laid upon his shoulders, and the punishment for that guilt was actually borne by Christ Jesus our Lord. God did not absolutely pass over sin; he punished it on Christ Jesus, his people's Substitute; and, henceforth, sin ceases to be punishable upon the persons of those for whom Christ died.

O ye who do not know how inflexible Divine justice is, stand at the foot of yon cross, and hear our Saviour's dying groans, see his looks of agony, mark his lineaments of woe; and then shall ye know how severe is the justice of God. No man ever thought Brutus so severely just as when he put his own sons to death. 'Surely,' the people said, 'he will spare *them.*' But, no; the inflexible senator said, 'They have broken the laws of my country, and they shall die.' And so, in a higher and more sublime sense, we might never have known how just God was, if he had not put his own Son to death for our sin. Bring forth the sinner, Justice! 'Nay,' saith Justice, 'the sinner may go free; for here is the sinner's Substitute.' Then bring him forth, O Justice! 'Art thou the Substitute for the guilty?' 'I am, my Father.' 'Well, my Son, I love thee, I have loved thee from all eternity; but since thou art become the Substitute for sinners, I must punish on thee every sin which they commit.' See! the lash is uplifted; will it not fall gently on his shoulders? He is the Son. See there! the sword is unsheathed. O sword, sleep in thy scabbard; he is the Son! He is the Son! Ay, but Son though he be, he is the sinner's Representative, and he must die. See how the cruel lash falls on him as they scourge him at Pilate's pillar; mark how he bleeds at every pore, while in the garden, under his Father's wrath against his people's sin, he sweats great drops of blood! Mark how the sword unsparingly smites him till he cries, 'It is finished.' O brethren, God is just; but we never know that truth half so well till, in Gethsemane's gloom, and in the midst of Golgotha's horrors, we have tarried for a while! What thinkest thou, O unpardoned man or woman? If God punished his Son for sins not his own, surely he will punish thee for thy sins if thou continuest an unbeliever. If Jesus Christ, who only had *imputed* guilt laid to his charge, must suffer like this, how wilt thou escape from suffering for *thine own sin?* If he, the perfect, the pure, the spotless One, must suffer so fearful an amount of agony, how shalt thou escape if thou dost 'neglect so great salvation'? How hopest thou to be delivered if, on the beloved Son's head, such vengeance fell? Where, O where, wilt thou find a covering for thyself? Know thou this, that God, who is infinitely just, having exacted, at the hands of Jesus Christ, the penalty for all his people, will surely exact the penalty at thine hands if thou diest impenitent, and if thou approachest his bar unwashed in the blood of the Saviour.

Next, I think we may also learn here *the omnipotence of love*. O Love, thou art the conqueror of all hearts! O Love, thou art the sum of Godhead, thou art the explanation of Divinity! What is this great world of ours, but 'Love' writ large? The stars, if we could read them rightly, would spell to us 'Love.' If we could interpret the language of the floods, we should hear them thundering 'Love.' And could we gather together all flowers, and distil their essence, and get the concentrated sweetness of them all, we should find that its fragrance was 'Love.' Everything in this world telleth of Love. But would you know the breadth, and length, and depth, and height of the love of God which passeth knowledge, come hither to the cross of Calvary, and 'behold the man.' We never know our love to our country till we are called to make some sacrifice for it. You remember that, in Russia, there was a law which exempted the only son of a widow from going to war; but it is said that, so closely were they driven for recruits, that the law was for a time rescinded, and the widow's only son was taken. Suppose such a thing happened here, and there should be a widow whose only son was demanded of her. See her come forward, saying, 'Ay, take him; my country is dearer to me even than he is.' She puts him forward, and says, 'Go forth, my son, to die if it be necessary; I give thee up right willingly.' You see the red eyes of the widow; she hath wiped them dry, but she hath wept in secret; and if we steal behind the door when her son is gone, and see her pouring out whole floods of sorrow, we can tell how great must have been her love for her country which made her give up him,—her all. Beloved, we never should have known Christ's love in all its depths and heights if he had not died; nor could we have told the depth of the Father's affection for us if he had not given his Son to die in our stead. As for the common mercies we enjoy, they all sing of 'Love,' just as the sea-shell, when we put it to our ears, whispers of the deep sea whence it came; but, ah! if ye desire to hear the ocean itself, if ye would hear the roarings of the floods, ye must not look at every-day mercies, but at the mercies of that night, that midday night, when Jesus Christ was crucified. He who would know Love, let him repair to Calvary, and see the man of sorrows die.

'See from his head, his hands, his feet,
  Sorrow and love flow mingled down!
Did e'er such love and sorrow meet,
  Or thorns compose so rich a crown?'

II. Now, beloved, let us 'behold the man' TO EXCITE OUR EMOTIONS.
We will again go, in imagination, to Calvary, and if God's Spirit shall

help us, it will be more than mere imagination; and we will endeavour there to hold fellowship with Christ, first, *that our emotions of sorrow may be excited*. We do not love a sorrowful religion, but we do not think anything of that religion which hath no sorrow in it. That which is entirely made up of sorrow, came not from God; for God loves happiness, he rejoices to see his creatures happy, and his religion has that tendency; but, still, he who never knew spiritual sorrow hath not known spiritual joy. If we have never shed the tear of penitence, we must not expect to sing the song of acceptance. Go ye to Calvary, if ye would learn to weep. There are times when we would give much to be able to shed a tear, for our icy hearts are so cold that all the heat of mercy cannot thaw them, and our souls are so hard that it seems impossible that they should ever be melted. Ye Christians, who have long walked in Christ's ways, have ye not sometimes cried, 'Oh, that we could weep as once we did, when we were young and tender in the fear of God! Then we could pour out our heart in tears, but now these rocky hearts will not weep; though there be things which we hear concerning Jesus that might make our souls run over at our eyes in perpetual torrents, yet we cannot weep a single tear just now.' Well, beloved, would you be made to weep? Come with me to Calvary. See there your Saviour with the thorns upon his brow; can you not afford a tear for him? See the wounds in his side; can you not drop a tear of grief there, especially when I remind you that he is your best Friend? Surely I might say, 'If you have tears, prepare to shed them now.' Ye ought to shed them while ye see his hands nailed to the accursed wood, his feet fastened there, too, and his side gushing like a fountain of blood. Ah! well may we sing,—

'Alas! and did my Saviour bleed?
    And did my Sovereign die?
Would he devote that sacred head
    For such a worm as I?

'Was it for crimes that I had done
    He groan'd upon the tree?
Amazing pity! grace unknown!
    And love beyond degree.

'Well might the sun in darkness hide,
   And shut his glories in,
When God, the mighty Maker, died
   For man, the creature's sin.'

Did he die? Ay, that he did. Then I may indeed weep; and I may say, with holy Herbert,—

'O who will give me tears? Come all ye springs,
Dwell in my head and eyes: come clouds, and rain:
My grief hath need of all the wat'ry things
That nature hath produc'd. Let ev'ry vein
Suck up a river to supply mine eyes,
My weary weeping eyes, too dry for me
Unless they get new conduits, new supplies,
To bear them out, and with my state agree.'

If, by any accident, I had killed my best earthly friend, I should go mourning all my days; but since, by my own accursed sin, I have slain my Saviour, oh! let me carry to my grave my grief,—not hopeless misery, but sincere sorrow that I slew my Saviour. Can I ever hear that word Calvary without remembering the sad tragedy connected with it? Shall I ever see the cross without shedding tears on account of its once heavy burden? Shall I ever hear the music of the Name of Jesus without mingling with it the plaintive notes of my own grief, crying yet again,—

'Thy body slain, sweet Jesus, thine,
   And bathed in its own blood,
While all exposed to wrath Divine,
   The injured Sufferer stood'?

Here let me weep myself away;—

'But drops of grief can ne'er repay
   The debt of love I owe;

Here, Lord, I give myself away;
    'Tis all that I can do.'

But, as I have already reminded you, true religion is not all sorrow; nor is much of it grief. True religion makes us happy; it lights up the eye like the lamps of heaven, it causes our feet to bound over this weary earth, it makes our souls elastic, and fills them with joy seraphic. They who have the most religion will have the least misery, for godliness will turn their bitterest cups of grief into sweetest chalices of joy. He who liveth near to Christ must be blessed, come what may; but he who wandereth from him, give him all the mercies of this life, and he cannot be happy, because he hath not God. Well, ye poor distressed, mourning souls, are you seeking to have joy in your hearts? Come, let me take you to Calvary; your desponding spirits cannot long mourn with the air of Calvary around you. Ready-to-Halt never leaned on his crutches when he went by the cross; for once, good man, he walked without them. Mr Fearing was not troubled with his fainting heart when he clasped that cross. No; his heart was as strong as that of Mr Valiant-for-Truth when he was there. Are you often given to depression of spirit? Do you labour under despondency of soul? Let me for once prescribe for you; let me recommend you something which will effectually cure you. When thou art low and miserable, go into thy chamber, and there, on thy knees, think of him who groaned in Gethsemane, and thou wilt say, 'What are all my sorrows compared with his?' Then, think of Calvary; and when thou hast, in thought, been there a little while, sing to thyself,—

'Oh! 'tis sweet to view the flowing
    Of his sin-atoning blood,
With Divine assurance knowing
    He hath made my peace with God.'

Or, if thou canst not reach so high a flight as that, still say,—

'Here I'll sit, for ever viewing
    Mercy's streams, in streams of blood;

Precious drops! my soul bedewing,
> Plead and claim my peace with God.'

The cross of our Lord Jesus Christ is an infallible remedy for thy misery. If thou wilt put the cross into thy cup, thou wilt find that it will be like the tree cast into the bitter fountain of Marah, it will make the water sweet. If thou wilt take some of the gall Christ drank, thou wilt find that it is marvellous in its power, for it maketh all other gall to be sweet. The happiest men are those who know most of Jesus Christ. Do not tell us that the epicure is happy; tell us not that the dissipated man is happy, he who says,—

'Fill, fill the glass to the brim,
Let the sparkling liquor kiss the rim.'

Say not that he is happy who runneth the mad career of lust; say not that he is happy whose whole soul is set on ambitious desires; he is miserable, and his conscience says that it is so. He is miserable; and, in the silence of the midnight hour, his trembling tells us that it is so. He is miserable, and in his inmost heart he knows it; though the upper floods of his soul do sometimes seem to leap with joy, down in the deep caverns of his heart there is darkness, compared with which midnight is as the blazing noonday. If ye would be happy,—if ye would rejoice with joy unspeakable and full of glory, 'Behold the man!'—the man of sorrows who hath died for you on Calvary's tree.

There is another emotion, which should always be excited when we behold the cross of Christ, that is, *the emotion of most ardent love*. Believe me, beloved, to hold on in this world, as a true Christian, requires much love to your Master. If you are content to conform to all the rules of Society even when you know that they are wrong, you may go on smoothly enough; but if you have a principle within you, which will not let you stoop to do that which is evil, if you have a soul which cannot be cramped or fettered, if you say, 'It is not folly to be singular so long as I am right; and even if I stand alone, and though the heavens fall, I must be true to my Lord;'—you will find that, to persevere in such a course of conduct, requires much love to the Saviour. If we could have read Martin Luther's heart, when he stood before the great assembly at Worms, and maintained the truth before them all, we might have seen deeply cut in it the Name of Jesus Christ, his Lord and Saviour; and if you could know the heart of those who labour for men's souls amidst obloquy, contempt, and scorn, you would see stamped in the very centre the Name of Jesus Christ. You cannot long persevere as a Christian, in the midst of persecution and trouble, unless you have much love to the Saviour.

But, alas! we often hear persons mourn that they do not love the Saviour as they ought. That is a common complaint, but there is an easy cure for it. The more you live with Christ, the better will you love him. There are some people in the world, of so unlovable a nature that, to see them once in seven years, is quite enough, if you wish to love them; the less you know of them, perhaps, the better you will like them. But of our Lord Jesus Christ, we may truly say, that the longer you live with him, the better you will love him. Ask the grey-headed saint whether he loves Christ now more or less than he used to do. If you could have asked one of the old martyrs in the Roman amphitheatre whether he still loved his Master, would he not have answered, 'These many years have I served him, and he has never done me an ill turn; I cannot deny him, but I can die for him'? Why do you not love Jesus Christ? It is because you do not live with him, and think enough of him, for—

'Living with Christ, his likeness we gain.'

Do not try to force yourselves up into a certain degree of love to Christ by some extraordinary means. Go and live with him; meditate upon him continually, picture to yourself his sufferings for you, and then you will love him; it will become easy to you. It would have been almost impossible for any of us to have seen Jesus Christ, when he was here below, without loving him, if we had any grace in our hearts. Alas! unless grace be within us, we may look at him for ages without loving him. One of the ardent desires of my soul is to see the Man Christ Jesus once more on earth. I do look for his premillennial advent. Oh! if we might but clasp his feet, if we might kiss his pierced hands, if we might see the pleasing lustre of his eyes which outshine the glories of the stars, then we should none of us be saying,

'We want to love him'; but we should indeed love him, for we could not help it. If we are in full fellowship with him, we shall never say, 'We cannot love him,' but we shall say,—

'Thou know'st I love thee, dearest Lord;
    But oh, I long to soar
Far from the sphere of mortal joys,
    And learn to love thee more;—'

and we shall add, concerning our Lord and Saviour,—

'His worth, if all the nations knew,
Sure the whole world would love him, too.'

III. Now we come to our last point. 'Behold the man' Christ Jesus that you may AMEND YOUR PRACTICE.

True religion is not merely emotional, or intellectual; it is also practical. That man has no real religion, however much profession he may make, if he does not carry out the principles of the gospel in his daily life. 'Be not deceived; God is not mocked: for whatsoever a man soweth, that shall he also reap.' Come with me to Calvary once more, and you will amend your practice.

Let me remind you of one thing, wherein your practice will be very much improved if you truly come to Calvary. Here are members of different denominations of Christ's one Church, but how often are we affected with *that deadly disease, bigotry!* How frequently are we set against one another! Now, if we would love all Christians, we must 'behold the man' Christ Jesus. We have seen Christians fight, and fight manfully against each other,—we say '*manfully*,' for we cannot use that other word we might have uttered; we have seen Christians fight *woefully* against each other; but there is one spot that never yet was profaned in this way, and that is, Calvary. There the command goes forth, 'Sheath your swords, combatants! The battle is over; this is holy ground, for here Jesus died.' There is something that touches our hearts, when we begin to talk of Jesus Christ. We care not who the man is, whether he be sweet George Herbert, of the so-called 'Church of England,' or the equally excellent Samuel Rutherford, of the so-called 'Church of Scotland,' whether he be Nonconformist or Conformist, when he comes to talk of Christ Jesus, then we all stand around him, and we say, 'We would fight each other about some points; but when we come here, we are all one in Christ Jesus.' Then out go our hands, for we feel that we are truly one. That touch, not of nature, but of grace, makes the whole Christian Church one. O poor little-souled man, if thou hast no love for any unless he belongs to thine own sect, thou knowest not much of Christ Jesus, for, if thou didst live near to him, thou wouldst have a heart full of love towards all those who love him.

Again, by going to Calvary, you will *amend your practice in regard to outward holiness*. Do not tell me that a man has any real sense of Christ's love to him, if he can wilfully sin against Jesus the Saviour. We do see some strange prodigies now and then; but the strangest of all would be a Christian who could afford to live like a worldling, and yet maintain communion with Jesus Christ. We have heard men talk of their experience, and say much about what they call 'godliness', that is, 'godliness' on the tongue; but when they come to practice, ah! then we find that their religion is not made to bear the pressure of every-day life. It is a kind of confectionery religion; not at all substantial. It was not made to be carried about in this rough world; but intended rather as an ornament for their drawing-room; a fashionable religion, to come out on a fine Sunday; but it was never intended for week-day business. What! would you have them take their religion to the exchange? Why, it would stand in the way of their dealing with their fellows! Have their religion in the shop? They never thought of such a thing; they thought religion was intended for the closet of communion, though even that has its door listed over so that no sound of it might be heard. They thought religion was intended for them simply when they were reading the Bible, or looking at other religious books. Do you imagine that such men know anything of Christ Jesus? Alas! no. Those who live near to him, those who 'behold the man,' will become like him.

There is no such thing as having an interest in the blood of Jesus, and holding fellowship with him, and yet living in sin. Be not deceived concerning this matter. The follies and the fashions of this world are not consistent with vital godliness; and he who hopes to have Christ, and to have the world, too, hath made a great mistake. Have you ever read that pretty fable, told by the Persian moralist? He took up in his hand a piece of scented clay, and said to it, 'Oh, clay! whence hast thou obtained thy perfume?' And it replied, 'I was once only a piece of common clay, but they laid me for a time in company with a rose, and I drank in its fragrance, and so became scented clay.' Believer, thou also art nothing but a piece of common clay; but if thou art placed beside the Rose of Sharon, if thou art much in the company of Jesus Christ, thou wilt be a piece of scented clay; and, wherever thou goest, thou wilt carry his savour with thee, and all men will know the company thou hast kept by the fragrance thou hast received. If thou hast lain in beds of spices, thou wilt smell of the myrrh, and the aloes, and the cassia. I cannot believe thee to be a child of God unless thou hast the lineaments of thy Father; nor will I think that thou hast been with Jesus unless I perceive that thou hast learned of him. O dear friends, if ye would reform yourselves, if ye would amend your lives, if ye would curb sin, and restrain the hot-mouthed steeds of your lusts, if ye would overcome your iniquities, and persevere in holiness, here is the means of doing it all, 'Behold the man!' Look continually at Christ Jesus on the cross.

Now I have only time to apply my text to you, and then I have done. 'Behold the man!' This is an exhortation which I will use to every one of you. I have some here, I trust, who are sorrowing on account of sin. You have discovered yourselves to be—

'Lost and ruined by the Fall.'

God's sovereign mercy has looked upon you, and taught you your own nothingness. You once thought your morality good enough, and that your own integrity would carry you to Heaven; but now a 'hue and cry' is raised in your soul concerning the fire of sin within you, and you have discovered that you are lost. I come to preach to you especially,—

'Not the righteous, not the righteous;
    Sinners, Jesus came to call.'

If now you acknowledge and feel yourselves to be sinners, 'the glorious gospel of the blessed God' is 'Behold the man!' Look to Jesus on the cross; behold your sin laid on his head; and see there the expiation of your guilt. So, the lesson for penitents is, 'Behold the man!'

Let me tell you an anecdote; I have often related it before, but I love to repeat it. A friend of mine, who has been a minister in Ireland, assured me that the narrative was true. The clergyman of an Irish parish said, 'I went round to visit all my parishioners, with the exception of one poor woman, who had been an abandoned character; I dared not go to visit *her*, because I thought it would ill become my position, so I passed by her house. Ah, brother! I know that it was an evil pride, or else I should have gone after the chief of sinners, for the care of her soul was in some measure committed to my hands.' One day, that clergyman saw the poor woman in his church, and thought he heard her repeating the responses, and fancied he saw big tears rolling down her cheeks. Oh, how intensely he yearned for her soul! He longed to speak with her, yet felt that he dared not venture to do so. She came there month after month, a constant worshipper, and yet he passed by her door, and did not visit her. At last, one day, as he was passing by, she came to the door, and said, 'Sir, I want to speak with you.' He went into her house then, and she put out her hand, and, taking hold of his, said, 'Oh, sir! if your Master had been in this village half as long as you have, I am sure he would have been to see me long ere this. I am the worst sinner in the parish, and therefore I want Jesus Christ's help the most; but though *you* have not been to see me, I know where it is written, "This is a faithful saying, and worthy of all acceptation, that Christ Jesus came into the world to save sinners: *of whom I am chief.*"' Ah, friend! you may never have sinned exactly as that woman had done; but you have sinned. You may not have openly transgressed as she did; but if God the Holy Spirit has been at work in your heart, you will be content to stand side by side with her, and to say at once,—

'I the chief of sinners am.'

Once more, I must remind you that Jesus died for poor sinners, even for *you*. I will not speak to any other character but to you; I will have an extra word with you now. Oh, that I could bring you, poor penitent, to the

Saviour's feet! Art thou not seeking rest, yet finding none? Where and how art thou seeking it? By the works of the law; endeavouring, by leaving off this sin, and reforming that error, to save thyself? Oh! I charge thee, do not seek thus to put a film over the wound, for all the deadly venom will still be within. Go not to Sinai, for on its rocky sides no mercy grows. Go not there, for the thunder from the mount declares, 'Sinner, thou shalt die.' But, ah! my hearers, if you are guilty now, and burdened with a sense of condemnation, let me beseech and implore you, by the love ye have to yourselves, to come to Jesus Christ, and believe in him, and you shall most assuredly find salvation. There never yet was a sinner spurned from his gate; shall you be the first? There never was a penitent sent away without a blessing; and if you now call on him, you shall not be rejected. Mercy's door is always open to the man who knocks with sincerity. Go thou and knock, and mercy shall be thine. What if thy sins are more than others? If they are, I have all the more reason to preach to thee. The only warrant to believe in Christ is that thou art a sinner. If thou knowest thy sinnership, thou mayest soon know the Saviour to be thy Saviour. 'Christ Jesus came into the world to save sinners.' Art thou a sinner? If so, I can tell thee, on Scriptural authority, that Christ Jesus came to save thee.

Ye good moral people, who trust in your own works; ye who are sewing fig leaves together, to cover your nakedness, and fashioning day by day the garments of your own righteousness, you will find your good works to be utterly insufficient. All that is of nature's spinning, death will unravel. All that nature ever girded about the sinner was vain, and worse than vain. Cast thy righteousness away, thou moralist; cast thy good works away, and 'believe on the Lord Jesus Christ, and thou shalt be saved, and thy house.' A good man, when dying, was asked what he was doing; and he answered, 'I am throwing all my good works overboard, and I am trusting wholly in Jesus; I am lashing myself to the plank of free grace, on which I hope to float into glory.'

I have done when I have told you the way of salvation. It is written in God's Word, 'He that believeth and is baptized shall be saved.' Do you ask me what it is to believe? To believe, is to trust yourselves, simply and wholly, on the blood of Jesus Christ for salvation. I know of no better utterance of faith than this,—

'Nothing in my hand I bring;
Simply to thy cross I cling;
Naked, come to thee for dress;
Helpless, look to thee for grace;
Foul, I to the fountain fly;
Wash me, Saviour, or I die.'

Come to Jesus, with this declaration; and then be immersed 'in the name of the Father, and of the Son, and of the Holy Ghost,' and verily you shall be saved. May God, of his sovereign grace, enable you thus to believe and to be baptized, for our Lord Jesus Christ's sake! Amen.

Christist, the rock

A sermon, delivered by C. H. Spurgeon, at New Park Street Chapel, Southwark, in 1856

FORWARDED BY T. W. MEDHURST, CARDIFF

'And that Rock was Christ.'—1 Corinthians 10:4.

IT is a fact, on record in Sacred Scripture, that there were two rocks, both of which gave forth water in the wilderness to supply the needs of the multitudes who were passing through the desert. Some have supposed that the apostle Paul stated that there was only one rock; whereas, on carefully reading what he says, you will see that he merely observed, they 'did all drink the same spiritual drink: for they drank of that spiritual Rock that followed them: and that Rock was Christ.' Whatever that rock might be of which the tribes of Israel drank, they all drank the same; there were not two rocks at one time; they all drank of the same rock which followed them, whichever of the two rocks it might be, and that rock, referring to either as you please, 'was Christ.' Whether you regard the first rock of Horeb, or the second rock at Kadesh, both were types of our Lord and Saviour Jesus Christ. Some may hint that, if there were two rocks, there may be two Christs. By no means, my friends. There was a fresh scapegoat every day of atonement, but that does not imply that there is to be a new Christ every year. A lamb was to be offered every morning and every evening, but who would infer from this that there were to be as many Christs as there were lambs? So, if there have been two rocks, there have been two types of Christ in different respects, and we may say, both of the rock in Rephidim and the rock in Kadesh, 'that Rock was Christ.' Understand, therefore, that there were two rocks, but not two rocks at one place; and, so, they did all drink of the same spiritual drink, which flowed from the same spiritual Rock: 'and that Rock was Christ.'

My object will be to show you that both the rocks were most eminent types of our blessed Lord Jesus Christ, who, being smitten, gives forth water for the refreshment of his people, and who follows them all the desert through with his refreshing floods. Let me trouble you to turn to the first passage, in the seventeenth chapter of Exodus, which I will endeavour to explain. I shall not tarry, even for a moment, to hint at the various views of Jesus Christ in which he might be regarded, as a rock, as being immutable, remaining constantly in the same position; as being a refuge from the stormy wind and tempest; and as being the place where all those who love him are hidden from the storms of avenging justice. That, however, does not happen to be the subject to which I invite your attention; the subject is not simply Christ as a rock, but Christ as a rock in the wilderness, from which the water gushed out.

Permit me now to request your attentive perusal of the following Scripture:—'And all the congregation of the children of Israel journeyed from the wilderness of Sin, after their journeys, according to the commandment of the Lord, and pitched in Rephidim: and there was no water for the people to drink. Wherefore the people did chide with Moses, and said, Give us water that we may drink. And Moses said unto them, Why chide ye with me? wherefore do ye tempt the Lord? And the people thirsted there for water; and the people murmured against Moses, and said, Wherefore is this that thou hast brought us up out of Egypt, to kill us and our children and our cattle with thirst? And Moses cried unto the Lord, saying, What shall I do unto this people? they be almost ready to stone me. And the Lord said unto Moses, Go on before the people, and take with thee of the elders of Israel; and thy rod, wherewith thou smotest the river, take in thine hand, and go. Behold, I will stand before thee there upon the rock in Horeb; and thou shalt smite the rock, and there shall come water out of it, that the people may drink. And Moses did so in the sight of the elders of Israel. And he called the name of the place Massah, and Meribah, because of the chiding of the children of Israel, and because they tempted the Lord, saying, Is the Lord among us, or not?'—Exodus 17:1–7.

I. This first rock was Christ personal.

In the first place, I remark that the rock at Rephidim, or Horeb, was a remarkable type of Christ, *from the very fact of its name*. It is called Horeb;

and, on referring to the dictionary of names, you will find that the word 'Horeb' signifies 'barrenness.' It is also called 'Rephidim,' which signifies 'beds of rest.' It is remarkable that these two names should belong to one rock, for both titles may be well applied to our Lord and Saviour Jesus Christ.

First, he was the Rock of Horeb; that is to say, he was a Rock in a barren and dry land. Isaiah prophesied of him that he should be 'a root out of a dry ground,' and so he was. He came out of a family which, although once royal, was then almost extinct. His reputed father and his mother were but common people of the artisan class; the glories of the royal line of David had been forgotten among the people; nevertheless, out of it came Jesus Christ, the man 'chosen out of the people,' that he might be exalted to be Ruler over God's chosen Israel. Isaiah said, 'When we shall see him, there is no beauty that we should desire him.' If anyone had looked upon the steep and rugged sides of Horeb, covered with thorn brakes and bushes, he would never have dreamed that there could be concealed within so stubborn a rock a flood of water sufficient to supply the wants of multitudes. He would have held up his hands in astonishment, and exclaimed, 'It is impossible: you may dig water out of barren sand; but I cannot suppose it possible that water can come out of that adamantine rock.'

So, looking on Jesus, the Jews said, 'Can he be the Saviour long foretold, to usher in the age of gold? Can the carpenter's son be the Messiah? Can this be he who comes to redeem us from our oppressors, and to found a Kingdom which shall never have an end? Is this the Jesus who is to come down like rain upon the mown grass, and as showers that water the earth?' They could not expect salvation from him; he seemed to be a rock of barrenness, and they would not believe that he could become the Saviour of a mighty nation, that he could be One from whose riven side should flow healing streams of blood and water to wash and purify his children.

Mark, also, the other name, Rephidim, or, the beds of rest. Doth not this title sweetly apply to the Lord Jesus? Although he is indeed as Horeb to his enemies, yet is he not a very Rephidim to his friends? He himself said, 'Come unto me, all ye that labour and are heavy laden, and I will give you rest;' and he does give us rest. We should little expect to find rest upon a rock, but there is no rest elsewhere. We may rest upon the softest earth, but we shall find it to be hard for our heads at the day of judgment. We may pile up for ourselves stately mansions of our own works, and hope therein to find rest; but there is no rest save that which remaineth for the people of God. Jesus is to us our only rest, the only one needed, and the only one possible. My dear friends, are you now regarding Christ as Horeb, that is, waste and barren; or can you look upon him as your Rephidim, your rest? Can you say, 'Lord, thou hast been our dwelling place in all generations'? Canst thou, like John, put thy head upon the bosom of the Lord Jesus? Canst thou say that thou hast believed, and so hast entered into rest? If so, then thou art a true child of God, and thou mayest rejoice that he who, to others, is without comeliness, is comely to thee: and that he who seemed to be everything save what men expected, is to thee all thy salvation and all thy desire.

It may be fanciful, perhaps, to refer to these names; but I had rather discover too much in God's Word than find too little in it. The names seem to me extremely significant, and therefore I have mentioned them both as applicable to Jesus Christ.

Notice, in the next place, that, like our Saviour, *this rock gave forth no water till it was smitten.* Our Lord Jesus was no Saviour except as he was smitten; he could not save his people except by his death. It is true that patriarchs, prophets, and priests ascended to Heaven before our Saviour died; but it was by the foresight of his death. If any of us shall be privileged to behold the City of the Most High in glory, we can only enter there through his agonies. I can have no trust for my eternal salvation in the simple man Christ Jesus, or even in the God over all, blessed for ever. It is not simply Christ, but Christ crucified, who is my salvation, it is Christ on the cross at Calvary who redeems my soul. Had he remained in Heaven, sitting on his lofty throne, he could never have been the Substitute for his chosen people. He could never have redeemed us unless he had been 'smitten of God, and afflicted.' He was our Saviour from before all worlds, he was so viewed in the eternal covenant; but it was because he was looked upon as the smitten Saviour, slain before the foundation of the world. There is no hope for thee, my friend, anywhere but in the smitten Jesus. Thou mayest bow down to worship his exalted Head, but that exalted

Head cannot save thee apart from the thorn-crowned brow. Thou mayest go to the Christ who grasps the sceptre; but remember, Christ with the sceptre could not be thy Saviour unless he had first been Christ with the reed. Thou mayest approach Christ whose robes are clouds of glory; but remember, he who is now arrayed in splendour could not have been thy Redeemer unless he had first of all been clothed in the scarlet of mockery, and brought forth with the infamous cry, *Ecce homo,* 'Behold the man!' It is Christ the Sufferer who redeems us. The rock yields no water till it is smitten, and the Saviour yields no salvation until he is slain. Learn then, believer, in all thy contemplations of thy Saviour, to consider him as the Smitten One, for it is thus, despised and afflicted, with the scars of his suffering upon him, that he becomes thy Redeemer.

Notice, again, this rock must be smitten in a peculiar manner; *it must be smitten with the rod of the lawgiver,* or else no water will come forth. So, our Saviour, Jesus Christ, was smitten with the sword of the lawgiver on earth, and by the rod of his great Father, the Lawgiver in Heaven. None but Moses might smite the rock, for he was king in Jeshurun. So was it with our Saviour. It is true that the Roman nailed him to the tree; it is true that the Jew dragged him to death; but it is equally true that it was his Father who did it all. It is a great fact that man slew the Saviour, but it is a greater fact that God slew him, too. Who was it said, 'Awake, O sword, against my Shepherd, and against the man that is my Fellow'? The prophet tells us, when he adds, 'Saith the Lord.' It was God who delivered up his Son for us, and who will now also with him freely give us all things. Christ would have been no Redeemer unless his Father had smitten him. There would have been no acceptable sacrifice, even if the Jew had dragged him to death, or the Roman had pierced his side, unless the Father's scourge had fallen on his shoulders, and unless the Father's sword had found a sheath in his blessed heart. It was the sword of the Lawgiver that smote Jesus Christ, and made him our acceptable sacrifice. Believer, take a view of this great fact; it will help thee most solemnly to adore both God the Father and God the Son. Remember, it was the Father who smote the Saviour; and it was the Son who bore the Father's stroke. It was not the cruel Roman lash, it was not the crown of thorns, it was not the nails alone that made Christ the Saviour; it was the great fact that made him cry, 'My God, my God, why hast thou forsaken me?' It was not Pilate and it was not Herod that put him to death as our Saviour; they put him to death as a reputed malefactor; but it was God who gave him up to die for us. His Father said, 'Take him, and let him die.' It was from Heaven that the death-warrant came; it was by God that the blow was struck; and if it had not been from the Father, we should all have been condemned. It was necessary that the rod of the Lawgiver should smite this Rock of Ages, to bring out from it plenteous streams of water, which should cause pardon and peace to flow out to dying souls.

Note, in the next place, that when this rock was smitten, *it was smitten publicly.* You read, in the fifth verse, 'And the Lord said unto Moses, Go on before the people, and take with thee of the elders of Israel; and thy rod.' It was not done in secret, in a dark place of the earth; but it was done before 'the elders.' Even so our Saviour, when he was put to death, was not executed in private, but he was taken to the summit of the hill of Golgotha, and there, amid the assembled multitude, amid jeers and ribaldry, contempt and mockery, he died. The elders of the people were there; the rich man was there, in his pride and pomp, looking up to a dying Saviour, and scorning him because he was of mean origin. Poor men were there, shouting with wicked voices, 'Crucify him! Crucify him!' and pointing with their fingers, and rudely wagging their heads at the mighty Prince who was then expiring. The wise man was there, the member of the Sanhedrim, the representative of earth's wisdom and philosophy, and he said, 'If he be the Christ, let him come down from the cross.' The unlettered man was there; he also laughed him to scorn, and thrust out his tongue in vulgar and ignorant jest. The righteous man was there; righteous in his own esteem, with the phylactery between his eyes, and the broad border to his garment. The chief of sinners was there, for there hung the thief expiring on the tree. All kinds of men beheld the smitten Lord. The Jews were assembled in multitudes; the Romans, too, taking a prominent part as the representatives of the Gentile race. In fact, being near the time of the Passover, there were gathered together Greeks, 'Parthians, and Medes, and Elamites, and the dwellers in Mesopotamia, and in Judæa, and Cappadocia, in Pontus, and Asia, Phrygia, and Pamphylia, in Egypt, and in the parts of Libya about Cyrene, and strangers of Rome, Jews and proselytes, Cretes and Arabians.' Persons out of all nations, standing as the representatives of the whole earth, saw the Saviour die, even as the elders stood with Moses as the representatives of all the tribes of Israel.

There is another thing which we cannot pass by. *This rock,* which was smitten, and thus represented the humanity of our Saviour offered up for our sins, *had Divinity above it;* for you will notice, in the sixth verse, that the Lord said to Moses, 'Behold, I will stand before thee there upon the rock in Horeb.' Although it was a barren rock, and so represented Christ's condition of dishonour; although it was a smitten rock, and so represented his suffering humanity; yet over that rock the bright light of the Shekinah shone. God stood over the rock, there was a manifestation of Deity upon the rock of Horeb. So it was at Calvary; albeit that it was Christ who died, very man of very man, yet there was enough of Deity about Calvary's smitten rock to show that God was there. There was the midday midnight; there was the swathing of the sun in clouds of darkness; there was the rending of the rocks, the tearing in sunder of the veil, the waking of the dead, the terrifying of the multitudes. God was there; Deity was there as well as humanity. 'I will stand before thee there upon the rock in Horeb.' I think God thus revealed himself to show us that Christ the Rock was Divine as well as human. Oh, how sweet it is to contemplate the complex person of our dear Redeemer, to behold him as truly man suffering for us, and yet to behold him as very God, sitting unsuffering in the highest Heaven! I remember what J. Harrington Evans sweetly says, that we make a great mistake when we deify the humanity of Christ, and we make an equal mistake when we bring down the Divinity of Christ to the level of his humanity. We should remember that the person of Christ was as much human as ours is, that it did suffer, was tempted, and was tried, even as we are tried. We must not suppose that the Divinity of Christ has taken away in the least degree from his humanity; yet while we behold him as the wayfaring man, full of sorrows and acquainted with grief, we must not forget that he was very God of very God at the same time that he was truly man. Though his manhood stood most apparent, suffering for the sin of man, yet there was also a sufficiently bright light in the cloud to let men see that God was there; and, though death had grasped the man, yet the God stood mightiest of the mighty, conquering for us. God was at that first rock to teach us that Christ was Divine as well as human.

I need scarcely hint at the other reason why this rock is like Jesus. *When smitten, the water gushed forth most freely*, sufficient for all the children of Israel, and following them through all their journeys, until it pleased God to stop it in order to open another fountain, to give us a further type of Christ in another fashion.

Christ smitten, my beloved, gives out water for all thirsty souls, affording enough for every child of Israel. Christ smitten gives forth a stream which doth not flow today nor tomorrow only, but which flows on for ever and ever; and, as this stream availed the Israelites wherever they went, so does Jesus Christ, by virtue of his atonement and his grace, follow his children wheresoever they journey. If they are brought to the wilderness of Sin, or to the realms of Kadesh, Christ shall follow them; the efficacy of his blood, the light of his grace, the power of his gospel, shall attend them in all their wanderings, however tortuous may be their paths, however winding the track in which the cloudy pillar shall lead them. O blessed Jesus, thou art indeed a sweet antitype of the rock! Once my thirsty soul clamoured for something to satisfy its wants; I hungered and I thirsted for righteousness. I looked to the heavens, but they were as brass, for an angry God seemed frowning upon me. I looked to the earth, but it was as arid sand; all my good works had failed me. I had no righteousness of my own, all my wells were stopped up; and when the rulers dug the wells with their staves, and sang, 'Spring up, O well,' still no water came. But I remember when my thirsty soul fainted within me, and God said, 'Come hither, sinner, I will show thee where thou mayest drink;' and he showed me Christ on the cross, with his side pierced and his hands nailed. I thought I heard his expiring death-cry, 'It is finished,' and when I heard it, lo! I saw a stream of water, at which I slaked my burning thirst; and here I am,—

'A monument of grace,
A sinner saved by blood;
The streams of love I trace
Up to that fountain,—God.
And in his mighty breast I see
Eternal thoughts of love to me.'

But this I know, had I never seen the open fountain, I had never lived; had I not beheld that mighty stream flowing there, I had never quenched my awful thirst. And now that water ever attracts my soul; and when I want to slake my returning thirst, still to that fountain, like the panting hart, I hasten. To the Incarnate God, I flee; here I may quench my raging thirst, and drink and never die. O sinners, do you want the living water? Christ gives it to you. Oh! wonder of wonders, he who said, 'I thirst,' says also, 'If any man thirst, let him come unto me, and drink.' He who had not a drop of water to moisten his parched lips, yet saith, 'He that believeth on me, out of his belly shall flow rivers of living water.' Come ye unto Christ, ye thirsty souls; come unto Jesus, ye who are thirsty, for it is written, 'Ho, every one that thirsteth, come ye to the waters, and he that hath no money; come ye, buy, and eat; yea, come, buy wine and milk without money and without price.'

You see, then, beloved, that this rock is a type of Christ personally; it is a type of him as dying, smitten for our sins. I have been brief on these particulars because I want to show you how both the rocks were types of Christ; and if I do so, it may be instructive to you.

I must now request your attention to the record concerning another rock, which is given to us in Numbers 20:1–13:—'Then came the children of Israel, even the whole congregation, into the desert of Zin in the first month: and the people abode in Kadesh; and Miriam died there, and was buried there. And there was no water for the congregation: and they gathered themselves together against Moses and against Aaron. And the people chode with Moses, and spake, saying, Would God that we had died when our brethren died before the Lord! And why have ye brought up the congregation of the Lord into this wilderness, that we and our cattle should die there? And wherefore have ye made us to come up out of Egypt, to bring us in unto this evil place? it is no place of seed, or of figs, or of vines, or of pomegranates; neither is there any water to drink. And Moses and Aaron went from the presence of the assembly unto the door of the tabernacle of the congregation, and they fell upon their faces: and the glory of the Lord appeared unto them. And the Lord spake unto Moses, saying, Take the rod, and gather thou the assembly together, thou, and Aaron thy brother, and speak ye unto the rock before their eyes; and it shall give forth his water, and thou shalt bring forth to them water out of the rock: so thou shalt give the congregation and their beasts drink. And Moses took the rod from before the Lord, as he commanded him. And Moses and Aaron gathered the congregation together before the rock, and he said unto them, Hear now, ye rebels; must we fetch you water out of this rock? And Moses lifted up his hand, and with his rod he smote the rock twice: and the water came out abundantly, and the congregation drank, and their beasts also. And the Lord spake unto Moses and Aaron, Because ye believed me not, to sanctify me in the eyes of the children of Israel, therefore ye shall not bring this congregation into the land which I have given them. This is the water of Meribah; because the children of Israel strove with the Lord, and he was sanctified in them.'

Of this second rock it may also be said, as of the first one, 'and that Rock was Christ.' I have already shown you that the first rock was Christ personal.

II. THE SECOND ROCK WAS CHRIST MYSTICAL.

You know what I mean by Christ mystical. You are aware that, in Scripture, the word Christ often stands for Christ's Church, for the whole body of Christ's people, for Christ the Head, and all his members. The first rock was Christ himself, the God-Man, smitten for us; the second rock is Christ the Church, Christ the Head and all his members together; and out of the Church, and out of the Church only, must always flow all that the world requires. There will never be any blessings given to the world except through the mystical body of Jesus Christ. As pardon and peace alone flow through the person of Christ smitten and crucified, even so the blessings given to the world can only flow through Christ the Head and his body, the Church. Now I am going to show you the parallels here, as I did in the case of the first rock.

First, note *the place where this rock was situated*. Two names are mentioned, at the commencement of the chapter, just as there were in the case of the first rock. 'Then came the children of Israel, even the whole congregation, into the desert of Zin in the first month: and the people abode in Kadesh.' So, this rock was called the rock of Kadesh. Kadesh signifies holiness, and that is just where Christ mystical dwells. Christ mystical may always be known by his holiness. We can tell Christ's Church by its being separated from the world; it dwells at Kadesh. It appears that it was in 'the desert of Zin,' which means 'a buckler' and also 'coldness.' It is true that the Church of God does stand in a double position. It stands in boldness and indifference with regard to the world, and it stands also secure, as in a buckler, with regard to its God. Observe the name, for it is significant; the second rock was not in Horeb,—barrenness,—as Christ was, personally, in a barren and dry land; but it was in Kadesh,— holiness,—as Christ is now in his Church; for the Church of Jesus Christ is a holy Church, justified through the righteousness of its blessed Lord; a holy Church, sanctified, and made free from sin, by the indwelling of the Holy Spirit. You may know the true Church of the living God, although it dwelleth in the tents of Kedar, and abideth amongst sinners, for it is always in reality distinct from them, and pitches its tent at Kadesh, being holy, sanctified unto the Lord.

Now, beloved, having only hinted at the name, I want to show you the parallel here. Notice the way in which the water was to be brought out of the second rock; *it was not to be by smiting, but by speaking.* That was God's plain command: 'Speak ye unto the rock before their eyes; and it shall give forth his water, and thou shalt bring forth to them water out of the rock: so thou shalt give the congregation and their beasts drink.' God would have this rock bless the people, not by being smitten, but by Moses and Aaron speaking. So, beloved, it is God's revealed will that Christ mystical should bless the world by speaking. Christ's Church sends forth rivers of living water every day by means of human speech. It is 'by the foolishness of preaching' that God has ordained 'to save them that believe.' He makes the Church to be a stream, pouring floods of living water upon all the barren lands of this world, and producing abundant verdure where, otherwise, all would have been, like the desert of Sahara, given up to barrenness. The Lord makes, or he intends to make, the Church a blessing to the world by means of speaking. How can I bless the world? By speaking out for Jesus. How can every Christian bless the world, and the Church at large be made a blessing to the inhabitants of the earth? By speaking. God has ordained the simple means of testifying the gospel of his Son, Jesus Christ, to make the living floods of his grace pour out upon the world. If any man wanteth life from Christ, he must, as a usual rule, get it by hearing the Word of God, and believing in Jesus Christ who is revealed therein; and if any of us desire to confer a blessing upon our fellow-creatures, it must be by speaking to them the inspired Word of the Lord.

Notice, next, that, while it was God's revealed will that Christ mystical should bless the world by speaking, yet, through the sin of Moses, *the rock did not produce water by speaking, but by smiting.* The rock was smitten twice. Now here is a significant parallel. Christ's Church was designed by God, in his revealed will, to bless the world simply by speaking; but the wicked men of this world have smitten Christ again in his Church. They have persecuted God's people; and a large part of the benefit which the Church now confers upon the world, speaking generally, comes through the smiting of persecution. Moses smote the rock in Kadesh,—not once only, as he struck the rock in Horeb,—but twice, to show that, if possible, the people of Christ should be even more persecuted, tormented, and plagued than was Jesus Christ, their Lord and Leader. Moses smote this second rock twice;—for, apparently, the water did not gush out at the first stroke;—to show that protracted persecution would be necessary to bless the world, and that the wicked world would be sure to smite the Church over and over again, before the world would be wholly blest.

But, although the smiting of the rock was a sinful act, the water came forth from it, to show that, by persecution, the Church has been made a blessing to this sinful world. The flames, that burned the martyrs at Smithfield, scattered sparks which have lit up a thousand fires all over this land and other countries, too. The smiting of God's gospel Rock, the Church, has caused floods of precious water to flow over lands where, otherwise, the stream might never have penetrated. It has been by persecution that the seed of life has been scattered, like the seeds which are blown about by the winds from plants which else might have died childless. Persecution takes up the words of God's children, and scatters them abroad everywhere. Never was there a more significant act performed than when the ashes of Wycliffe were dug up, and cast into the river, whence they were carried out to the sea, and so were wafted to the shores of every land. Thus is it still with Christ mystical. His influence must be scattered abroad, his ashes, as it were, must be cast to the winds of heaven, that he may give life to distant nations, and that men in all lands may hear the truth of his blessed gospel.

You see, dear friends, what I have intended to explain to you; I hope I have made myself clearly understood. This second rock is a type, not of Christ personal, but of Christ in his Church;—the Saviour of the world instrumentally, not mediatorially. It was not God's revealed will that his Church should be the means of blessing to the world by smiting, but by speaking. Wicked men have run counter to the Divine will, and have smitten the Church; but, nevertheless, it has been found that the smiting of the Church has produced the best possible results, for the living water has gushed out, and many thirsty ones have been refreshed. The more persecution and the more trial the Church of Christ has to endure, so much the more mighty are those streams of blessing which flow from it far and wide throughout the earth. I believe, my brethren, that there is nothing in the world better for a man, or for a church, than a measure of persecution. Where should *we* have been now, had it not been for the slander, abuse, and contumely, which have been continually heaped upon our head? I believe that our prosperity is, in no small degree, owing to our enemies. We should not have been nearly so well known unless they had charged us falsely with all manner of evils; we should not have been anything like so influential unless they had attempted to put us down; but they cannot put us down by all that they may say or do. The more they try to oppress us, the more do we multiply, as the children of Israel did in Egypt, when their tasks were made heavier, and their burdens were increased. So, my brethren, never be ashamed or afraid of persecution. Remember that you must be smitten. It is true that God did not intend—he did really intend it secretly, but it was not according to his revealed will—that you should be smitten. He is never pleased with those who smite you; he said you were to bless the world by speaking. Moses erred, and a wicked world has erred. God foresaw that Moses would smite that rock, though he did it sinfully; and God also foresaw that you would be smitten, in order that you might be of more use to the people in the world. The fig ripens by being bruised, and thou wouldst not have ripened if thou hadst not felt the rod. The fountains of the earth would never send us up their waters unless they were bored deeply; and, in like manner, the Christian must often be pierced with trouble, and trial, and persecution, to make him give forth living water. It is said that the oyster hath no pearl unless it be sick, so it is true of the Christian that he will have no pearl unless he be persecuted. There will be little good done by any of us, unless we have some trials and troubles. The rock must be smitten; if it hath a double blow, do not be grieved; for the rock at Kadesh was smitten twice, and then the waters gushed forth from it.

I want you also to notice that the rock, although smitten wrongly, *was smitten with the rod of the lawgiver*. This delighted me, when I first thought of it, that the second rock, Christ mystical, was smitten with the very same rod which smote the first rock, Christ himself. If I suffer *for* Christ, my sufferings are, in effect, the sufferings *of* Christ; and, although they are occasioned by man as the second cause, yet they do really spring from God. 'The rod of the wicked shall not rest upon the lot of the righteous;' and when the wicked smite us, unwittingly to themselves, they do not smite with their own rod, but with the rod of God. The Lord himself measures out our trials and our troubles; and let the enemy do what he may against us, he cannot smite us with anything except our Father's rod. The Lord could make even Rab-shakeh the rod of justice to Hezekiah, but Rab-shakeh could not smite with his own rod. It is God's rod that falls on his children; no child of his is ever smitten with any rod but that of his Father. It may be that we think some terrible blow comes from hell, but in truth it comes from Heaven. Even though Judas wickedly betrayed his Master, he did by that very act fulfil the Scripture which had foretold his infamy. If our most intimate friend lift up his heel against us, it is because God permits it. God has given the dog leave to bark, or he would have to be silent. No devouring lion roars against a child of God until the Lord unchains his lips. No fierce leopard comes out of his den against an heir of Heaven until God allows him to do so. Even the devil himself becomes the servant of God, and he cannot smite God's child with anything but God's rod. He had to go and ask leave of God to oppress one of his children; he had to ask whether he might afflict Job; and even then, Satan could not afflict Job himself, but he besought God saying, 'Put forth thine hand now, and touch all that he hath, and he will curse thee to thy face.' It was, after all, the hand of God that smote Job, even though Satan seemed to be the instrument in the

Lord's hand. So, beloved, though thou art smitten by a rod, it is the same rod which fell upon the back of Christ Jesus thy Lord and Saviour.

Once more, observe, you who are the persecutors of the children of God, that although great results flowed from the smiting of the rock, yet *Moses was punished for smiting it.* He was not allowed to enter the Promised Land, because he smote that rock. It was the emblem of Christ mystical, and even in the smiting of the emblem there was significance. Moses was commanded to speak, not to smite; he rashly and wickedly did smite, and therefore he was punished. Mark that, persecutor! Thou shalt be punished for thy persecution, whether it be by word or by deed. Whatsoever thou doest against a child of God shall be fearfully returned into thine own bosom. 'Whosoever shall offend one of these little ones that believe in me, it is better for him that a millstone were hanged about his neck, and he were cast into the sea.' I tell you, men and women, there is pardon for all kinds of sins against the Son of man, even for the sin of persecution; but if there be anything which, when God doth punish, he visiteth with severer vengeance than other transgressions, it is this sin of persecution. Do you not remember how Herod, the proud persecutor, was eaten of worms? Have you never read of the fate of Antiochus Epiphanes, who put to death the brave Maccabees, the testifiers of the truth? Have you never heard how Bishop Bonner, who persecuted the Lord's children, died? Do you not know that persecutors seldom die in their beds; or, if they do, they die as if the flames of hell were kindled about them even before they entered their eternal prison? To be a persecutor, is indeed a horrible thing; a sinner of any kind must be damned, if unsaved; but a persecutor must be sunk into the lowermost depths of the pit that is bottomless. Tremble, ye who slander, and jeer, and ridicule, and oppress the children of God; remember that their Father is almighty. They cannot avenge themselves; they do not wish to avenge themselves; but recollect that text, 'Vengeance is mine; I will repay, saith the Lord.' It may be, concerning some of you who are persecutors of the children of God, that the sentence of exclusion has been pronounced; and if so, O man, thou shalt never enter into the Promised Land, because thou hast smitten that Rock! Yet, if thou art a persecutor, hear yet more of the truth of God. Paul says, 'I was before a blasphemer, and a persecutor, and injurious: but I obtained mercy, because I did it ignorantly in unbelief. And the grace of our Lord was exceeding abundant with faith and love which is in Christ Jesus. This is a faithful saying, and worthy of all acceptation, that Christ Jesus came into the world to save sinners; of whom I am chief. Howbeit for this cause I obtained mercy, that in me first Jesus Christ might shew forth all long-suffering, for a pattern to them which should hereafter believe on him to life everlasting.' Have you persecuted the children of God ignorantly? Have any of you been persecuting God's children, not believing them to be his, but supposing them to be hypocrites? Or have you thus wilfully and wickedly acted? Hear this! Return, ye persecutors, return, ye who have sinned against God, for with him is plenteous redemption. He is able to blot out all your transgressions, and to wash you from all your sins; yea, he will pass by all your iniquities, receive you graciously, and love you freely, if you will but turn unto him with your whole heart. Oh! believe me, there is no sin which can damn a man if he only has faith in Jesus Christ. There is no crime, however black, which can exclude a man from Heaven, if he doth but believe on the Lord Jesus; but if thou goest on to thy grave a hoary-headed sinner against God, how awful will be thy fate when the fierce lions of his vengeance shall have the mastery over thee, and shall break all thy bones in pieces ere ever thou comest to the bottom of the den where thou hadst hoped to have destroyed Daniel! Thou shalt see him delivered, and thou shalt thyself be cast into the midst of demons fiercer than thou hast ever imagined, and into flames more terrible than thou hast ever dreamed of. Then tremble and repent. 'Kiss the Son, lest he be angry, and ye perish from the way, when his wrath is kindled but a little. Blessed are all they that put their trust in him.'

May God bless, to all your souls, what I have said to you, for our Lord Jesus Christ's sake! Amen.

The deaf and the dumb

A sermon delivered at Westbourne Grove Chapel, London, on Friday morning, 5 February 1858, by C. H. Spurgeon

FORWARDED BY T. W. MEDHURST, CARDIFF

'And they bring unto him one that was deaf, and had an impediment in his speech; and they beseech him to put his hand upon him. And he took him aside from the multitude, and put his fingers into his ears, and he spit, and touched his tongue; and looking up to heaven, he sighed, and saith unto him, Ephphatha, that is, Be opened. And straightway his ears were opened, and the string of his tongue was loosed, and he spake plain.'—Mark 7:32–35.

SIMPLICITY seems to be one of the indispensable requisites of sublimity. Why then did our Lord detract from the apparent simplicity of this cure by thus connecting together such a round of services? There never was a greater piece of sublimity than when God said to the world all swathed in darkness, 'Light be,' 'and light was.' Surely, if Christ would make his cure sublime, he should act in the same way. Being God, if he had said, 'Be opened,' straightway the man's ears would have been opened, and the strings of his tongue would have been loosed. What need then that he should thrust his fingers into the man's ears? Why the spitting and the touching of his tongue, and the lifting of his eyes to Heaven, and sighing? All these seem to be actions which detract from sublimity. Why did Christ do all that? We are quite certain that he did not act without a wise motive. My answer to the question I have suggested would be this:—Our Lord Jesus, when he was on earth, as the greatest of preachers, was wont to preach continually by parables. He never taught an abstract truth in its abstract form. He breathed it in a figure, a metaphor, or simile. He continually said, 'The Kingdom of God is like' unto this, or like unto that. He did not thrust forth truth in its most simple form. He himself was Divinely Incarnate; and the truths he uttered were incarnated in symbol and figure. It was his wish that his ministers should be imitators of him in this respect; and he would have us teach the people by allegories, metaphors, and pictures; but, alas! we are but little skilled in this heavenly art; we have few of us much ability or genius for making allegories; and it is a happy thing that Christ has provided for our want of ability. He has given us this great Book, the Bible, which, if it were sent only to teach us doctrine, might have been one-tenth of the size it is. This great Book is full of incidents and narratives, that out of these we might continually dig a vast wealth of metaphor and figure. I look upon all the Historical Books of Scripture as being books of verity and fact, but as being especially given to us to illustrate the doctrinal part of Scripture.

I think that, in using these various services narrated in this case of the deaf and dumb man, our Saviour did so in order that he might furnish us with an allegorical representation of the way in which he saves souls. I think he has presented to us a picture of the sovereign work of his Holy Spirit upon the hearts and consciences of men, when he brings them to know his truth. Believing so, I shall start by *comparing this man to all men by nature.* He was deaf and dumb; so are men naturally. I shall then notice *how Christ went to work in his cure,* and try to show that it is the same way in which he works in restoring the spiritually deaf and dumb; and then, by God's help, I would try to *ask some solemn questions,* which, if answered by our consciences, may lead us to a thorough self-examination.

I. First, then, here is a man deaf and dumb; and I am going to COMPARE HIM TO HUMAN NATURE IN ITS FALLEN STATE.

Perhaps someone asks, 'Would you for a moment assert that man is deaf?' Certainly not, in a natural sense; his ears are open widely enough as a rule. We find people generally have quite sufficient ear, and power of hearing, if there is any scandal to listen to. If there is an ill report concerning their neighbours, there are seldom persons who cannot listen to *that.* Or if there be aught that is amusing, or to our personal advantage, we are all ready to catch its faintest echo, however softly it may be said. Oh, no; man is not deaf in that sense! It would be well for some men that they should be deaf. If, in certain company, they could hear much less than they now do, there might be far less grief of heart for them, and much less contamination of mind. It is in a spiritual sense that we assert the fact of man's deafness; and in asserting it, we are certain that we have the Spirit of God with us. We are sure that men are deaf, for we have proof positive of their spiritual deafness. Have we not ascended to our pulpits, many a time, burning with zeal for the salvation of our fellow-creatures? We have gone from our closets, where we have wrestled with God, to our pulpits, where we have endeavoured to wrestle with men. We have selected for our subject the terrors of the law, and we have laboured like Paul to persuade men; and, as though God did beseech them by us, we have prayed them, in Christ's stead, to be reconciled to God. We have brought before them the great commands of God; we have shown how exceedingly broad the commandment is; we have proclaimed the curse of the law; we have not hesitated to utter the dread sentence which we have found in God's Word: 'Cursed is every one that continueth not in all things which are written in the book of the law to do them.' We have spoken like old Moses, till believers present have thought that all who heard us must be exceedingly afraid, and must have quaked and trembled. But, instead of being moved, they have sat under our ministry unconscious and unstirred; or if, under a momentary sense of terror, they have dropped the passing compliment of a tear, they have speedily stolen out, and forgotten what manner of men they were; and so have they proved to us that they were deaf, for no one is so deaf as the man whom Sinai's thunders cannot awaken and alarm. Those hearers must be deaf indeed who cannot be awakened by the curses, and thunders, and condemnations of God's holy law.

Another Sabbath we have gone into our pulpits with equal desires after man's salvation, and we have selected another subject, and we have said, 'Surely, those who will not be awakened by the threatenings of the law, may be aroused by the invitations of the gospel; those who will not be driven may be drawn;' and we have preached of the boundless mercy and love of God. We have declared that 'God so loved the world, that he gave his only begotten Son, that whosoever believeth in him should not perish, but have everlasting life. For God sent not his Son into the world to condemn the world; but that the world through him might be saved.' We have tried to describe the Father's love in the gift of his Son. We have then tried to depict Christ on the cross of Calvary in all his woe and agony. Tears have run down our own cheeks, and our hearts have been melted with sorrow while we have been painting that mournful picture of the sufferings of the Son of God. We have lifted up our hands, and cried,—

'Is it nothing to you, all ye that pass by,
Is it nothing to you that Jesus should die?
   For sins not his own,
   He died to atone;
Was love and was sorrow like his ever known?'

Yet still we have seen the same deafness manifested by our hearers. Their hearts, which would not be split in pieces by the hammer of the law, were not to be melted by the soft oil of the gospel. They would not come to Christ when driven by Sinai's thunders, and they would not come to him when the turtledove of Calvary was gently wooing them. No; men will not hear us, they will not regard us, plead we never so mightily; charm we never so wisely, they are like the deaf adder that will not listen to the music of the charmer. This is a truth which every minister will have to learn sooner or later to his own sad disappointment, that, unless God the Holy Spirit shall supernaturally speak to the hearts of men, all our preaching, and warning, and pleading must be utterly in vain. I am conscious that I might as well stand, this morning, and talk to the waves of the sea, or address the rocks upon its shores, as try to reach your hearts, if you are unconverted, unless God the Holy Spirit shall speak by me. I might as well ascend the summit of a hill, and speak to vacancy, and address the air; or go to the top of some lofty mountain, and speak to the pathless snows; for I should have as good hope of a lasting effect being produced there as by addressing you, unless God the Holy Spirit shall come and bore the deaf ear so that the spiritual sound shall enter into your hearts. It is not in our power to get at men's hearts; that must lie with our Master. It is ours to speak his Word; it is not ours to make men hear it. We speak to the natural ear; he alone can make the Word penetrate the conscience, and the heart. Thus, then, man is spiritually deaf, just as this man was physically deaf.

He also 'had an impediment in his speech,' or, as the last verse of the chapter says, he was 'dumb.' I suppose he could make a little noise, but he was 'dumb' in this sense, that his speech was not articulate, it was of no use for conversational purposes. He had such 'an impediment in his speech' that he could not make other people understand what he meant. Now, shall anyone say that men by nature are dumb? Certainly we should be laughed at to all eternity if we were to say this in a natural sense, for we are all quite ready with plenty of tongue for all our wants. We can talk quite fast enough, sometimes too fast. If we said half as much, we might only sin half as much. If we were twice as silent as we are, perhaps we should have only half as many sins to confess; for, as Solomon truly says, 'In the multitude of words there wanteth not sin: but he that refraineth his lips is wise.' There is sure to be much iniquity where there is much speaking.

Yet is it true in a spiritual sense that man is dumb. Until God the Holy Spirit opens his mouth, he cannot speak a word spiritually. You know that Paul wrote to the Corinthians, 'No man can say that Jesus is the Lord, but by the Holy Ghost;' and when Simon Peter said to Jesus, 'Thou art the Christ, the Son of the living God,' Jesus answered and said unto him, 'Blessed art thou, Simon Bar-jona: for flesh and blood hath not revealed it unto thee, but my Father which is in Heaven.' The very first letters of the gospel alphabet must be put into our mouths by the Holy Spirit, or else we shall be dumb for ever. Of our own power and strength, we cannot speak spiritually; nay, in a spiritual sense, a man cannot think; he cannot think a good thought unless he is taught by the Holy Spirit. The whole of salvation, from the first tiny rill of desire to the broad ocean of eternal holiness in glory, is all from him.

Man as he is by nature, till God the Holy Ghost renews him, is incapable of prayer; he may fall upon his knees morning and night, and repeat a form of prayer; but that is not praying. A man may regularly use a form of prayer for fifty years, and yet he may not have prayed even once. I tell you, friends, though you try never so much, you cannot utter a single syllable of true prayer, unless you are taught by the Divine Spirit. In vain, then, your many petitions and supplications, unless the Spirit of God hath instructed you how to pray. Though your prayers be garnished with the trappings of oratory, and though they be brilliant with the ornaments of eloquence, they shall never reach as far as Heaven; for they are not prayers at all, unless they are prayers breathed into your heart by the Holy Ghost.

Nor can man by nature speak in praise. It is true that he can sing a song very sweetly, but he cannot sing in God's sense of the term. No; true praise can come from no man's soul until the Holy Spirit has given him a new heart and a right spirit. He may labour never so well, the music-master may instruct him never so skilfully; but not one note, which will be fit to join in the choral symphonies of angels before the throne, can ever come from an ungodly heart, from a soul that has not been renewed by the Holy Spirit. Men are dumb, by nature, in this sense; they have nothing of spiritual prayer or praise to offer, they are silent before the throne of God.

The description I have given of man is not at all exaggerated; I will show you that it is not. The fact is, it only goes part of the way, for Holy Scripture not only teaches us that man is spiritually deaf and dumb, but it also says that believers are quickened, they 'who were dead in trespasses and sins,' are made alive. Now, none are so deaf as are the dead; none are so dumb as are those who sleep in the silent grave. Imagine not, ye formalists, that I am uttering harsh things, this morning; fancy not, ye chapel and church-goers, who are wrapped in the outward garb of religion, but are destitute of the heart thereof, that I am saying harsh things which I have myself invented; God forbid that I should ever do that! It is not my business to alarm the conscience unnecessarily; but, as this Bible is true, the words I have uttered are inspired by the Spirit, and therefore they have life in them. And except ye know them, and have felt their power in your hearts, how dwelleth the love of God in you? We must first know our ruin in the fall, before we can know our restoration in the redemption by Christ Jesus, We must first know nature's inability, nature's death, nature's corruption, before we can know the omnipotence of the Spirit, and the infinity of the mercy of God.

II. I proceed now to point out to you Christ's usual method of saving souls. It is illustrated in the thirty-third verse: 'And he took him aside from the multitude, and put his fingers into his ears, and he spit, and touched his tongue.'

Let me first utter this word of caution before I speak fully upon this part of the subject. Do not consider or imagine that I would lay down any uniform method of experience, or any constant and unvarying way in which God deals with his creatures. There are certain men who make their own experience like the bed of Procrustes. They stretch every man upon it; and then, if he is not long enough to reach their standard, they stretch him a little; and if he is taller than they are, he must be cut short; for they think that their experience is to be the standard by which everyone is to be measured. They bring every man, not to the infallible test of the Word of God, but to the very faulty test of their own feelings. According to their judgment, it is all in vain for you to know that your Redeemer liveth, and to talk of the things which you have tasted and handled of the good Word of the Lord, for you have not tasted and handled these things in their way. If you have not been in all respects conformed to them, they will not be so uncharitable as to say to you, 'You will perish everlastingly;' but they commit you to what they call 'the uncovenanted mercies of God,' thinking that there is just a possibility that you may get into Heaven edgewise; but that there is no very great likelihood of it, unless you are in every way conformed to their model and pattern. They think that all must be like themselves, or they shall never see the gates of glory, except the outside of them. But I am preaching concerning an experience which is the general rule, not one that has no exceptions, but one that embraces the major part of those who are brought to a saving knowledge of the Lord Jesus Christ.

The first thing that Christ did to this deaf and dumb man was, '*He took him aside from the multitude*.' This is usually the way that Christ begins the work of conversion. Like a wise hunter, he singles out a man or a woman, and when he has smitten him or her with his arrow, like the deer that is stricken, which seeks the deepest glades of the forest where it may bleed and die alone, so does the Saviour, by his gracious Spirit, move the wounded heart and conscience to seek a place of secrecy and seclusion where it may weep by itself. Children of God, turn over the pages of your diary till you come to the day of your salvation. Do you not remember that you entered the house of God, and that, on that day, the minister seemed, somehow or other, to preach at you? You had heard him on many previous occasions, but then he had preached *before* his congregation. That day, however, he preached *at* them, and *to* them; and he seemed specially to fix his eyes on you, as if the words he was uttering were meant in a special manner for your case. When he pleaded, he seemed to plead with you; his arguments were arguments to your conscience. You were solitary and alone. Perhaps it was in some neglected village church, and you sat down in the farthest aisle near the porch; but, even there, every word of the minister reached you; and the arrow seemed to come straight from the bow of the mighty man to your heart. Or, possibly, it was in some crowded sanctuary, and there seemed to be a great black wall of human beings all round you, and you were shut within; but the minister's eyes met yours, his message went right to your heart, and, as you went out of the sanctuary, you said to your friends, 'Come, see a man, which told me all things that ever I did.' You went to your home, but how solitary you were! There were good people there, but you felt that you dared not join them. You feared that you never could be a child of God, for you felt yourself to be so unworthy. There were, perhaps, some wicked persons there, but you could not join them, for their songs were like vinegar upon nitre to you, they were sung to a sad heart. You felt that you were weaned from the society of the wicked, although you were not yet one of the children of God, and you were too humble to venture into their company. The members of your family began to taunt you with being unsociable; you were almost always alone in your own room, or you would take a walk secretly and quietly, that your heart might muse with its Maker. Ah! young man, you told your sister every secret that you ever had before; but you did not tell her this one. Yes, young woman, you told your mother everything before, but you could not tell her this; you felt as if your tongue had been sealed up, so that you could not speak. You could perhaps have talked to a stranger about it, but you could not speak of it to any members of your own family. You were smitten by one of the King's arrows, and you desired to be alone. Like the man mentioned in our text, you were taken 'aside from the multitude.'

It is a happy circumstance when a man feels himself to be thus solitary. It is often the way in which God begins the work of salvation, taking us out from the masses of our fellow-creatures. We must recollect that we shall be judged alone, each of must die alone, and we shall be condemned alone, or saved alone, every man for himself, every woman for herself; so, as a general rule, we must each of us be convicted of sin alone. Do you not often find yourself falling into the habit of hearing for other people? Do you not sometimes say to yourselves, 'Well, certainly, I thought that sermon would do very well for Mr Green,' or 'it was the very message Mrs Grey needed'? Happy is the man who just listens for himself, and who goes up to the house of God with this prayer on his lip and in his heart, 'Lord, meet with me now, speak to me through thy servant! Behold, I lay myself by the pool of Bethesda. Lord Jesus, send an angel down to trouble the water; and when it is troubled, give me strength that I may be able to step down into the water, and be cured.' Happy are you if, during the sermon, you are crying to God, 'Grant, O Lord, that there may be a word for my soul! Bring me to Jesus Christ, that I may be blessed for ever.' This is one of the first indications that God has begun the good work in you when you are taken 'aside from the multitude,' and begin to look into the things of the Kingdom for yourselves.

I must not, however, enlarge upon any one point, but pass over them all briefly and quickly. The next thing that Jesus did to the deaf and dumb man was, '*He put his fingers into his ears.*' He did not immediately open his ears; mark that. The man's ears and mouth were opened by the word, 'Ephphatha, that is, Be opened.' This was the expression that Jesus Christ used before he worked the cure; it was not necessary for him to employ it, but it pleased him to use it. Generally, the Lord Jesus thrusts his fingers into the ears of those who are spiritually deaf, and they are thus enabled to hear.

People often have a desire to hear the Word before they hear it to profit. Let me just put it in the way I heard a poor man put it the other day. 'Now, sir,' said he, 'for thirty years, I never went inside the walls of church or chapel; but, one day, I was induced to go and hear a certain preacher. I could not understand him, I confess; he talked about the new birth, and about election, and about final perseverance, and other things, which I had never heard of before. But, sir, that man made me cry; and when I went out of the building, my views of places of worship were quite changed. I thought that people went there just to put their legs up, and go to sleep, or to sit down and listen, and think of nothing at all. But I found it quite the reverse; I felt a desire to *hear,* so I went again that evening; and when I heard that there was to be a prayer meeting or a service during the week, I went again; and when I could not go on week-nights, I longed for Sunday to come that I might go then. Before that, no preaching would have induced me to go to the house of God; but, now, I felt such a desire to hear that I would stand all the time, or lean against a pillar. Before, the most comfortable seat would not have tempted me; but, now, I would squeeze into the gallery, or go anywhere if I could but hear. And yet,' added this poor man, 'I was not converted then; I did not understand what I heard. I felt certain, sir, that I did not know spiritually what it was to be lost and to be saved; and yet I had the hearing ear, and I would walk any number of miles to hear a gospel sermon.'

I trust no wise person will ever speak contemptuously of the intense desire to hear the Word which is apparent in London just now. Perhaps, never since Paul's times were there such immense congregations assembled to listen to the truths of the gospel as there are in our day. Look at the crowds that gather in St Paul's Cathedral, and Westminster Abbey, and Exeter Hall; these are, to my mind, most blessed tokens for good. You may depend upon it that, when the heart is aroused to hear the Word, and when men and women desire to listen to the gospel, there is a blessing coming upon them. When I know that men are longing to go to the house of God, and are pressing into it in crowds, I am reminded of our Saviour's words: 'And from the days of John the Baptist until now the Kingdom of Heaven suffereth violence, and the violent take it by force.' When men have no desire to hear the truth, how can we get at them? But when they come within the sound of the ministry, then is the time for us to use our most weighty and telling arguments, and to urge them to 'flee from the wrath to come.' O dear Christian people, do everything you can to get your ungodly friends to hear the Word of God! Are you a gentleman? Well, then, let some poor man have your comfortable seat. Have you an ungodly relative? Stand in the most inconvenient place behind a pillar, and give him your place, where he can both see and hear the minister of the gospel. The man who is the most often in battle runs the greatest risk of being shot; and if I may speak of any comparison in such things, it does seem to me that the man who is most often under the sound of the gospel is the one who is most likely to be converted by its influence. Do your utmost, then, that the men and women with whom you come into contact may have the opportunity of hearing the Word, and pray the Lord Jesus to be pleased to thrust his fingers into the ears of the multitude, that they may come, and hear, and that, hearing, they may be saved.

But this is not salvation; this is only the method by which it often comes to sinners, the way in which our Lord Jesus Christ goes round about, as it were, to compass his purpose of love and mercy. So, next, we read, '*and he spit.*' O ye fastidious, ye exquisitely polite and proper people, ye superfine, hot-pressed sons and daughters of elegance, how this would shock you! 'He spit.' How vile and vulgar! 'He spit.' What did he mean by this action? Why, this man was deaf, and therefore Christ could not tell him anything by word of mouth; but he was not blind, and therefore, though Christ could not address him in words which he could hear, he could speak to him by signs. Now, suppose you wished to communicate to a deaf man the thought that, if he was to be cured, it must be in a way which would bring contempt upon him, in what better way could you do it than by the act of spitting? Or, if you wished to show him that it was not the means of grace, but the application of the means of grace that would save him, in what better mode could you do it than by touching his tongue? And if you wished to show him that the power of salvation was not in man, but in the God of all grace, how could you do so better than by looking up? And if, afterwards, you wished to teach the man that, though the blessing seemed easy to attain, yet it was granted at great cost, how could you do it better than by sighs and groans? So we have all these actions here: '*and he spit, and touched his tongue; and looking up to heaven, he sighed.*' And then, afterwards, he said, '*Be opened.*' It was all in dumb show; a sermon preached in figures, not in words; but, in some respects, more potent and more suggestive than words would have been.

First, '*He spit;*' and I think this was to convey to the man the fact that he must be saved in what worldly men think *a contemptible manner.* Christ crucified is still, just as in Paul's day, 'unto the Jews a stumbling-block, and unto the Greeks foolishness.' When the gospel is preached in simplicity, those who are proud of their mental powers, those who are educated in worldly learning, and yet so little educated that they think nothing excellent but what is unintelligible to the masses, will generally turn away from it in contempt. 'What!' they say, 'is that the gospel? The man talks so plainly that my servant girl could understand all he says; what is the good of my being educated if I cannot understand the gospel better than she can? I will not hear that man again; I will seek out some *intellectual* preacher.' (That is, a man whom nobody can understand at all.) 'I will attend the place where I can hear a preacher who goes to the very bottom of his subject.' (That is, one who stirs up the mud so that he cannot see his own way, or point out the path to anyone else.) 'He will flatter me by making me think that I am highly intelligent, but I cannot endure that simple preacher, who keeps on quoting texts of Scripture in his sermons, and who stands up in his chapel, and speaks with unstudied eloquence, and endeavours to lead the poor simple souls, who come to hear him, where they may find the Saviour.'

But perhaps the objection does not relate so much to the man's manner as to his *matter*. 'What!' says one, 'is that the gospel,—"Believe and live"?' 'Oh!' they say, 'it is ridiculous. "Believe; simply believe, and you shall be saved;" that is absurd. I like a religion that has a thousand rubrics, each of which must be carefully attended to, or else the soul will be lost. I love that kind of religion which demands a host of bowings of the body, and the saying of a vast number of prayers, and the offering of a variety of things that give a gaudy appearance to religion, even if they have little good in them. "Believe and live!" Why, my blood boils within me, like that of old Naaman when he was told to go and wash in Jordan. "Are not Abana and Pharpar, rivers of Damascus, better than all the waters of Israel? may I not wash in them, and be clean?" What! is my tongue to be loosed by spittle? It cannot be; such a plan of salvation may do very well for the masses; it may do to preach to common people, but to preach that to a respectable and educated congregation is ridiculous.' Yet, my friend, that is the way by which you must be saved, or else you will be for ever shut out from salvation. There are no two roads to Heaven; the Queen and her subjects must tread the same path. The richest and the poorest must enter the Kingdom of Heaven in the same way, for there is no exception here. 'Except ye be converted,'—be ye never so moral, never so exceptionable,— 'except ye be converted, and become as little children, ye shall not enter into the Kingdom of Heaven.' We have for a long time had special sermons for the working-classes, but we need quite as much sermons for gentlemen and ladies. There are many preachers who speak against the vices of the lower orders; we want some equally strong speaking against the vices of the upper classes. We must preach a gospel that has no knowledge of any class whatever, we must preach as man to man; and whether we are preaching to ladies in satin, or to servants in calico, it is our duty to make no distinction or difference, but just to say to all alike, 'Ye must be born again.' Jesus said to Nicodemus, 'Verily, verily, I say unto thee, Except a man be born again, he cannot see the Kingdom of God;' and we are to proclaim the same truth to you. If you turn away from this simple gospel, you are infinitely more foolish than this deaf and dumb man would have been if he had turned away from Jesus Christ, because he used spittle to cure him. O blessed Master, use what means thou wilt, only do save us! If thou wilt break the neck of our pride before thou wilt heal our broken hearts, even so let it be done, and we will love thy method as well as the gift conferred upon us thereby.

'He spit,' and there was much instruction in that dumb show; and then he 'touched his tongue,' *to teach him that there must be an application of the remedy*. Let us learn that it is not the means of grace that can save us; it is not the number of sermons that we hear, but the application of the truth contained in them, that can save us; and that application is the work of God alone. The gospel must be brought to the dumb lip by the finger of Christ, or else there will be no blessing to us from the means of grace, and we shall still remain as deaf and as dumb as ever we were. Jesus 'touched his tongue.'

I must, however, diverge here a little, and show that usually in salvation the tongue desires to move before it can move aright. You may ask many Christians their experience, and they will tell you that, before they put up an acceptable prayer to God, they had many desires to pray; Christ had touched their tongue. 'Oh!' says one, 'I used often to long to pour out my heart in supplication before God. I said, "Oh, that I could believe! Oh, that I could but pray!" I used to try to pray, but it did not seem to be prayer. I know now that it was true prayer; but it did not seem like prayer to me then. Somehow or other, I could not utter the words I wanted to use; and I sometimes was afraid I could not believe the gospel, and that my desires and longings after salvation were only the result of temporary enthusiasm or excitement, and not a real work of grace. If I could but have groaned my heart out before God, then I thought I should have found peace.' It is a good sign when you can talk like that. It is a most blessed evidence that something has been done when the tongue is touched; when it is, if I may use so expressive a word, set itching to speak, when it would go if it could. This is a sure sign of something better to come.

Then, next, we see Christ 'looking up to heaven,' to show the deaf and dumb man that, not the means, nor even the application of the means in itself was sufficient, but that *it is the power from on high that must save us.* And this is one of the hardest things in theology, always to keep ourselves looking up. Why, even after you have known the Lord,—and some of you have known him these fifty years, mayhap,—you will find it very difficult always to remember that the blessing comes from above. I question whether, even when on our dying bed, this lesson can be learned too well, that all must come from above. We often find ourselves relying upon the mere act of prayer, or looking to our sermons, and to our services, for a blessing, instead of remembering that every good gift must come from God. There is a sweet passage in the eighty-fourth Psalm, which we ought to remember: 'Who passing through the valley of Baca make it a well.' That is our business; but did you ever notice the way in which the wells were filled? They were not filled as many of our wells are, from the bottom, but from the top: 'the rain also filleth the pools.' We are to dig the well, but we must always direct our eyes up, and remember that the grace must come down upon the means. I must not go to my church or to my chapel, to baptism, or to the communion table, expecting a blessing from the means, looked upon alone and in themselves; but I am to use the means, looking up all the while, and praying to God to send down a blessing upon them. Say, my hearers, have you come as far as this? Have you learned that all your help is laid on him, on the shoulders of the Lord God of your salvation? Are you stripped of all creature strength? Are you obliged to say, 'I can do nothing without thee; all my strength is in thee'? Then, verily, I may safely say, 'Thou art not far from the Kingdom of God.'

There is one thing more; that is, '*He sighed*' Jesus sighed; and that was to teach the deaf and dumb man, or the disciples, and any other onlookers, that, though the cure seemed easy, *yet it cost the Saviour many groans to heal him.* So Christ Jesus, when he gives us the priceless jewel of his grace, always likes us to see the hole in the hand that won that jewel for us. When he saves us, he will let us know the price he paid for our salvation. I shall never forget when, as a weary pilgrim, I went about my sad and mournful way, seeking rest, and finding none. Heavy was the burden on my back, and doleful were the forebodings of my fears. 'Lost, lost, lost!' was my continual cry. But as I wandered far, one day I heard a cry, a bitter and a mournful one, and I turned aside to listen; I heard the cry again, in accents too awful to be imitated, but in words like these, 'Eloi, Eloi, lama sabachthani?' I wondered whence it came, and I turned aside to see the sad sight; and, lo! there stood a cross, and on it hung a man, his head all crowned with thorns, and ruby drops ran down his cheeks from the temples that were pierced with them; and I saw his hands all stained with blood, his feet the same, and his back was a mass of crimson gore. I looked into his face, and I never saw sorrow like unto his sorrow, while pity floated in his languid eye; yet he looked as if he needed pity rather than to give it. As I stood there, I began to weep, the sorrows of Christ had melted my heart; and as I stood and wept, methought Christ's lips opened, and he looked as if he would begin to speak, and I wondered much what he would say. He spake, and oh, how sweet it was to my soul to hear him say, 'It is finished!' Then he bowed his head, and died. My spirit lost its burden, my eyes forgot their tears, my heart began its never-ceasing song, and I went on my way the happiest of mortals; no more to mourn or sigh, for at that cross I found my Saviour. There is a sweet hymn of Keble's, in his *Christian Year;* I do not remember the exact wording of it, but one of the first ideas of it is, that it is strange that Calvary, which was the very Palace of Misery, should be the birthplace of all our joys. How strange that the mournful sigh of the Saviour should be the mother of our songs, that his sobs and tears and agonies should be the parent of the sweetest hallelujahs of souls redeemed!

O poor heart, wouldst thou find salvation? The cross is just there; and 'tis there, 'tis there, 'tis there, that thou canst get thy sins forgiven! I cannot preach you to Christ, poor sinners; I can only preach Christ to you. If you will not go to him, yet I must again lift up his cross before you, and bid you, 'Look and live.' Do you not know that Jesus Christ, the Son of God, was born of the Virgin Mary, that he lived a life of sorrow, and that, at last, he suffered under Pontius Pilate, was crucified, yea, that he died for your sins, and was buried for you? Oh! I beseech you, turn not away your eyes, and though they be dim with the tears of sorrow, look upon that man Christ Jesus, who for your sins died upon the cross of Calvary, look, look, look unto him, and be saved. He himself is saying, 'Look unto me, and be ye saved, all the ends of the earth; for I am God, and there is none else.' Sinner, art thou looking to Christ? If so, the word of Omnipotence is already spoken, and the Divine 'Ephphatha' hath gone forth.

This brings me to the concluding thought. After all, it was not the spittle, it was not the thrusting of Christ's fingers into the man's ears, it was not the looking up to Heaven, or even the sighing, that absolutely produced the cure, though all these were necessary concomitants of the cure, in the Saviour's way and method. It was, after all, the command, '*Be opened,*' that did it. So, in salvation, it is the one effectual word that saves the soul. The doctrine of effectual quickening grace must be held by those who read the Scriptures aright. It is by that grace that men are really saved. The teaching of Scripture is, that men are not saved by the means, but by the omnipotent fiat of God the Holy Spirit speaking in the heart. Christ finds us dead. He does not ask us for anything; he says to us, 'Live,' and straightway we live. He finds us deaf; he says to us, 'Be opened,' and at once our ears are opened. He finds us weak; he says to us, 'Be strong,' and we are. Though he would always have us use the means, yet would he always have us recollect that the real saving power lieth in his own almighty Word. So, then,—

'Give all the glory to his holy Name,
  For to him all the glory belongs.'

III. And now, lastly, I have been stating doctrines, yet I cannot apply them to your hearts,—the Holy Spirit must do that; but I CAN ASK A QUESTION OR TWO OF EACH OF YOU.

Mark, the questions that I ask you, I shall also ask myself; I shall not exempt any one of my congregation. Minister, speak to thyself now; speak to thy brother-ministers present, to the deacons, to the church-members, to one, to all. Friends, *do you know anything about salvation?* I would not venture to question you as to what else you know. Doubtless, most of you have received sufficient education upon other subjects; but what do you know about salvation? What do you know concerning your own ruin? Do you know no more than the schools have taught you, or than your preacher has declared to you? Say, dost thou know, by experience, anything about thy lost estate? Hast thou ever been made to weep over sin? Hast thou ever seen thy total inability to offer an adequate atonement for thine offences? There are some of you, my hearers, who would lie to your own consciences if you should say, 'Yes,' to these questions; for you have lived, up to this hour, hearers only, but not doers of the Word. These things have never been part and parcel of your inner being. You have never felt that Jesus Christ has been precious to your souls. Oh! let me affectionately warn you, to whatever church you belong, it matters not to me; you may in one church have received the so-called christening in your infancy, and the confirmation in your youth; but, oh! I beseech you, do not trust in these things; they are vanities, utterly worthless, as a ground or hope for salvation. They are a rotten foundation for your spirit to build upon. Or you, members of another communion, have perhaps been baptized after the New Testament pattern,—upon a profession of your faith in Jesus Christ, and you have partaken of the Lord's supper; but I beseech you to recollect that even this, however we may believe that you have followed the teaching of the Scriptures in a more excellent manner, is just as unsound a ground of trust as any other. If you rely upon any or all of these things, although your practice were as orthodox and your doctrines as sound as even the apostle Paul could desire, you are a lost soul unless the love of God dwelleth in you.

This is a searching question,—what am I? Let me ask you each one to breathe this prayer: 'O gracious God, let me know the very worst of my case, let me not go blindfolded into perdition thinking that I am saved! O Lord, my God, let me know whether I am thine or not; and if I be not this day a saved man, a saved woman, Lord, if my heart be not broken, break it; and if it be broken, heal it now.'

I think I hear one say, 'Sir, I want to know whether I am a child of God.' I will put to you one question, and if you can answer it truly, I will tell you what I think about you, '*Can you say that you have no hope save in Jesus*

Christ?' If so, I can assure you that there was never yet one who perished who had faith in the Lord Jesus Christ. You may ride in the gallant ship of your own good works, but you will go in it to destruction; but on the sorry plank, as some think it, of a simple faith in the Lord Jesus Christ, you shall float securely. There is no fear of shipwreck when faith in Christ is the barque in which you sail. Oh, trust him, trust him, trust him! He is worthy of your trust. Cast your soul on him. He gave his soul unto death for you. Come unto him, all ye that labour and are heavy laden, and he will give you rest. Come to Jesus now; come to Jesus Christ, O ye wanderers! O ye sin-smitten, ye sin-defiled sinners, come ye to the Saviour's arms this day! He is ready to receive you.

'Bow the knee, and kiss the Son,
Come, and welcome, sinner, come!'

Chapter 24

Jesus communicating his riches

An early meditation by C. H. Spurgeon

'For ye know the grace of our Lord Jesus Christ, that, though he was rich, yet for your sakes he became poor, that ye through his poverty might be rich.'—2 Corinthians 8:9.

O UR glorious Lord was in the beginning ordained to be the Husband of his Church, and it therefore became necessary that he should in due time fulfil the duties of that relationship. He had voluntarily chosen his bride, and had of his own free grace taken her into union with himself. Love was the only compulsion which moved him to the deed, but that was a power so strong that he did not hesitate to yield to its influence. When he had thus graciously entered into affinity with his Church, the same constraining power impelled him to the faithful discharge of all the responsibilities which his position involved. From no part of his office did he shrink, in no point was he found wanting. Whatever was incumbent upon him through the relationship which he had assumed, he did most cheerfully engage to do or bear for his beloved.

Among the acts which are inseparably connected with the conjugal state, that of loving communion holds a high position; and hence the Lord Jesus was bent upon establishing communion between himself and his chosen, knowing as he did that, without this, his marriage union would be but a mere form, and not a blessed reality. This communion he has effected in a most excellent and admirable manner, leaving no stone unturned to secure the most intimate fellowship between himself and his Church. Let our mind, for an instant, consider the history of the Redeemer's love, and a thousand enchanting acts of affection will at once suggest themselves, all of which have had for their design the weaving of the heart of believers into Christ, and the intertwisting of the thoughts and emotions of their soul with the mind of Jesus. Among these loving endeavours to bring us near to himself, we give prominence to his communicative acts by which unspeakable blessings are bestowed upon us.

The Lord Jesus Christ was eternally rich, glorious, and exalted; for, saith the text, 'though *he was rich,* yet for your sakes he became poor.' Now, as the rich saint cannot be true in his communion with the poor brethren unless out of his own substance he ministers to their necessities, so (the same rule holding with the Head as between the members) it is impossible that our Divine Lord could have had fellowship with us unless he had imparted to us of his own abounding wealth, and had become poor to make us rich. Had he remained upon his throne of glory, and had we continued in the ruins of the fall without receiving of his salvation, communion would have been impossible on both sides. Our position by the fall, apart from the covenant of grace, was not one whit preferable to that of the apostate angels, nor was our character much superior, and therefore it would have been as impossible for fallen man to commune with God as it is for Belial to be in concord with Christ.

In order, therefore, that communion might be compassed, it was necessary that the rich Kinsman should bestow his estate upon his poor relatives, that the righteous Saviour should give to his sinning brethren of his own perfection, and that we, the poor and guilty, should receive of his fulness grace for grace, and by his Spirit partake of his holiness; that thus, in giving and receiving, the One might descend from the heights, and the others ascend from the depths, and so be able to embrace each other in true and hearty fellowship. Poverty must be enriched by him in whom are infinite treasures before it can venture to commune; and guilt must lose itself in imputed and imparted righteousness ere the soul can walk in fellowship with purity. Jesus must clothe his naked friends in his own garments, or he cannot admit them into his palace of glory; and he must wash his poor and filthy brethren in his own blood, or else they will be too defiled for the embrace of his fellowship.

How the Lord Jesus communes with us in donation, and how we commune with him in reception, it is now our delightful business to explain. May God the Holy Spirit bless us with a profitable meditation! We use the verse at the head of our paper rather for suggestion than for exposition, and now propound the doctrine which the text admirably illustrates.

The Lord Jesus Christ in a most precious manner communes with us in his gifts. As his blessings are of infinite value, so his fellowship in bestowing them is profound and unparalleled. Never man communed like this man; for never man had such riches to confer upon his friends, and such poor friends to receive them. The incomparable excellence of his gifts is but proportionate to the peerless fulness of his fellowship. Inasmuch as he did endow his Church with immeasurable riches, it is certain that he hath with her an unbounded union of spirit. It shows the strength of Christian brotherhood when the crowned monarch grasps the beggar's hand, bows his knee upon the same floor, sits at the same table, and gives a portion of his luxury to relieve the poor man's need; but the fellowship of Jesus is stronger far, for it leaps the leagues of separating distance, makes him become bone of our bone, and flesh of our flesh, and completes the communion by giving us the dignity, the glory, and the righteousness with which our King is himself surrounded, in order that we may feel that the distance is not simply forgotten, but destroyed. It is impossible sufficiently to admire the God-like love which has established a communion so complete by a succession of gifts of priceless value. Turn aside, O saint, and view this great sight!

I. First, observe THE COMPLETENESS OF THY LORD'S COMMUNICATION: 'Ye know the grace of our Lord Jesus Christ, that, though he was rich, yet for your sakes he became poor.'

In our remembrance of the poor saints, there is but a partial communion; for however hearty may be our charity, we give but a portion of our substance for their benefit. We do not bestow *all our goods* to feed the poor, nor does God require us to do so; nevertheless, as the communication is limited, so must the communion be. The Church realized the fulness of this species of fellowship in her earliest days, when her members had 'all things common.' A reference to the original text of Acts 2:44, and 4:32, will suggest to the reader the connection between this community of possessions and communion of heart; for the Holy Spirit has employed the word κοινά, which is the root of the word κοινωνία, as if to teach us this very doctrine of communion in gifts. Since that halycon period, we have devoted a portion to the Lord's poor; but, in many cases, the pittance has been too small in proportion to our means to allow the spirit of fellowship to develop itself in any notable measure. Doubtless there are some who, though they are themselves poor, drop their last mite into the treasury, and so come near to a complete fellowship; but the most of us have only a slender degree of it, for our alms are scanty; and those among us who are the most considerate and bounteous, have yet cause to lament that we have done too little for the tried children of God.

Behold, then, the superlative excellence of the Lord Jesus, for he hath given us his all. Although a tithe of his possessions would have made a whole universe full of angels rich beyond all thought, yet he was not content until he had given us all that he had. It would have been surprising grace if he had allowed us to eat the crumbs of his bounty beneath the table of his mercy; but he never does anything by halves, so he makes us sit with him, and share the feast. Had he given us some small pension from his royal coffers, we should have had cause to love him eternally; but no, he will have his bride as rich as himself, and he will not have a glory or a grace in which she shall not share. He has not been content with less than making us joint-heirs with himself, so that we might have equal possessions. He has emptied all his estate into the coffers of the Church, and hath all things common with his redeemed. There is not one room in his house the key of which he will withhold from his people. He gives them full liberty to take all that he hath to be their own; he loves them to make free with his treasure, and appropriate as much as they can possibly carry. From the sandals on his feet to the crown upon his head, he reserves nothing.

The boundless fulness of his all-sufficiency is as free to the believer as the air he breathes. Christ puts the flagon of his love and grace to the believer's lip, and bids him drink on for ever; for could he drain it, he is welcome to do so, and as he cannot exhaust it, he is bidden to drink abundantly, for it is all his own. What truer proof of fellowship can Heaven or earth afford? What higher honour can any created being receive? Unto which of the angels said Jesus at any time, 'Thou art co-heir with me'? Remember the eternal stores of grace which are thus opened to us. Review the shining armies of mercies which are thus enrolled in our cause. Compute the immeasurable, enumerate the countless, weigh the infinite, and fathom the bottomless; then mayest thou attain to the understanding of the abyss of fellowship, out of which these great communications have been digged. In a few words, let us reckon up the all which Christ hath given us, and may the blessed Spirit inspire us with gratitude in so doing!

Consider *the greatness of those riches which for our sake he laid aside.* The wealth of all the worlds that swim in the ether of the boundless universe, the homage of the myriads who inhabit the various provinces of his dominion, the hallelujahs of the angelic hosts who wait perpetually before him,—all these, he resigned in the hour of our redemption. 'From the highest throne in glory' he descended 'to the cross of deepest woe,' all the way unrobing himself of the garments of glory, happiness, and brightness, with which he had been eternally arrayed.

If we were capable of conceiving the majesty and honour with which our Divine Lord had been invested before his incarnation, how great would the contrast appear to be when we see him, as the 'Man of sorrows,' 'a reproach of men, and despised of the people.' Without house or home, the Saviour wanders through the land of Judæa; without food, he hungers; without water, he cries, 'Give me to drink;' without a helper, he wrestles with his fiercest foe in the Garden of Gethsemane; and, without a garment, he expires upon the cross of Calvary. When he would ride into Jerusalem in triumph, it must be upon a borrowed ass; and when he must sleep in the tomb, the sepulchre must be lent by another. See, then, the greatness of his love, when thou hearest him, who was God's equal, crying, 'My God, my God, why hast thou forsaken me?' Say, like Bernard, 'O love that art so sweet, why wast thou so bitter to thyself?' and remember that the only answer is, that Jesus communicated his sweetness unto us, and himself drank all that was in our bitter cup.

All his attributes as God and man are at our disposal. 'In him dwelleth all the fulness of the Godhead bodily;' and whatever that marvellous term may comprehend is ours. He cannot make us gods, we cannot partake in the attributes of Deity; but he has done for us all that could be done, for he has made even his Divine power and Godhead subservient to our salvation. His omnipotence, omniscience, omnipresence, immutability, and infallibility, are all engaged upon our side, and are all combined for our defence. Arise, believer, and behold the Lord Jesus yoking the whole of his Godhead to the chariot of salvation! How vast his grace, how firm his faithfulness, how unswerving his immutability, how infinite his power, how limitless his knowledge! And all these are, by the Lord Jesus, made to be the pillars of the temple of salvation; and all, without any diminution of their infinity, are covenanted to us as our perpetual inheritance. The fathomless love of the Saviour's heart is every drop of it ours; every sinew in the arm of his might, every jewel in the crown of his majesty, the immensity of Divine knowledge, and sternness of Divine justice, all are ours, and shall be employed for us. There is no golden attribute, however incomparable in its Divinity, which Christ hath withheld from us. The whole of Christ, in his adorable character as the Son of God, is by himself made over to us most richly to enjoy. His wisdom is our direction, his knowledge our instruction, his power our protection, his justice our surety, his love our comfort, his mercy our solace, and his immutability our trust. He maketh no reserve, but openeth the inmost recesses of the Mount of God, and biddeth us dig in its mines for the hidden treasures. 'All, all, all are yours,' saith he, 'be ye satisfied with favour, and full with the blessing of the Lord.'

His *manhood* also, which he took upon him for us, is ours in all its perfection. To us, our gracious Lord communicates the spotless virtue of a stainless character; to us, he gives the meritorious efficacy of a devoted life; on us, he bestows the reward procured by obedient submission and incessant service. He makes the unsullied garment of his perfect life to be our covering and beauty; the glittering virtues of his character, our ornaments and jewels; and the superhuman meekness of his death, our boast and glory. He bequeaths us his manger, from which to learn how God came down to man; and his cross, to teach us how man may go up to God. All his thoughts, emotions, actions, utterances, miracles, and intercessions, were for us. He trod the road of sorrow on our behalf, and he hath made over to us, as his heavenly legacy, the full results of all the labours of his wondrous life. And since he still appears in the form of manhood in the world above, he is as much ours now as heretofore; and he blushes not to acknowledge himself 'our Lord Jesus Christ,' though he is 'the blessed and only Potentate, the King of kings, and Lord of lords.' As one has well said, 'There is that in Christ which answers to all our wants, and an all-sufficiency for all degrees of happiness. Christ is all marrow and all sweetness; all the several graces and comforts we have, and the several promises whereby they are made over and conveyed to us, are but Christ set forth in several manners, as the need of every Christian shall require. Christ himself is the ocean issuing into several streams to refresh the city of God.'

Oh, how sweet thus to behold him, and to call upon him, with the certain confidence that, in seeking the interposition of his love or power, we are but asking for that which he has already given! It is as we receive, day by day, more and more help from Jesus, and more constantly recognize it as coming from him, that we shall be able to behold him in communion with us, and enjoy the felicity of fellowship with him. Let us make daily use of our riches in Christ Jesus, and ever repair to him as our Lord in covenant, taking from him the supply of all our need with as much boldness as men take money from their own purse.

Let us remember, too, that *all the offices of Christ are ours.* He is King for us, Priest for us, and Prophet for us. Whenever we read a new title of the Redeemer, let us appropriate him as ours under that name as much as under any other. The Shepherd's staff, the Father's rod, the Captain's sword, the Priest's mitre, the Prince's sceptre, the Prophet's mantle, all are ours. Christ hath no dignity which he will not employ for our exaltation, and no prerogative which he will not exercise for our defence. Christ everywhere and every way is our Christ, for ever and ever for us most richly to enjoy.

He hath given us all his grace. He hath grace without measure in himself, but he hath not retained it for himself. As the reservoir empties itself into the pipes, so hath Christ emptied out his grace for his people. 'Of his fulness have all we received, and grace for grace.' He seems to have only in order that he may dispense it to us. He stands like the fountain in the market, always flowing, but only running in order to supply the empty pitchers and the thirsty lips that draw nigh unto it. Grace, to pardon, to cleanse, to preserve, to strengthen, to enlighten, to quicken, or to restore, is ever to be had from him 'without money and without price;' nor is there one form of the work of grace which he has not bestowed upon his people. As the blood of the body, though flowing from the heart, belongs equally to every member, so the influences of grace are the inheritance of every saint who is united to the Lamb; and herein there is a sweet community of interest between Christ and his Church, inasmuch as they both receive the same grace. Christ is the head upon which the oil is first poured; but the same oil runs down to the very skirts of the garments, so that the meanest saint has an unction of the same costly moisture as that which fell upon the head. This is true, living communion when the sap of grace flows from the stem to the branch, and when it is perceived that the stem itself is sustained by the very nourishment which feeds the branch. The Mediator, Jesus, knows as much of the value of grace as we do, for as man he was sustained by the very influence which supports us.

Further, *Jesus rules the kingdom of Providence for us.* He is the sole Arbiter of all events; in everything, his sway is supreme; and he exercises his power for the good of his Church. He spins the thread of events and acts, from the distaff of destiny, and does not suffer those threads to be woven otherwise than according to the pattern arranged by his loving wisdom. He will not allow the mysterious wheels to revolve in any way which shall not bring good unto his chosen. He makes their worst things to be blessings to them, and their best things to be better still. As all things are working together for his glory, so all things are working together for their good.

The boundless stores of Providence are all engaged for the support of the believer. Christ is our Joseph, who has granaries full of wheat; but he does not treat us as Joseph did the Egyptians, for he opens the doors of his storehouses, and bids us call all the good thereof our own. He has entailed upon his estate of Providence a perpetual charge of a daily portion for us; and he has promised that, one day, we shall clearly perceive that the estate itself has been well farmed on our behalf, and that it has always been ours. The axle of the wheels of the chariot of Providence is infinite love, and Gracious Wisdom is the perpetual charioteer. Even when, to the eye of reason, all things seem to be contrary to us, they are really serving our cause; and there are special seasons when this is made apparent to a believer, when he sees his very trials blossoming with comfort. As

Rutherford says, 'The thorn is one of the most cursed and angry weeds that the earth yieldeth, and yet out of it springeth the rose, one of the most sweetly-smelling flowers, and most delightful to the eye.' Yes, believer, Christ Jesus thy Lord presents to thee thy crosses, and they are no mean gifts of his love.

Yet further, *all the goodness of the past, the present, and the future, he bestows upon us.* In the mysterious ages of the past, the Lord Jesus was his Father's first elect; and in his *election* we have the deepest possible interest, for we were 'chosen in him before the foundation of the world.' He had, from all eternity, the prerogatives of *Sonship,* as his Father's only-begotten and well-beloved Son; and he has, in the riches of his grace, by adoption and regeneration, elevated us also to sonship; so that to us he has given 'power to become the sons of God.' The *Eternal Covenant,* based upon suretyship and confirmed by oath, is ours for our strong consolation and unfailing security. In the everlasting settlements of predestinating wisdom and omnipotent decree, the eye of the Lord Jesus was ever fixed upon us; and we may rest assured that, in the whole roll of destiny, there is not a line which militates against the interests of his redeemed. The *great betrothal* of the Prince of Glory is ours, for it is to us that he is affianced, as the sacred nuptials shall one day declare. The *marvellous incarnation* of the God of Heaven, with all the amazing condescension and humiliation which attended it, is ours. The bloody sweat, the scourge, and the cross, in all their plenitude of power to bless and save, are ours for ever. Whatever blissful consequences flow from perfect obedience, finished atonement, resurrection, ascension, or intercession, are all ours by his own gift. Upon his breastplate, he is now bearing our names; and in his authoritative pleadings at the throne, he remembers our persons, and pleads our cause. The advantages of his high position, his dominion over principalities and powers, and his absolute majesty in Heaven, he employs for the benefit of all them that trust in him. His high estate is as much at our service as was his condition of abasement. He who gave himself for us in the depths of woe and death, doth not withdraw the grant now that he is enthroned in the highest heavens.

And as for the future, we may rest content that, through our Lord Jesus, it is all on our side. The delay of the coming Bridegroom has a kind intention in it; and as for 'the coming' itself, it is love made perfect. The splendours of the approaching reign, the glories of the golden age, the enthroned Church, the triumphant gospel, shall contain a portion for us. Ay, and the reeling earth, the withering stars, the extinguished sun, and reddened moon, shall bear us blessings. The trump of doom, the throne of judgment, the tremendous pomp of that awful day, all are ours, to anticipate, not with terror, but with joy.

In all Christ's triumphs, he permits us to share;—in fact, he seems but to triumph for us. He bids us hurl defiance at *death,* and expect a certain victory over the last enemy,—

'For as the Lord, our Saviour, rose,
So all his followers must.'

The apostle Paul claims the victory over death as ours: 'Thanks be to God, which *giveth us* the victory through our Lord Jesus Christ.' His is the sole glory, but the halo of it enlightens us.

His conquest of sin and Satan, though accomplished by his single-handed efforts, is presented to us as the means of our own triumph, for, concerning the great adversary of the redeemed, it is written, 'they overcame him by the blood of the Lamb.' His bruising of Satan's head he transfers to us, and promises that the God of Peace shall also bruise Satan under our feet shortly. To each believer, he says, 'Thou shalt tread upon the lion and adder: the young lion and the dragon shalt thou trample under feet.'

The august ascension of the Conqueror is ours, for we have risen with him; yea, and in him we are 'made to sit together in heavenly places;' and we are told that the unrivalled splendours of his ultimate and complete triumph are to be shared by us. When he shall ride through the streets of the new Jerusalem, amidst the plaudits of Heaven, when he shall render up the Kingdom to God and his Father, he shall grant us a share in the presentation before the Divine presence, exclaiming, 'Here am I, Father, and the children thou hast given me.'

He hath given us his royal robes. It was a high proof of hearty fellowship between David and Jonathan when 'Jonathan stripped himself of the robe that was upon him, and gave it to David, and his garments, even to his sword, and to his bow, and to his girdle;' but, truly, our Lord hath outdone this brotherly act, for he made himself naked for our sake, insomuch that he was exposed before the face of the sun without a rag to cover him, and by this stripping he hath clothed us in a garment of perfect righteousness and surpassing beauty. Our court-dress in Heaven, and our garments of sanctification for daily wear on earth, are the condescending gifts of his love.

But he hath exceeded all this by the next deed, for *he hath crowned us with his crown*. The crown-royal he hath placed upon the head of his Church, appointing unto her a Kingdom, and calling her sons a royal priesthood, a generation of priests and kings. He did uncrown himself that we might have a coronation of glory; he would not sit upon his own throne until he had procured a place upon it for all those whom he had purchased by his blood. Crown the head, and the whole body shares the honour. The foot of a Cæsar was as royal as his brow; and so the meanest saint is as truly possessed of royal dignity as is our glorious Lord. Mark well this community of honour, and be not backward to perceive that, where the Lord hath given so much, he must have communed much.

His very life he has not withheld from us. His Deity could not be subject to death; but as his humanity was mortal, he gave up the vital spark of its existence on our account. In order that we might live for ever, he 'even dared to die.' We do not usually think it our duty to resign our lives for the welfare of our neighbours; but the Lord Jesus, that he might prove the infinity of his love, laid down the life of his body at the bidding of our necessity. The silver cord was loosed, the golden bowl was broken, the pitcher was broken at the fountain, and the wheel broken at the cistern; they that looked out of the windows were darkened, the keepers of the house trembled, and the strong men bowed themselves; the dust returned to the earth as it was, and the spirit was commended to its God, and all this for us, his dearly-beloved.

His possessions he holds jointly with us. The boundless realms of his Father's universe are his by prescriptive right. As 'heir of all things,' he is the sole Proprietor of the vast creation of God, and he has permitted us to claim the whole as ours; for 'all things are ours,' by virtue of that deed of joint-heirship which the Lord hath ratified with his chosen people. The golden streets of Paradise, the jewelled walls, the pearly gates, the river of life, the living fountains, the transcendent bliss, the inconceivable happiness, and the unutterable glory are, by our thrice-blessed Lord, made over to us for our everlasting possessions.

Well has one written:—'Behold here the reward of every Christian conqueror! A throne, a crown, a sceptre, a palace, treasures incorruptible, robes which wax not old, an inheritance that fadeth not away,—all are yours. Christ's throne, crown, sceptre, palace, treasure, robes, heritage, are all yours. Far superior to the jealousy, selfishness, and scorn, which admit no participation in their advantages, Christ deems his happiness completed by his people sharing it. To his Father he said, "The glory which thou gavest me I have given them," and to his disciples he said, "These things have I spoken unto you, that my joy might remain in you, and that your joy might be full." We can almost hear him saying, at this moment, "The smiles of my Father are sweeter to me, because my people shall share them. The honours of my Kingdom are more pleasing, because my people appear with me in glory. More valuable to me are my conquests, since they have taught my people to overcome. I delight in this throne, because on it there is a place for them. I delight in these robes, since over them their skirts are spread. I delight the more in this joy, because I can call them to enter into it."'

Where the catalogue containeth all things, who can go through it? I feel that I have but skimmed the surface of the unfathomable sea of wealth which the Saviour has conferred upon us as the pledge and means of communion with us. I have but, as it were, numbered the doors of the chambers which enclose the countless riches which the Lord Jesus has laid up in store for his people. Believer, here remember that, in every cup of thy Lord's blessing, a thousand pearls are dissolved; and recollect that there is a boundless ocean of the same richness, and that thy deepest draught is but one cupful out of a shoreless, bottomless sea of lovingkindness. Hold up thine hands in wonder at the unlimited love of thy Lord, and guess at thy surprise if thou couldst be able to estimate in full the unsearchable riches he has conferred upon thee. Oh, sad poverty of a willing pen that it cannot even find words in which to tell the mercy of the Lord! Surely, ye angels, ye would lose yourselves in this unexplored expanse of grace; your mighty wings would tire ere ye had flown half-way across this sea of love.

'God only knows the love of God.'

We can admire, but we cannot measure the depths of the lovingkindness of Jesus.

II. Next, mark well, O believer, THE CONTINUANCE OF THY MASTER'S COMMUNICATIONS, and, consequently, the immutability of his communion.

Our fellowship with the poor saints, so far as it is expressed in our contributions to their needs, is necessarily, from our own want of means, if not from lack of love, of a broken and interrupted character. It is not every day that we visit the sick, and feed the hungry, or at least it is not every hour that we are engaged in such pious acts. We must rest even from the pleasure of relieving our needy brethren; the eye must close for sleep, even if hand and purse could be ever open. But our Lord Jesus is ever giving, and does not for a solitary instant withdraw his hand. As long as there is a vessel of grace not yet full to the brim, the oil shall not be stayed. He is a sun ever shining; he is manna always falling round about the camp; he is a rock in the desert, ever sending out streams of life from his smitten side; the rain of his grace is always dropping; the river of his bounty is ever flowing, and the well-spring of his love is constantly overflowing. Daily we pluck the fruit from this Tree of Life, and daily its branches bend down to our hand with a fresh store of mercy. As the King can never die, so his grace can never fail. He keeps open house, and kills his fatted calf every day. There are seven feast days in his weeks; and as many as are the days, so many are the banquets in his years. Who has ever returned from his door unblessed? Who has ever risen from his table unsatisfied, or from his bosom un-emparadised? His mercies are new every morning and fresh every evening. Who can tell the number of his benefits, or recount the list of his bounties? Every grain of sand that drops from the glass of time is but the tardy follower of a myriad of mercies. The wings of our hours are covered with the silver of his gracious kindness, and with the yellow gold of his ardent affection. The river of time bears from the mountains of eternity the golden sands of his favour. The countless numbers of the stars are but as the standard-bearers of a more innumerable host of blessings. Who can count the dust of the benefits which he bestows upon Jacob, or the number of the fourth part of his mercies towards Israel? How shall my soul extol him who daily loadeth us with benefits? Surely Addison may be forgiven the extravagance of his expression when he sang,—

'Through all eternity to thee,
    A joyful song I'll raise;
But, oh! eternity's too short
    To utter all thy praise.'

III. Thirdly, ponder over THE HEARTINESS OF CHRIST'S COMMUNICATIONS, as expressive of the intensity of his fellowship.

The chilling heartlessness, with which some professors bestow their alms upon their afflicted brethren, is the death of fervent communion; and it must ever be a source of lamentation, to the most eminent of the saints while here on earth, that their acts of charity are seldom so lovingly performed as to afford the delightful warmth of soul which is the native atmosphere of true fellowship. To give our hearts with our charity, is to give well; but we fear we must often plead guilty to failure here. Not so our blessed Lord. His favours are always perfumed with the love of his heart. He does not give us the cold meat and broken bits from the table of his luxury; but he dips our morsel in his own dish, and seasons our provisions with the spices of his fragrant affection. When he puts the golden tokens of his grace into our palm, he accompanies the gift with such a fervent pressure upon our hand that the manner of his giving seems to be as precious as the boon itself. He comes into our houses upon his errands of kindness, and he does not act as some austere visitors do, for he sits by our side, not despising our poverty, nor blaming our weakness. And with what smiles does he speak to us! What golden sentences he drops from his gracious lips! And what embraces of affection does he bestow upon us! If he had but given us farthings, the way of his giving would have gilded them; but as it is, the costly alms are set in a basket of silver by his pleasant and gracious demeanour.

It is impossible to doubt the sincerity of his charity, for there is a bleeding heart stamped upon the face of all his favours. He giveth to us liberally, and upbraideth us not. He never drops even a hint that we are burdensome to him, nor does he ever give one cold look at his poor pensioners. Like as a mother giveth nourishment to the child at her breast, smiling all the while, and taking pleasure in its feeding, so doth the Lord Jesus rejoice in his mercy, and press us to his bosom even while he is pouring out his life for us. There is a fragrance in his spikenard which nothing but his heart could produce; there is a sweetness in his honeycomb which could not lie in it unless the very essence of his soul's affection had been mingled with it. Oh, rare communion which such singular heartiness effecteth! May we taste and know the blessedness of it continually!

IV. Finally, child of God, mark THE FREENESS OF THY LORD'S BOUNTIES, and see therein how spontaneous is his communion with his people.

Some Christians, before they will assist the needy saints, require much persuading. They are like deep wells which need much labour before the bucket can be brought to the surface; and many of them have so small a bucket that, when we at last procure their charity, it is such a niggardly portion, that we regret our much-ado-about-nothing, and resolve never again to draw at that well. Indeed, if only 'the liberal soul shall be made fat,' it is no marvel that we have so many of Pharaoh's lean kine in all our pastures. There are a few generous hearts, which survive the selfishness of the age, and still exist, like bright spots upon the tawny skin of the sterile desert on which this generation appears to have fallen. They are the harbours of refuge where the ship of charity has found a haven from the prevailing tempests of worldliness and self-aggrandisement. Peradventure, even these good angels sometimes feel the chilly air of a niggardly world, and wrap themselves, in some moments of temptation, in a part of the robe of him 'that withholdeth more than is meet.' It cannot be wondered at if they sometimes hint that they have done their share, and that it would be well if others were willing to bear part of the burden.

But here is one unique excellence of our adorable Jesus. He is ever free with his gifts; he needs no urging, and requires no pressure. Prove your need, and claim his bounty, and he will as soon think of denying his own Name as of refusing to relieve your wants. Often does he give before we ask, and never is he behind his promise. He does not dole out his mercy as if he desired to restrain it; but he lifts the floodgates of his kindness, and bids the stream of blessings rush forth in an exuberant torrent of generosity. As a King, he gives right royally. You cannot grieve him more than by doubting the freeness of his love. Like the sun, he rises upon a sleeping world, and does not stop until the matin prayer has invited him to come. As the world revolves without a hand to turn it, so his favour is in perpetual motion without the need of constraint.

True, he loves to hear our prayers, but our supplications are not the cause of his goodness. Prayer may be the rope which binds the vessel of his mercy to our shore, but the wind that floated it hither blows from no quarter but his own voluntary love. When our ingratitude and unbelief, like windows bespattered with mire, have done their best to shut out the sunlight of his grace, he has darted rays of light and heat so marvellously powerful that they have shone into our hearts despite all the filthiness that did hinder them; nay, more, they have even dispersed the obstructing impurities, and have cleansed away the uncleanness of our spirits. We have never found his door bolted on the inside, although our own baseness has often locked it from without. When the hand of Divine mercy encloses a blessing, it never needs much labour to unloose the fingers. Christ's grasp of us is firm and unyielding, but his hold upon his own mercies is so slight that a babe in grace may open his hand, and obtain the blessing. How sweet it is to believe that Christ's fellowship with us is just as free and unconstrained as his gracious gifts; how pleasant to know that we may always seek his company; and how cheering to remember that he sometimes visits his children when they are not looking for him!

Believer, if thou art not in communion with thy Lord, blame not the Master. His door is ever on the jar. An earthly monarch is hard to approach; Esther trembled to go to the king even though she could call him husband; but no such difficulties lie in thy path; thou hast the privilege of constant admittance, and none dare stay thee at thy Saviour's door. When thou art at a low ebb in thy communion, thou art not straitened in him, but in thine own bowels. He will offer no objection to thine approach, however much thine unworthiness may display itself. Thou mayest come in thy low estate, and be as cheerfully welcomed as in the day of thine honour; yea, thou mayest come with all thy backslidings about thee, and still find the cleansing fountain freely flowing.

Sinner, if thou also desirest to be blessed, look not for anything in thyself to qualify thee for receiving the Lord Jesus. He is his own preparation. Come as thou art, and receive of the fulness of his grace. Satan will labour to make thee think so much of thine own emptiness as to doubt the all-sufficiency and freeness of the Saviour's grace; but be sure to remember, as an antidote to so vile a temptation, that '*this man receiveth sinners, and eateth with them,*' and that '*this is a faithful saying, and worthy of all acceptation, that Christ Jesus came into the world to save sinners; of whom I am chief.*' Surely, *sinners* can have nothing of merit to bring to Jesus; and if such persons are the recipients of his mercy, it cannot be on account of their own deservings. Come then, O soul, conscious of sin, and full of unbelief, look to the covenant storehouse, and rest assured that all thy wants have been forestalled in the abundant riches of the Redeemer!

How sweet it is to behold the Saviour communing with his own flesh! There can be nothing more delightful than, by the Divine Spirit, to be led into this fertile field of meditation. When I behold the all-glorious Kinsman of the Church endowing her with all his ancient wealth, and bestowing upon her all his infinite riches, my soul fainteth for joy. Who is he that can endure such a weight of love? That partial sense of it, which the Holy Spirit is sometimes pleased to afford, is more than the soul can contain; how transporting must be a complete view of it! When the soul shall have understanding to discern all the Saviour's gifts, wisdom wherewith to estimate them, and time in which to meditate upon them, such as the world to come will afford us, we shall then commune in a nearer manner than at present. But who can imagine the sweetness of such fellowship? It must be one of the things which have not entered into the heart of man, which God hath prepared for them that love him. Oh, to burst open the door of our Joseph's granaries, and see the abundance which he hath stored up for us! This will overwhelm us with love. By faith, we see, as in a glass darkly, the reflected image of his unbounded treasures; but when we shall, with our own eyes, actually see the heavenly things themselves, how deep will be the stream of fellowship in which our soul shall bathe itself! Till then, our heartiest love and loudest sonnets shall be reserved for our loving Benefactor, Jesus Christ, our Lord.

Chapter 25

Christ glorified in his people

An early sermon by C. H. Spurgeon

'I am glorified in them.'—John 17:10.

THERE are many people who profess to admire the perfect humanity of the Lord Jesus Christ, but who deny his Divinity. They are willing to admit that he was a good man, and the best of men, but only a man. Yet if he was not 'very God of very God,' he was a base impostor, for he said, 'I and my Father are one.' There are many allusions, made to him in the Scriptures, which could not be true if he were not the eternal Son of God, co-equal and co-eternal with the Father; and amongst the rest of the passages to that effect which I might quote, I should adduce the verse from which our text is taken: 'All mine are thine, and thine are mine; and I am glorified in them.' Now, glory can never rightly be given to a creature. In the model prayer which our Lord taught his disciples, he bade them say to their Father in Heaven, 'Thine is the kingdom, and the power, and the glory, for ever. Amen.' To God alone belongeth glory; he only is to be worshipped, and adored, and to be had in reverence by all the intelligent creatures whom he hath made. All angels round about the throne worship God, saying, 'Blessing, and glory, and wisdom, and thanksgiving, and honour, and power, and might, be unto our God for ever and ever;' and John tells us that he heard every creature in Heaven, and on earth, and under the earth, and in the sea, saying, 'Blessing, and honour, and glory, and power, be unto him that sitteth upon the throne, and unto the Lamb, for ever and ever.' So that glory is equally ascribed to the Father and to his equal Son. A mere creature cannot in this sense be glorified; it is utterly impossible. A creature may be loved and honoured by its fellows; but it cannot rightly receive glory; and if any man shall ascribe glory to his fellow-man, he will be ascribing to him that which is not properly his. It is only Jesus Christ our Lord and Saviour who counts it not robbery to be equal with God; it is only he who can take glory unto himself, and who can rightly say concerning his people, 'I am glorified in them.' Glory is the prerogative of the Godhead, no creature has the right to claim it; and since Jesus Christ declares himself to be glorified in his people, it manifestly appears that he is the Son of God, that he who is glorified is Divine, and not a mere man.

Ah! my friends, you and I, who believe the gospel of Christ, can never be Socinians. We cannot accept the teaching of those who assert that Christ was only a great, and good, and wise man; for we know better than that. When we have been on the bed of sickness, and have seemed to be about to die, and have thought that we had but a few moments more to live, when he has put his blessed arms around us, and made this mortal frame feel indescribable joys, we have had the assurance that he was more than a mere man, and we have enjoyed blessed rest of heart in the confidence and trust which we have been able to repose in him as our Divine Lord and Saviour. We may not be able to bring forth all the proofs and arguments which can be adduced respecting the Divinity of the man Christ Jesus; we require none for ourselves, for we have the clear evidence within; and that, after all, though it may not be perceptible by the world without, is the source of dependence for the Christian himself. We know that Christ is God, and we are glad to find any allusion to this great truth, as we have it in our text, where glory is ascribed to Jesus: 'I am glorified in them.'

We know, then, that Jesus Christ is God; and, being God, nothing whatever can increase his glory; yet he says, in our text, 'I am glorified in them.' Now, God is so glorious that nothing can ever make him more glorious than he is. The stars, that are countless, are but as the smallest pieces of the bright needles that produce night's tapestry; they cannot make him more glorious than he is. The clouds do not make him more glorious, for they are but 'the dust of his feet;' the lightning, when it flashes in all its wondrous brilliance, is unable to add more glory to him. All these things he throws from his hand without the slightest effort; what glory can they bring to him? Great worlds of light he scattereth through the heavens as though they were but common pebbles; comets are only so much sparkling incandescent matter, sent forth by him to accomplish some mysterious purpose; but there is no power in all of them to add to his glory. He was glorified before the world was created. He is God alone, requiring none to add to his magnificence; God Most High, great, glorious, unsearchable.

Yet, in our text, Christ says of his people, 'I am glorified in them;' so here we must draw a distinction which the old Puritans used to make. People may laugh at the idea of going back to Puritan times to learn the meaning of Scripture; but there were intellectual giants in those days, at whose feet we may well sit. I find that some of them say that this passage refers to God's 'declarative glory', and not to his 'essential glory.' His essential glory is just what it always was. He is as glorious now as he was before the foundation of the world; but his people increase his declarative glory, that glory which is manifested through the spread of his cause upon the earth. In this sense, then, we understand the Lord Jesus Christ to say that believers increase his declarative glory: 'I am glorified in them.'

There are three things of which I am going to speak to you. First, there is *the great fact:* 'I am glorified in them.' Secondly, we shall consider *the corresponding duty,* that Christ should be glorified in all his people; and, thirdly, we will *regard the text as a promise,* for though it is here in the present tense, anyone who will examine the original will agree with me that it may be also read in the future tense: 'I shall be glorified in them.'

I. Here is THE GREAT FACT that the Lord Jesus Christ is glorified in all his people.

Not merely is he glorified in a few of them who are endowed with great talent, nor in those alone who are gifted with eloquence, upon whom he has laid his hands, and sent them out as apostles; not simply in a few who call themselves archbishops and bishops, who seek to rule as lords over God's heritage; but Christ says, 'I am glorified in them,'—meaning, all of them, the poorest, the weakest, the most miserable of those who are truly his people. He is glorified in the most unlearned and feeble ones who trust him in all parts of the world: 'I am glorified in them.' I will try to show you in what respects Christ is glorified in all of them.

First, *in their conversion,* for that is the great means of bringing glory to Christ. Nothing manifests God's glory more than the conversion of a soul. Who but he can accomplish the conversion of a single soul? We have heard of engineers who could bridge the widest gulfs; we have seen men who could force the lightning's flash to carry a message for them; we know that men can control the sunbeams for their photography, and electricity for their telegraphy; but where dwelleth the man, where even is the angel, who can convert an immortal soul? Let any one of them try if he thinks he can accomplish this great work. Bring hither the drunkard, who has just been dragged from his cups; let expostulation be used, let the man speak with all the powers which compassionate humanity can command, let him earnestly plead while the tears roll down his face, let him pour out his very heart, yet the drunkard shall remain unmoved. He may assail him with the law and its loudest thunders, or preach to him the gospel with sincerest tenderness; but he will sit unmoved;—or if, perchance, he may be to some degree stirred, his goodness will be as a morning cloud, and as the early dew which quickly passes away.

Ah! my brethren, it is a mercy that the work of the conversion of sinners is not committed to us. If we had to do it, if we had to convert so many before we could enter Heaven, hard—nay, impossible—would be our task. But see what happens when Christ undertakes the great task. With the softest touch of one of his gentle fingers, the door of the sinner's heart flies open, and he enters. He has but to speak to the rocky heart, and at the sound of his voice it melts away. Behold, he scattereth the seed, and it speedily ripeneth unto the harvest. He breatheth upon the iceberg, and it dissolveth. And as he looks upon all the trophies of his gracious work, he says, 'I am glorified in them.' However poor, however feeble, however mean they may be, it will glorify Christ if they are converted. That poor drunkard may become a sober Christian, and so he will glorify Christ. And if you moral men and women,—you who have so often professed to glorify God, but have not really done so,—if even you shall be converted by his grace, and become humble followers of the Lamb, you also shall bring glory to Christ. You, who are aliens from the commonwealth of Israel, may become fellow-citizens with the saints, and of the household of faith; and ye prodigals and profligates, ye also can be converted by Christ, and when you are, you shall bring great glory to him. All Heaven will ring with the praises of Jesus when you are saved by his grace, for 'there is joy in the presence of the angels of God over one sinner that repenteth.' What though the millions of mighty stars shall magnify him, one converted soul doth glorify him more than all these wondrous worlds ever can.

'I am glorified in them,' says Jesus. Pause then, Christian, and consider that, though thou art of such small account that thou seemest to be as nought in thine own eyes, yet thy Lord and Saviour, Jesus Christ, was positively honoured by thy conversion. This is the great fact which I am attempting to set forth: 'I am glorified in them.' Hear this, poor despairing one! Christ is glorified if *thou* art saved! Dost thou say, 'I am too bad to be saved'? Nay, but God will be glorified by thy conversion. 'I am too foul, too vile, ever to hope to be saved.' But it will magnify God's mercy all the more if thou art the very chief of sinners, and yet he saves thee. This is the very time for thee to trust the Saviour when thou knowest that thou hast nothing of thine own goodness to plead. I tell thee, sinner, that thy salvation will put another gem in Christ's crown; the deliverance of thee from thy sin will add glory even to the Eternal. Would not a beggar feel very bold in going to a gentleman's door if he knew that he could truly say, 'Whatever he gives me, I can give him more'? It will add fresh glory to the all-glorious One if thou art saved. Jesus will not have to die again in order to save thee, poor sinner. He will not have to endure more agonies in order that he may save thee. He died once, 'the just for the unjust;' and if thou, unjust as thou art, dost trust him, he will get something even by thee, for he will get love, praise, glory, honour, from thee, and because of thy salvation. And this is what he desires, for of old he said, concerning his great work of grace, 'It shall be to the Lord for a name,'—and he loves such a name as this,—'it shall be to the Lord for a name, for an everlasting sign that shall not be cut off.'

Now let me give you another thought. Our Lord Jesus Christ is glorified in the conversion of sinners, and he is also glorified *in their perseverance*. You know that there are many people who are said to be converted, after a fashion, yet they do not hold on to the end. I remember what a minister once told me, though I did not believe it. Pointing to a man who was passing by, he said, 'There's a man who has been converted three times, to my certain knowledge.' I expressed my astonishment at the announcement, for I knew that he could not have been regenerated three times, and there is no true conversion without regeneration. The minister was an Arminian, who did not seem to know what the conversion of a soul involves; and I am afraid that, if the man had been 'converted' in that fashion a fourth time, or a fortieth time, it would have been no good to him, and it would have brought no glory to God. I thank God that we do not believe in any 'conversions' of that sort. We count it to be the uttermost folly and falsehood to talk of the Christianity of such persons; for, by-and-by, they go back to the world, as Demas did, showing that the root of the matter was never in them.

We hold that, when once a man becomes a Christian, he is bound to walk in holiness, and in the fear of the Lord; that, when once he is a Christian, he is the sworn soldier of the King of kings, and that he must never desert from Emmanuel's army. Mighty is the power that regenerates dead sinners, and makes them living saints; and equally mighty is the grace of God which will keep them steadfast even unto the end. And herein is the power of Christ revealed, and his declaration fulfilled, 'I am glorified in them.' By preserving all who have believed in him, and by presenting them faultless before the presence of his glory with exceeding joy, Christ is indeed glorified. Alas! many of them fear, poor souls, that they will fall away, and perish; they think that God will not keep such worthless creatures as they are. They may be wrong in their theory; but, by his grace, they will be right in their practice. The Lord will keep the feet of all his saints, and none of them that trust in him shall be lost. Amidst trials fierce and fiery, amidst temptations sharp and strong, they shall war a good warfare, and overcome their triple foe, the world, the flesh, and the devil. As Job said, 'The righteous also shall hold on his way, and he that hath clean hands shall be stronger and stronger.' And in their perseverance Jesus Christ is glorified, and he can say, 'I am glorified in them.'

II. Now for the second part of our subject, THE CORRESPONDING DUTY: 'I am glorified in them.' This is what we should be constantly doing, seeking to glorify Christ at all times.

Alas! my dear friends, it is hard work for us to *keep from glorifying self;* continually denying ourselves. If any man were to say that he is not proud, he would thereby display his pride most plainly. If anyone were to say, 'I have no desire after self-love, I have no ambition for self-glory,' he would be giving the lie to what he was saying, he would be denying that which is his very aim in life, for in all men there still lurks some love of self-glory. I am afraid that some of us will not cast aside all our pride until we are clothed in our winding-sheet.

But, notwithstanding this evil tendency, beloved Christians, it is our duty in all cases to glorify Christ, and to endeavour always to honour him. We should *glorify him in public,* and we should *glorify him in private.* Some people seem to think that there is no way of glorifying Christ unless we have great powers of speech, and are able, with flaming tongue, to preach from a platform or a pulpit. Why, there are many who have never seen a pulpit, and whom the world doth not know, who yet glorify Christ from the heart. There are many who, for years, have been languishing in pain without a murmur, and enduring much sorrow without a sigh. They have been able to direct their eyes up to Heaven, and to pray, 'Grant, O Lord, that thy will, not ours, may be done! Give us, O Father, the grace to lie passive in thine arms, knowing no will but thine!' I tell you, friends, that those patient sufferers have glorified Christ as much as any of us have ever done. Brethren, never despise the sick and the poor of God's family.

Then there are the duties of public life in which we can equally glorify Christ. Some persons seem to fancy that we can do nothing to glorify God except in the performance of ecclesiastical duties; but I sometimes think that those who have to fulfil ecclesiastical duties are apt to be pious in an inverse ratio. Some people suppose that there is nothing that is holy except the services in churches and in chapels; but a man, who diligently attends to his daily business, and then devotes what time he can to the service of Christ, is really as holy as the minister is in the pulpit. There are many who look like Christians, and who talk like Christians, yet they do not follow the right course; they are not glorifying Christ. But the man, who goes to his occupation, in the morning, determined to honour Christ in every transaction all the day through, and who, not only once, but habitually, is charitable, benevolent, and true, and is especially kind to all who are of the household of faith, is far more a child of God than those others are.

In some sense, and in a certain measure, the glory of Christ depends upon his people. He says, 'I am glorified in them.' Therefore, they should seek, in their whole life, and walk, and conversation, to glorify and magnify Christ. Let me put this question to each one in this congregation. Sister, how much glory did Christ ever get from you? Brother, how much glory did Christ ever get from you? Let the enquiry go to all in the gallery as well as to all downstairs. Just take out the book of memory, and see how the account stands. How much have you glorified Christ this week? Did you glorify Christ on the Sabbath-day? That is often a bright day in the record; but did you glorify him on Monday, or did you devote the day to worldliness and carnal pleasures? 'No,' say some, 'we had the sweet enjoyment of devotion, and we did Christ honour, for we came to this house of prayer, and we rejoiced exceedingly as we spent the time with our Lord and with his people.' Can you say, concerning each day of the week, 'We glorified Christ in it'? I am afraid, dear friends, that some of us could write in a very small book, which we could carry in our waistcoat pocket, all about the glory which we have brought to Christ; yet it ought to be a volume as large as our life. I say, it *ought* to be, yet it is not usually so; for we often go astray from our Lord instead of glorifying him. Let each one of us follow Paul's example, and say, 'This one thing I do, forgetting those things which are behind, and reaching forth unto those things which are before, I press toward the mark for the prize of the high calling of God in Christ Jesus.'

III. Now, lastly, let us REGARD THE TEXT AS A PROMISE: 'I will be glorified in them.' For Christ's 'I am' must also be 'I will be,' for what he is today he is tomorrow, and he will be for ever. But even the original itself allows this rendering: 'I will be glorified in them.'

Believer, Christ shall be glorified in you as long as you live; and by his grace he will keep you so that he may continue to be glorified in you. He will not suffer you to fall, he will not allow you to perish; but he will be glorified in you. Shall I tell you when he will be glorified in you? Specially, when you come to die. That is a time when the true Christian greatly glorifies his Lord and Saviour. I need not paint the scene—as I have often done—during the last hours on earth of a dying Christian. I need not show you the warrior as he takes off his helmet, as he ungirds his coat of mail, and sheathes his sword for eternal rest. I need not let you see him when he unrobes himself, and waits in readiness to go through the narrow stream of death. I need not picture him when the floods surge around him, and when he is grasped by the chilly hand of death. I need not bid you listen to his dying voice as he ascends to Heaven saying, 'God is my strength and song, and is become my salvation.' I need not,—nay, I could not, if I would, show you the glory of his hallowed rest where, unseen by us, but seen of angels, he is with God himself. It is then that Christ is glorified in his people. The man, who lives wholly to God, glorifies Christ in whatever he does even while he is in this world; and he who nobly lives, triumphantly dies, glorifying Christ in everything, undeterred by the sufferings which begirt that death. Oh, may each one of us be able then to say, 'I am glorifying my Master,' and take off this armour to view no more the marks of the conflict with which it is indented, to feel no more those fierce thrusts of our old enemy, the devil, but to leave this world of sin and sorrow, and to rest in Heaven, for ever there to glorify Christ!

Above all, the Christian shall glorify Christ when he shall be with his fellows safe on the other side of the flood, and march in the triumphant procession of the King of kings. Methinks, in fancy, I see that great procession of the slain but risen Lamb, with all his happy followers. They have all again put on their garments of flesh. The massive books have been opened. The wicked have been cast away in their final condemnation; and now the righteous are gathered around their King. Methinks I hear the Lord Jesus say to them, 'Come, ye blessed of my Father, inherit the kingdom prepared for you from the foundation of the world.' He points upward, and he takes the first step, and quickly they all follow him. He is clothed in a robe of light and unspeakable radiance. 'Come,' saith he, and what a crowd of rejoicing ones ascends Heaven's high hill one after another! The procession seems never to have an end; still on they go, and as they come near to Heaven, the angels above shout and say, 'He comes! He, who stooped to conquer, comes again; and see what trophies of his grace, what vast numbers of followers he has brought back with him!' Then shall be realized to the full that glorious scene of which David sang so many centuries ago, as the singers within and without the gates of glory answer one another in the words of the ancient choruses: 'Lift up your heads, O ye gates; even lift them up, ye everlasting doors; and the King of glory shall come in. Who is this King of glory? The Lord of hosts, he is the King of glory.' And may you and I, dear friends, all be there when the King says, in that great day, 'I am glorified in them,' for his dear Name's sake! Amen.

Four most gracious things

An early sermon by C. H. Spurgeon

'Ho, every one that thirsteth, come ye to the waters, and he that hath no money; come ye, buy, and eat; yea, come, buy wine and milk without money and without price. Wherefore do ye spend money for that which is not bread? and your labour for that which satisfieth not? hearken diligently unto me, and eat ye that which is good, and let your soul delight itself in fatness. Incline your ear, and come unto me: hear, and your soul shall live; and I will make an everlasting covenant with you, even the sure mercies of David.'—Isaiah 55:1–3.

MARTIN LUTHER used to give the name of 'little Bibles' to certain texts of Scripture, because they seemed to contain, in a small compass, the whole of Revelation. I think I might, with much appropriateness, give that title to my text, for it certainly is a little Bible. Perhaps there are no words in Scripture which are more full of gospel truth, and which have been more blessed to the sons of men, than those which I have just read to you.

In speaking upon the text, I shall have to divide it into four parts, each of which contains something of a most gracious character. First, you will perceive that we have here *a most gracious invitation:* 'Ho, every one that thirsteth, come ye to the waters, and he that hath no money; come ye, buy, and eat; yea, come, buy wine and milk without money and without price.' We have, in the second place, *a most gracious reproof,*—a reproof, but one that is very tenderly worded: 'Wherefore do ye spend money for that which is not bread? and your labour for that which satisfieth not?' Then we have, in the third place, *a most gracious direction:* 'Hearken diligently unto me, and eat ye that which is good, and let your soul delight itself in fatness. Incline your ear, and come unto me;' and the verses conclude with *a most gracious encouragement:* 'Your soul shall live; and I will make an everlasting covenant with you, even the sure mercies of David.'

I. In the first place, we have here A MOST GRACIOUS INVITATION.

In speaking upon it, I would have you note, first, that *it is most earnest in its manner.* It begins with the word 'Ho,' which is the exclamation that the salesman uses when he wants to catch the ear of the passer-by, to attract his attention to the wares he has to sell. 'Ho,' saith he. 'Ho, such an one, turn in hither.' Thus the shopman cries to his neighbour when he sees him likely to pass by. It is strange, yet strangely true, that man, by nature, is not in earnest to be saved from the wrath to come. Though his danger is so great, his carelessness is still greater. Though his sin, if he did but feel it, would be to him an intolerable burden, yet, like the dead man, who has a weight upon him, and yet slumbers quietly in the tomb, feeling nothing of the load, such is the sinner in his natural state. But however careless men may be about salvation, God is in earnest. He cries, 'Ho.' As Solomon says, 'Wisdom crieth without; she uttereth her voice in the streets: she crieth in the chief place of concourse, in the openings of the gates: in the city she uttereth her words, saying, How long, ye simple ones, will ye love simplicity? and the scorners delight in their scorning, and fools hate knowledge?' For wisdom is in earnest, let folly play as it may.

I pray you, who are not saved, to observe the great love of God towards man, that he should condescend, as it were, to become a beggar to his own creature,—to beg one of his own creatures to lay hold on that which he himself is willing so freely to give; and observe also the folly of the human heart that it should need to be entreated to seek God's mercy. No mere human entreaties will bring you to him; and until God puts out his gracious power, and, to use our Saviour's words, compels you to come in, you would rather starve than enter the festal hall where the marriage feast is to be enjoyed for ever. At which shall I marvel the more,—the insanity of the sinner, or the graciousness of God? I cannot but remind you that, if the invitation is so earnest in its manner, you should be at least as earnest in listening to it. When God pleads, who will stop his ears? When he, who might have been dressed in robes of vengeance, puts on the garments of love, and gives a gracious invitation, who will be so ungrateful and so foolish as to turn a deaf ear to it?

Then, observe, in the next place, that *this invitation is most condescendingly addressed:* 'Ho, every one that thirsteth, ... and he that hath no money.' It would be great condescension on God's part to invite the angels to feast upon the good things that he has laid up in store, but here he invites sinful, fallen men to come to the feast of love. If God had been pleased to call the righteous to himself,—the good and gracious ones, if such there be,—it would have been a great stoop for him, and a high honour for them; but when he condescends to call the sinner,—the sinner conscious of his sinnership, panting and thirsting under a terrible sense of it,—the sinner who is naked, and empty, and with nothing like goodness about him, for that is what is meant by the expression, 'he that hath no money,'—oh, this is condescension indeed! Surely I must have, in this house, some to whom God thus personally speaks: 'Ho, every one that thirsteth.' Have you no longings after God's grace,—no desires towards your Creator? Do you not wish to be reconciled to him whom you have offended? Do you not want to have your sins forgiven? Would you not escape from the wrath to come if you could? Do you not desire to be found written among the living in Zion? Alas! there are many, who are like sick persons that are greatly in need of healing, yet they do not feel their need. Some men, puffed up with ill humours and various diseases, have no hunger when they ought to eat, and no thirst, though their body may require drink. The psalmist describes these people when he says, 'Fools because of their transgression, and because of their iniquities, are afflicted. Their soul abhorreth all manner of meat; and they draw near unto the gates of death.' And, in like manner, self-righteous fools, who need the living waters of which our text speaks, have no thirst; on the contrary, they say that they are full of all that heart could wish. They are 'wretched, and miserable, and poor, and blind, and naked;' yet they boast that they are 'rich, and increased with goods, and have need of nothing.' If there be a soul here that feels its poverty, that desires to feel it more, that is brought low before God, to such a soul, the voice of mercy speaks, 'Ho, every one that thirsteth, come ye to the waters.'

That other description, 'he that hath no money,' refers to the sinner who is emptied of all self-sufficiency; he has no merit to plead before God, no natural power, no good thing of his own. He is the one to whom this invitation is given: 'he that hath no money.' Those who will perish are those who think they have much money; they imagine that they could buy Heaven itself if they wished to do so. They expect that their tears, their prayers, their Bible-readings, their alms-givings, their respectability, their church-goings or their chapel-goings, their observance of the ordinances, and so on, will procure them a seat before the eternal throne of God. They have much money according to their mode of reckoning; but, to such people, God never gives the right to drink of the river of the water of life. Unless his grace should prevent it, they will perish, with all their supposed wealth, and go down, like the rich man in the parable, to lift up their eyes in hell, being in torments. But if you, dear friend, have nothing of your own,—no merit, no power, no strength, no atom of anything that can recommend you to God,—there comes to you the gracious invitation of our text: 'Ho, every one that thirsteth,'—ye who are old, and ye who are young; ye who are rich, and ye who are poor; ye who are educated, and ye who are illiterate; ye who earn your bread by the sweat of your brow, and ye who gain it by the sweat of your brain,—'Ho, every one that thirsteth, come ye to the waters;'—and if you have no money, you are bidden a second time to come, and 'buy wine and milk without money and without price.'

The invitation is also most liberal in its provision. A thirsty soul needs water, and it is already provided; all that your soul can need is provided in the covenant of grace. God has not to make a feast for you. His oxen and fatlings are killed, and he has sent out his servants to say to you, 'Come, for all things are now ready.' Everything is ready except yourself. The fountain filled with blood is ready, the robe of righteousness is ready, the ring for your hand, the shoes for your feet, the music and those that shall make merry with you, all are ready and waiting. There is no unreadiness in the Kingdom of God's grace; the unreadiness is all in your poor unready soul. You need not remain unready any longer; remember how good Joseph Hart sings,—

'All the *fitness* he requireth,
   Is to feel your need of him:
      This he gives you;
   'Tis the Spirit's rising beam.'

Notice, too, in our text that there is not only water provided for the thirsty, but there is wine for those who are not only thirsty, but so faint that they say they have no power to drink. Well, then, here is wine to revive them. They are faint and feeble, but God's grace shall be as strengthening medicine to them, to put new life into them. The grace of God is not only a blessing to you who feel that you can receive it; but to you who seem utterly powerless, it gives the power which enables you to receive itself.

The text also speaks not only of wine, but of wine and milk. If you are such a little child that you cannot endure wine, it being too strong for you, then here is milk, milk for babes.

And as if that were not enough, the Lord further says, 'Eat ye that which is good, and let your soul delight itself in fatness.' You are invited to 'buy, and eat;' so both food and drink are provided for you. In fact, poor sinner, all you can desire or need, for the benefit of your immortal soul, you will find treasured up in Christ. We sometimes sing, when we are praising our Lord,—

'All my capacious powers can wish
   In thee doth richly meet;
Nor to mine eyes is light so dear,
   Nor friendship half so sweet;'—

and it is even so. There is nothing that is needed to make you fit for Heaven but what you can find in Christ. He will be both Alpha and Omega to you,—the first letter of the alphabet of grace and the last letter of its triumph in glory. You shall find Christ to be food suitable and convenient for the nourishment of your spiritual nature. You strong men can 'buy, and eat,' for in the gospel there is an abundance of strong meat provided for you; and you weak ones can 'buy wine and milk,' for here is the reviving cordial, and also the strengthening milk from the breast of Divine love all ready for you. So, you see, there is liberal provision for you; and where God is so liberal with his provision, shall we be stinted in our desires? If we are straitened at all, it is not in him; but in our own bowels.

Notice yet again, for herein much of the graciousness of the text consists, that *the invitation is very pressing*. In the first verse, the Lord says three times, 'Come,' 'come,' 'come.' We shall not err if we declare that the Father says, 'Come;' and that Jesus says, 'Come;' and that the Holy Spirit saith, 'Come.' O sinner, may the Holy Spirit say it effectually in your soul now! The Triune Jehovah thus calls you again, and again, and again; and he does not say, 'Come tomorrow;' or 'Postpone your coming until the hour of your death;' but he just says 'Come.' The verb is in the present tense, and it means, 'Come to the waters now,' 'Come now, buy and eat;' and even though you are without money, yet still 'Come, buy wine and milk without money and without price.'

A great part of the graciousness of the invitation lies *in its being free and unfettered with conditions*. It is simply, 'Come.' The description of character, which is given, is not meant to limit the invitation, but rather to entice and attract more to accept it. If thou wantest Christ,—that is what is meant by being thirsty after him,—and if thou hast no goodness of thine own to plead before the Lord, thou art the man intended by the expression, 'he that hath no money.' Whatever thou mayest not be, if thou art needy, come; if thou art guilty, come; if thou art bowed down and distressed, come. Remember how the Lord put the invitation in the first chapter of this Book of the prophet Isaiah, 'Come now, and let us reason together, saith the Lord: though your sins be as scarlet, they shall be as white as snow; though they be red like crimson, they shall be as wool.'

Was there ever a text that threw open the door of mercy to the sinner more widely than the one on which I am now preaching? It does not merely invite some thirsty one, but 'every one that thirsteth.' It does not call to a man here or there who has no money, but every one who has no money is bidden to come and 'buy wine and milk without money and without price.' The Holy Ghost is himself infinite in understanding; but when he would express the freeness and richness of Divine grace, and invite the needy, trembling sinner to come to Jesus, he could find no tenderer, no richer, no more encouraging word than this text contains. I will read it again, and then we will leave this first part of our subject: 'Ho, every one that thirsteth, come ye to the waters, and he that hath no money; come ye, buy, and eat; yea, come, buy wine and milk without money and without price. Wherefore do ye spend money for that which is not bread? and your labour for that which satisfieth not? hearken diligently unto me, and eat ye that which is good, and let your soul delight itself in fatness. Incline your ear, and come unto me: hear, and your soul shall live; and I will make an everlasting covenant with you, even the sure mercies of David.'

II. Now, secondly, the text has in it A MOST GRACIOUS REPROOF: 'Wherefore do ye spend money for that which is not bread? and your labour for that which satisfieth not?'

I know that I am addressing some who have been for a long time spiritually hungry, and needing bread for their soul; yet it is not bread that they have bought with their money. They have been longing to be satisfied, but they have laboured for that which has not satisfied them, and which never will satisfy them. Now, who are these people? I will try to describe them.

There are some, who seek to get satisfaction to their souls *by the outward formalities of religion.* They are very attentive to all the exernals of religion; they go often to a place of worship, they think there is a blessing in being in places which they regard as sacred, and in what they call 'sacraments.' Let me at once assure them that there is nothing in all these things, in and of themselves alone, that can save a soul. If one could, by the space of a thousand years, eat and drink in Christ's presence, and hear him talk in the streets of the city, yet still he might say to such an one at the last, 'I never knew you; depart from me.' We still need to hear the apostle Paul say to us, 'They are not all Israel, which are of Israel.' They are not all Christians who profess to be Christians. It is not all prayer that is called prayer, nor all praise that is called praise, nor all worship that is called worship. If you could go the whole round of Ritualism, whether it be Dissenting Ritualism, or the Church of England variety, it would never bring you peace with God. There is nothing in priestcraft, with all its inventions, that can possibly be a balm to a wounded soul. Truly did Dr Watts write,—

'Not all the outward forms on earth
    Nor rites that God has given,
Nor will of man, nor blood, nor birth,
    Can raise a soul to Heaven.'

And he rightly adds,—

'The sovereign will of God alone
   Creates us heirs of grace;'—

for nothing else can do it. The bread that the soul needs to satisfy its craving must be procured from him, and not from external ceremonies.

But others of you are trying what you can do to obtain satisfaction *by seeking to reform yourselves;* and, truly, when a man has been utterly ungodly and careless, it is something, when he comes under the sound of the Word, to find him changed in his outward morals, endeavouring to conquer his evil temper, and to behave justly toward his fellow-men. Yet many have told me that they tried this plan for a long while, but never got any solid comfort from it; and, at last, when the Word of the Lord came with power to their souls, the fair tower of works which they had built fell to the ground; and they realized the truth of the apostle's words, 'By the deeds of the law there shall no flesh be justified.' The law brings the knowledge of sin home to the human heart, but it cannot bring deliverance from sin; nor can anything which we are able to do effect our emancipation. There is no escaping from the wrath of God by all that we can do; and each one of us must sing, with Toplady,—

'Not the labours of my hands
Can fulfil thy law's demands,
Could my zeal no respite know,
Could my tears for ever flow,
All for sin could not atone;
Thou must save, and thou alone.'

There are others of you who spend your money for that which is not bread in another way. *You are going round and round the mill of feelings.* Sometimes you feel bright and happy, and therefore you get a little comfort; but when you do not feel thus, then you have not any hope left. You read this book, or that, and try to put yourself into the state which the writer describes; and then you read another author's work, and you try to get yourself into the condition which he describes; or, possibly, you look into your own heart in the hope of finding comfort there. You might just as well go and peep under the ice, and expect to find fire. Do you not know that, if you are to be saved, it is a stronger arm than your own which must do the mighty deed? If you are ever to be washed from your sin, it will not be by thine own tears, nor even by the tears of Christ, but by his precious blood. When will you give up, guilty, lost, and ruined sinner, trying to make yourself better, and to put yourself in a gracious state? Come, just as you are, a graceless soul, and cast yourself on Jesus, who is full of grace. It is not in thyself, but there, where the eternal Son of God sweat as it were great drops of blood falling to the ground, and there, where he at last surrendered his life for guilty man, that thy hope is to be found. Trembling sinner, look to him, and live. Say not that thine eyes are bleared and dim; look unto him, and though thou canst not see him, yet still that look shall bring thee blessing, for—

'There is life for a look at the Crucified One;
    There is life at this moment for thee;
Then look, sinner—look unto him, and be saved—
    Unto him who was nail'd to the tree.'

Still, it is the hardest thing in the world to get people out of this foolish habit of spending their money for that which is not bread, and relying upon that which can never satisfy their immortal spirit. If you are not resting upon your feelings, there is something else, just as unsatisfactory, in which you are trusting. Some of you are more difficult to unearth than a fox would be, for he has only one hole to run into, but you have ever so many. If we drive you from one hiding-place, straightway you run to another. I do not suppose a condemned murderer raises so many objections to his being consigned to the rope as you do to being saved from hell; does it not appear strange to you that you should virtually become advocates for the devil, setting yourselves up to plead against the Lord Jesus Christ, so that, while he urges reasons why you should live, you give reasons why you should die? Oh, this is madness indeed! May God stop us from continuing in it! This is the meaning of spending your money for that which is not bread, and giving your labour for that which satisfieth not.

If you will only become like little children, and put your hands into

God's hands, and go where he leads, you will be safe and right enough; and if you feel yourselves to be like very little children, just ask him to carry you in his arms, and then all will be well. The smaller you are, the greater he will be. The more there is in you, so much the less room will there be for him. It is a blessed thing to be like a vessel turned upside down, and drained of every drop, so as to have nothing of your own left within you, for then you will be in the way of being filled from his fulness, and he will have all the glory of it. Are you hopeless because you are such a great sinner? You are ten thousand times worse than you think you are, yet that need not keep you away from Christ, for he is many millions of times better than you think he is; and he is able 'to save them to the uttermost that come unto God by him, seeing he ever liveth to make intercession for them.' Although you are driven almost to despair by what you know about your own sinfulness, and although you are overwhelmed at the thought of how great your debt is, yet remember that, as soon as we have nought to pay, God freely forgives us all our debt, if we do but trust his Son, and take him to be our All-in-all.

So I leave this most gracious reproof with you, praying God to impress it upon your hearts, that you may feel its power: 'Wherefore do ye spend money for that which is not bread? and your labour for that which satisfieth not?'

III. Thirdly, the text contains A MOST GRACIOUS DIRECTION.

The direction is very simple: '*Hearken.*' There is more to be got by listening to the Word of the Lord than by all the works of the law. It is an easy thing to hearken. 'He that hath ears to hear, let him hear.' 'Faith cometh by hearing.' An anxious soul is never in a better position than when it is really hearing the gospel. I would be very careful, dear friends, where I spent my Sabbaths; with so few as we may have, we certainly have none to waste. I implore you not to attend an unprofitable ministry; a ministry is unprofitable when it merely feeds the vanity of the natural man, or tickles his fancy, but does not impress his conscience, and lead him to Christ. If the ministry you attend has a sweet savour of Christ about it, do not let anyone draw you away from it; but if the Name of Christ be not as ointment poured forth, it is at your peril that you waste your time by listening to anything else that may be proclaimed there. Take heed what you hear, and take heed how you hear. 'Faith cometh by hearing, and hearing by the Word of God;' not by the word of man. If our hearts hearken to Christ's gospel, God's truth, the gracious Evangelical system of truth revealed to us in the inspired Word, we are following the direction God gives us in our text: 'Hearken.'

Then, next, '*hearken diligently;*' that is to say, try to catch every word, do not miss a single syllable. Seek also to drink in the meaning of the truth. Many hear the Word, but not so many 'hearken diligently' to it. A little boy heard his father say that, if ever there was a part of a sermon that was likely to bless a soul, he was quite sure the devil would make somebody distract the congregation, so as to take away their attention from the preacher for fear the Word should go home to the heart. So the child listened with both his ears, and all his heart, because he did not know what part of the discourse God might bless to him. Let us do likewise: 'Hearken diligently.'

'Hearken,' but 'hearken diligently *unto* me,' saith the Lord. Hearken not to the minister, for he may mislead you; but hearken to God. Read his Word. Keep close to that; let it be the test of all our teaching. 'To the law and to the testimony;' if we speak not according to God's Word, do not hearken to us. I pray you, my dear hearer, if at any time I do, through error of judgment, teach you that which is not in accordance with the Scriptures, reject it at once. Take not the message on my word, but on the Master's Word. But, if it be the Master's Word that I deliver, I charge you, by the living God, who shall judge the quick and the dead, not to reject it, for you will do so at your peril.

'Hearken diligently unto me,' saith the Lord. Yet many men do not think of what God says. Some rely on what the Prayer-book says; and that is very often the very opposite to the teaching of God's Word. Others ask what such-and-such a Magazine says; yet that Magazine may be tainted with the teaching of a set of heretics. Many ask what such-and-such a minister says, or what a monarch says; but God's command is, 'Hearken diligently unto me.' Let it be your sincere desire that God may speak to you, and that what he speaks, you may hear in the very depths of your spirit. If you are in such a state as that, you are far more likely to be on the road to the Eternal Kingdom than are those who are following their own devices instead of hearkening diligently unto the Lord.

But the text says, 'Hearken diligently unto me, *and eat.*' Now, eating is much more than merely hearing. To hear the plates rattle, does not satisfy hunger; you must eat if you are to be nourished and strengthened. To hear the sound of the jingling of glasses, will not satisfy a thirsty soul; he must drink if his thirst is to be quenched. So, we are bidden, not only to hearken diligently unto God, but to eat; that is, to receive into our very soul that which God presents to us in the gospel. When a man is eating, he is simply a receiver. He does not give anything out from himself, but he takes it all in. It is just so in relation to the act of faith by which Christ becomes ours: 'As many as received him, to them gave he power to become the sons of God, even to them that believe on his name.' The blessing comes from what you take into your soul by faith. Therefore, believe God's Word, trust his Son, rely upon his grace.

Then you are further told, in the text, that, if you do take God at his Word, if you do hearken diligently unto him, and do eat what he sets before you in his Word, you shall find that what he gives you is really good; that it is no mere dream of a feast, no unsatisfactory delusion, no sham bread, but you shall '*eat that which is good.*' When a soul trusts in Jesus Christ, it soon finds out the difference between the sham of walking by sight and the reality of trusting in the Lord Jesus.

You shall not only eat, but you shall '*let your soul delight itself in fatness.*' Joy will follow the reception of Christ, and you shall delight yourself in the best of the best,—in the marrow and fatness of the gospel provision. There shall be the best food, the most savoury food, the most angelic food, the most strengthening, life-giving, celestial food that you could possibly have: 'let your soul delight itself in fatness.'

Then, for fear you should not have understood the previous messages, the Lord has repeated his gracious direction and invitation: '*Incline your ear, and come unto me.*' Your ear is now turned away from God. You hear the din of the world, the noise of its pomp and vanity. Now turn your ear the other way: 'incline your ear,' try to catch God's meaning, seek to hear his Word in your very soul. 'Incline your ear;' keep it turned towards God. You know how, when people are a little deaf, they put their hands up to their ears, and lean forward, anxiously listening lest they should not catch the sound they wish to hear. Be you just as anxious to hear every syllable of

God's message: 'Incline your ear.' I remind you again that it is through hearing that faith comes; so always hear with a longing desire that faith may come to you through what you hear.

But do not be satisfied with hearing; for God says, 'Incline your ear, *and come unto me.*' That coming is the great soul-saving act. You know that all that is meant by that oft-repeated invitation, 'Come to Jesus,' is simply trust him, and especially trust in his great atoning sacrifice. I have told you the gospel, over and over again; but, unless the Holy Spirit himself shall teach it to you, I am afraid my poor words will be of no avail. Anyone who knows anything about the Christian life knows that the plainest possible preaching is mystical and obscure to the soul that has not had its spiritual apprehension quickened by God the Holy Ghost. Yet, dear hearer, I tell you once more that there is nothing for you to do, nothing for you to feel, nothing for you to be; there is nothing, in fact, expected from you,—it would be vain to expect it, for it would be like looking for something to come out of nothing. All you need for your soul's salvation is in Jesus Christ; and if you will but repose upon him,—and oh, may his sovereign grace bring you so to do!—then a full Christ becomes the joy of the empty sinner, and the riches of Jesus belong to the poor sinner who has nothing whatever of his own.

IV. Now I close by speaking briefly upon the fourth point, which is, A MOST GRACIOUS ENCOURAGEMENT: 'Hear, and your soul shall live; and I will make an everlasting covenant with you, even the sure mercies of David.'

You fear that you will die in despair; but if you hear the gospel diligently, and come unto Christ, *you shall live;* you shall truly live, you shall live with the life of Christ in you. When the time comes for you to die, it shall not really be death to you, but it shall be the full development of your life; you shall not die, but live, and declare the mighty works of the Lord; you shall not go down to the pit amongst his enemies, but angelic convoys shall bear you up to live for ever at his right hand in glory. Your soul, though deserving to be cast into hell, shall, through pardoning mercy, live for ever with the holy and the happy.

The Lord adds, 'and I will make an everlasting covenant with you, even the sure mercies of David.' Amongst all the great blessings of the

Christian religion, there is nothing more full of comfort, nor more delightful, than that thought of the new covenant of grace. The old covenant was a covenant of works: 'Do this, and you shall live.' Our father Adam could not keep it; it is thought by some that he was in Eden for only a very little while. 'Man being in honour abideth not.' Adam fell from his high estate; and if you and I were standing on the footing of our own works, and our salvation depended on our merits, we should perish before the sun rose tomorrow morning, or almost before it has gone down this evening. But God has made another covenant;—not with the first man, Adam, but with the second man, the Lord from Heaven; and it is on this wise: if Christ shall keep the law, then his obedience shall be reckoned to be the obedience of all whom he represents, and they shall live. Now that Christ has been obedient, there is no soul that is in him that can perish, for the covenant cannot be broken. If our first father Adam had been obedient, we should have lived through him; but, as he was disobedient, we died in him, not because of anything we did, but because of what Adam, our federal head and representative, did. Our salvation is on the same footing of representation; for we are not saved through what we have ourselves done, but through what our Lord Jesus Christ did, and through his obedience the covenant is made sure to all the chosen seed. Now, every soul that trusts Christ is one of the seed of Christ. Every man, however guilty he has been aforetime, who leans with his whole heart on the blood and righteousness of Jesus Christ, is in Christ; and God has made a covenant with Christ on their behalf, which is on this wise: 'I will put my laws into their hearts, and in their minds will I write them; and their sins and iniquities will I remember no more.' 'And they shall be my people, and I will be their God: and I will give them one heart, and one way, that they may fear me for ever, for the good of them, and of their children after them: and I will make an everlasting covenant with them, that I will not turn away from them, to do them good; but I will put my fear in their hearts, that they shall not depart from me.' This everlasting covenant you cannot break because it was not made with you in the first place, but with Christ your Covenant Head; and it was so established in him that it could not be broken. If you are in that covenant, you can never fall out of it.

What sayest thou, sinner? God says, 'Hearken diligently unto me; hear, and your soul shall live; and I will make an everlasting covenant with you.' Does it not cause your heart to leap for joy, even to think that God should make a covenant with you, and a covenant of such a sort that it can never be broken, an everlasting covenant? Does it not make you feel as if you must come to him when he says that he will give you 'the sure mercies of David'? You know what they are; you remember David's swan song, 'Although my house be not so with God; yet he hath made with me an everlasting covenant, ordered in all things, and sure: for this is all my salvation, and all my desire.' Now, such a covenant as that God has promised to make with every guilty and needy sinner that comes to him through Jesus Christ his Son, and rests upon him.

Thus have I once more given you the gospel. I know not how to preach it more simply, nor how to press it more earnestly upon you. I commend you to God, and to the effectual working of his Spirit; and I ask all believers to join me in praying that this simple message may be applied with power to all to whom it is addressed, that blind eyes may be opened, that deaf ears may be unstopped, and that the dead may be raised to life. To every unconverted hearer, I say,—You have had set before you life and death. You have been warned against the eternal consequences of continuing in your sin; see that you put not away from yourselves the mercies of which I have spoken. Remember the apostle's warning: 'Therefore we ought to give the more earnest heed to the things which we have heard, lest at any time we should let them slip. For if the word spoken by angels was stedfast, and every transgression and disobedience received a just recompense of reward; how shall we escape, if we neglect so great salvation?' You are still on praying ground and on pleading terms with God,—

'Not in torments, not in hell.'

Still doth the Spirit strive with you, even though you are the chief of sinners. Oh, that you may incline your ear, and come unto the Lord this very hour! Then shall you have all the mercies of the everlasting covenant, and his shall be the praise for ever and ever. Amen.

Spiritual Samsons

An early sermon by C. H. Spurgeon

'Tell me, I pray thee, wherein thy great strength lieth.'—Judges
16:6.

OFTEN as I have repeated that sentence, 'The best of men are but
men at the best,' it has not lost any of its meaning or force, and the
truth of it is impressed upon my mind and heart more deeply
every day. No child of God should ever forget that, even when he is nearest
Heaven, there is nothing but the grace of God that keeps him from being
equally near to hell. When he is most diligent in his Master's service,
instead of pluming himself upon that fact, this reflection should arise to
humble him, 'I should have been quite as diligent in the service of Satan,
and perhaps even more so, if the grace of God had not prevented me.'

We ought to be very thankful that the Holy Spirit, as a biographer, is
very different from most of the writers of the memoirs of men; for, if you
purchase a volume containing the life of any good man recently deceased,
as far as anything there is in the book, you might conceive that he was not
of the same flesh and blood as ourselves. There is a great display of all his
virtues, but his failings—if, indeed, they are mentioned at all,—are
recorded as though they leaned to virtue's side. All that was deficient in the
man's character is forgotten, and all that might have been told to the
dishonour of his poor human nature is generally left out. I do not know
that, constituted as we are, these memoirs could be written in a different
style, but I thank God, the Holy Spirit, that he did not write the memorials
of the men of faith in the olden times according to this rule. He has given us
a full and a fair picture of them. He has not done as Apelles did with
Alexander when he put the warrior's finger over the scar; he has shown us
the scars, and given us the weak points of the strong man, the foolish points
of the wise man, the sinful points of the holy man; in fact, he has shown us

that, while they were men of God, they were not gods, and that, while God helped them, and was with them, the highest glory of all the good that they did was due to him, for if it had not been for his sovereign grace, they would not have been able to do anything at all that was good.

I. Coming to the consideration of our text, we shall notice, first, that THE BELIEVER IS, OR OUGHT TO BE, A MAN OF GREAT STRENGTH.

Of course, no one will imagine that I mean that believers should always be distinguished for great physical strength, or even for extraordinary mental development, for there are many true believers who have no great powers of mind or body; but there is a wonderful strength which dwells in the believer as the result of his possessing the inner spiritual life which is the gift of God's grace. He is, or at least he ought to be, and might be, a man of great and even gigantic strength.

This strength will be shown, first, *in overcoming afflictions*. When the young lion roared against Samson, the Spirit of the Lord came mightily upon him, and he rent the lion as he would have rent a kid; and afterwards he found a swarm of bees and honey in the carcase. So is it often with the Christian, if he be indeed a man of God, and filled with his Master's spirit; when affliction roars upon him, he does not turn from it as though some strange thing had happened unto him, but he faces it boldly, wrestles with it bravely until he overcomes it, and then, ere long, he finds unexpected sweetness in the trial which he had conquered. It shows great strength of heart when a man can meekly bear severe trials and troubles. Many people are like reeds shaken with the wind as soon as ever affliction falls upon them. Like ships that are without moorings, they are driven out to sea; like the vane on the church spire, that turns round with every breeze, they have no strength of character, no force of will with which they can stand against the storm. But the Christian has learnt to spell the word 'patience'; and, though trial should succeed trial till all God's waves and billows have gone over him, yet will he cry, with David, 'Why art thou cast down, O my soul? and why art thou disquieted within me? hope thou in God: for I shall yet praise him, who is the health of my countenance, and my God.' The Christian, who is what he should be, is a man who looks at affliction as being only light, and but for a moment, and not worthy to be compared with the far more exceeding and eternal weight of glory which is yet to be revealed. He knows that, through much tribulation, he must enter the Kingdom; so he lifts up his song unto Jehovah from the midst of the floods, even in the furnace of affliction his trials do not overwhelm him.

Next, the believer proves that he is a strong man *by overcoming difficulties*. Samson was in the city of Gaza, surrounded by foes who sought his life; he desired to come forth, but there stood the huge gates,— probably, massive structures, like the gates of many Eastern cities still are, it would take several men even to open and shut them. They were so great, and so firmly fixed in their sockets, that they could not be moved by anyone possessing only ordinary strength. But Samson, instead of lifting them from their hinges, pulled up the doors, and the two posts, 'and went away with them, bar and all,' and carried them up to the top of the hill that is before Hebron. Vast was his strength, and grandly was it displayed in overcoming the difficulties that stood in his way. It is the same with the Christian when he is 'strong in the Lord, and in the power of his might.' Whatever may oppose him, when he is serving his Master, he always reckons every difficulty as a thing to be overcome; and if it be an impossibility to all human power, he relies the more completely upon the Divine strength, and then nothing is impossible to him. It is a true saying that 'there is nothing so hard but what it can be cut with something that is harder;' and there is nothing in this world, which the Christian is ever called to do, that is so hard, but that a firm resolution, importunate praying, and unfaltering faith can cut right through it. Talk of Hannibal melting the Alps with vinegar,—'tis but a legend! But the true Christian, with his passionate tears, and his vehement pleading, and his earnest faith, can bore the rocks, and make them melt like wax. Each believer, if he leaned upon his God as he should do, might, like Samson, take away the gates of any Gaza where an attempt might be made to shut him in. The Christian has great strength, in the third place, *to overcome enemies*. In the chapter preceding the one from which our text is taken, we find that Samson was bound, by his own countrymen, with two new cords, and delivered up to the Philistines, but he fearlessly contended alone against the whole host of them, 'for the Spirit of the Lord came mightily upon him.' There might be thousands of them, but what cared he when filled with a faith that perhaps has never been equalled? Notwithstanding all the sin that was in Samson, his faith was glorious. He rushed upon his foes,—one solitary man against thousands of them;—and with no other weapon than the jaw-bone of an ass, he laid them prostrate. Exulting in his victory, he cried, 'With the jawbone of an ass, heaps upon heaps, with the jaw of an ass have I slain a thousand men.' Then he lifted up his heart in prayer to God to give him relief from the thirst engendered by the extreme exhaustion resulting from the conflict; he said, 'Thou hast given this great deliverance into the hand of thy servant: and now shall I die for thirst, and fall into the hand of the uncircumcised?' Like a man who knows the holy art of prayer, he uses past mercies as an argument for further favours yet to come. So the Christian, if he be living near to God, is strong to meet his spiritual foes. Doubts and fears assail him,—doubts concerning the authenticity of Scripture, doubts concerning the Deity of Christ, doubts concerning the doctrine of atonement, doubts concerning the power of the blood of Christ, doubts about his being elected, doubts about his being called, doubts about his perseverance, doubts about his ever seeing the face of God. O friends, the doubts that assail some Christians are far too numerous to be catalogued. They go in hosts, as the Philistines were before Samson; but, with simple faith in the promise of God, the Christian meets them, and puts them to the rout, and piles his enemies in heaps till, like Deborah, he can say, 'O my soul, thou hast trodden down strength.' The strong one he leads captive, and the mighty one is utterly overturned by the vehemence of his triumphant faith. He that hath faith like this will not only have strength enough to disperse his own doubts, but he will, oftentimes, also put to flight the falsehoods and false teaching of errorists without. He may not be able to meet them in argument, and overthrow them according to the rules of logic. He may not be able to disentangle their subtleties and sophistries; but, like Alexander, who could not untie the Gordian knot, but cut it with his sword, so will the Christian, often, profiting by his own experience, cut through the knot that another man cannot unloose; and thus he will overcome some of those who have overturned the faith of the unwary. It is grand to see a believing Christian, by his godly life, and by his holy example, put to the rout all adversaries, even though they be armed to the teeth, and conquer them with a most despicable weapon, as they esteem it, but which really is far too strong for them to stand up against it.

The Christian has great strength when he is as he should be, when he has not told his secret, when the secret of the Lord is with him, as it is with all them that fear him. And when God, the Holy Spirit, continually supplies strength to him, then is he strengthened indeed to overcome those three things which I have mentioned, affliction, difficulties, and adversaries.

I must also add that, like Samson, the Christian man, when he is as he should be, is wondrously strong *in snapping his bonds*. It may be that the attempt is made to strap the Christian down tightly with the bond of custom. 'This is the rule in the trade.' 'This is the manner of buying and selling which is current in dealing with this kind of merchandise.' The true believer will break that bond as Samson snapped the seven green withes with which Delilah bound him. 'No,' he will say; 'I cannot and I will not lie, neither will I act the part of a deceiver, whatever others may do.' Perhaps an attempt will be made to entrap him into sumptuous forms of worship, glittering with show, and fascinating with all manner of sweet musical sounds; and, for a while, his ear may be entranced, and his feet may be almost gone; but presently he remembers the words of his Master to the woman of Samaria, 'God is a Spirit: and they that worship him must worship him in spirit and in truth.' In an instant, away go the bonds of Ritualism and Romanism, and the man is free once more.

Possibly, he is bound, for a time, with the fetters of fear of man, which is a snare to many. He is in the presence of one of whom he is afraid; so, for a while, he holds his tongue, and does not reveal his own sentiments with regard to Christ and his cross. Or else he has the fear of losing his business; or—such fools are many in England,—the greater fear of 'losing caste in Society.' It is that fear which makes slaves of half our population,—the fear of not being thought 'respectable.' But the true man of God very soon snaps that bond, for he regards it as an honour to be accounted dishonourable for Christ's sake; he feels that, if it be vile to be a servant of the Lord Jesus Christ, he will be viler still; and that if the fact that he is a Christian will bring him into contempt, he will be willing to be in even greater contempt, for he will serve his Lord.

If you want a good specimen of a spiritual Samson snapping his bonds, look at Martin Luther. In that day when he rose up from the Santa Scala, and would no longer go up and down those stairs on his knees in the vain hope of winning salvation by his own good works,—in that moment he snapped his bonds. At the gates of Wittemberg, on that cold December day when his friends had piled together a little heap of wood, and it was blazing away right cheerily, Martin thought that nothing would make the fire burn so well as one of the Pope's bulls, so he threw it on, amidst the wondrous gaze of all the spectators of the daring deed, and the hope or fear of some that he would drop down dead while performing so dangerous an action. He was, by that defiance of the Pope, a real Samson breaking all bonds that still held him to Popery. And such freemen should all Christians be. If they were, you would not see them—as so many of them still are,—fettered with absurd notions about holy days, and holy places, and priests, and I know not what beside of Papistical trumpery. The true believer in Christ breaks away from all this nonsense and error, and goes forth, even though he stands alone, and says, 'The Son of God hath made me free, and I am free indeed.' I might give you many other illustrations of the way in which the Christian uses his God-given power; but I will simply repeat what I have already said, that he is, through the grace of God, made to be a man of great strength.

II. Secondly, THE SOURCE OF THE GREAT STRENGTH OF THE BELIEVER IS A SECRET, even as the source of Samson's strength was a secret from Delilah and the Philistines.

For, first, *it doth not lie where the strength of other men lies.* In some men, all the might they have to boast of lies in their body; yet a lion, or an elephant, or an ox, has more of that kind of strength than they have, so there is nothing for them to glory over in that respect. Let a man be as strong as he may be, you can make a steam-engine as powerful as a thousand men like him. Mere mortal strength is not a thing to boast of; the Lord 'taketh not pleasure in the legs of a man. The Lord taketh pleasure in them that fear him, in those that hope in his mercy.'

Some reckon their wisdom to be their strength, and boast a great deal of it. They have had a wonderful education; and, besides, they have had the benefit of their observation and experience, so they are exceedingly wise men. But the Lord says, 'Let not the wise man glory in his wisdom, neither let the mighty man glory in his might, let not the rich man glory in his riches: but let him that glorieth glory in this, that he understandeth and knoweth me, that I am the Lord which exercise lovingkindness, judgment, and righteousness, in the earth: for in these things I delight, saith the Lord.' The true Christian, in the matter of wisdom, is as a little child; it is his wisdom to learn of Christ; and what the men of the world count to be foolishness he reckons to be the highest form of wisdom. The words of the Lord Jesus are quite enough for him; and though these may not seem to be consistent with the current philosophy, he is quite content not to be known as a philosopher, and is even willing to be called a fool for Christ's sake that he may be accounted truly wise in the sight of God. The Christian Church, my brethren, was never really strong when she was puffed up with worldly wisdom. In Paul's day, when he preached, not according to the wisdom of words, but in the power of the Holy Spirit, the Church grew strong in the Lord, and in the power of his might; but when the Gnostic heresy prevailed,—which I might, popularly speaking, call the heresy of knowing a great deal without really knowing the truth,—when texts of Scripture came to be spiritualized, and the doctrines of grace were refined almost to nothing, and education was cried up in the Church as the main thing,—from that hour, Christianity lost much of its real strength. I suppose that there never was a time, after the coming of Christ, when the whole world was in greater darkness than under the reign of the schoolmen. Yet those schoolmen were wondrously wise men, so far as earthly wisdom was concerned. In the days of those word-choppers and hair-splitters, the men who could argue at great length about nothing at all, and who could write elaborate treatises upon subjects that never ought or needed to have engaged anybody's attention, but which were only intended to show the extreme wisdom of the writers,—in those times, the force of the Church was gone. Aristotle was considered to be greater than the apostle Paul, and an attempt was made to show that the whole of the Aristotelian philosophy might be found reproduced in Paul's Epistles. In this kind of folly, away went the strength of the Church at once. The pity is, that this foolishness is still being repeated; but, whenever you have seen a professedly Christian minister pretend to be wonderfully wise,—and, especially, to be wise above what is written,—when he has begun to explain away the Scripture, have you never noticed how he has also explained away his congregation at the same time? So it always must be. I speak not against education and learning; when they are in their right place, at the feet of Christ, the more of them that we have, the better; but when they become the pillars of our strength, and we lean upon them, they are simply like an arm of flesh on a broken reed, and God's curse has gone forth against all who rely upon such things instead of trusting alone in the Lord. Most manifestly was this the case in the early Church; if there is anything that can be proved by positive facts, it is this, that the great strength of the Church does not lie in carnal wisdom.

Nor does the strength of any Christian, or of the Church of Christ as a whole, lie in eloquence. It is a good thing that a Christian minister should be able to speak well; there have been men, endowed with matchless powers of speech, who could make an audience listen entranced as they delivered the Gospel message; but, my brethren, I have yet to learn that brilliant orators have ever been any very great help to the Church of God. Those have done far more lasting good who, eschewing rhetoric, have preached simply, as their Master did, so that the common people heard them gladly. Where the mere orator has, perhaps, been used to the winning of one soul, the man who laid eloquence aside for Christ's sake has won his hundreds, or even his thousands. True eloquence is not necessarily rhetorical; the eloquence that speaks from the heart disdains the meretricious ornaments that are so highly recommended in certain quarters, and which are so eagerly sought after by many who would fain be accounted great preachers of the Gospel. But it is not the wisdom of words, it is not the charm of human language, it is not the attraction of glowing periods, it is not the fascination of beautiful metaphors, it is not the blaze of rhythmic poetry, that is the secret of the Church's strength; but it is the preaching of the truth in love, it is the power of the Gospel itself as applied by the Holy Spirit, that is the true source of success. So, the Christian's great strength does not lie where others might think that it does, and it does not lie where other men's power lies. He may have similar strength to what they have; but he also has another kind of force over and above theirs, whose sources are out of sight, whose deep springs are not open to the eye of every passer-by,—celestial springs, fountains from the deep that lieth under, vast wells supplied from the great deeps of God himself, who keeps them always fed with fresh and powerful streams.

The Christian's great strength, then, is a secret. I will tell you the secret; but when I have told it, it will still remain a secret to those who know it not. They will only know the words, as they might see certain Masonic signs without understanding the meaning of them. The strength of Christians lies in the fact that God, who first made us, has made us anew; and after we are new-made, all the strength which we have, which is worth having, that is, our spiritual strength, comes alone from him; and it comes from him, through the merits and death of the Redeemer, by the effectual working of the Holy Spirit. He is with us, and he is in us. 'The Spirit also helpeth our infirmities.' He gives us strength; yet his modes of operation are like the wind, of which our Lord said to Nicodemus, 'Thou hearest the sound thereof, but canst not tell whence it cometh, and whither it goeth.' The Holy Spirit imparts to us a strength which is, like himself, mysterious, and beyond the ken of ordinary eyes.

Still, *the way in which the Christian obtains this strength will be found to lie in certain things which can be traced.*

It lies, first of all, *in his faith.* In proportion as a man believes, he is strong. The very backbone of a Christian is confidence in God. Weak faith means weakness everywhere, but strong faith means spiritual strength in all the faculties of our being. Love is always fervent where faith is active and vigorous. Patience is perfect, hope is bright, and zeal is lambent, when faith is firm and strong. It is by believing God that we receive God. Faith's hand layeth hold on the eternal arm, and then strength is imparted to us by God, and so our hands, like Joseph's, are 'made strong by the hands of the mighty God of Jacob.'

Further, faith is greatly assisted by *prayer;* and, therefore, the Christian's strength lies, secondarily, in prayer. Prayer made Jacob, externally, go halting upon his thigh; but, internally, prayer made the feeble Jacob into a prince who could prevail even with God. You can gauge the measure of your strength by your prayers. If you have importuned God, if you have waited upon him in prayer, if you have wrestled with him in prayer, if you know what 'praying in the Holy Ghost' means, if you know what it is to come to close quarters with the Infinite, and by faith to enter into that which is within the veil, and to stand before the uncovered mercy-seat, all sprinkled with the Saviour's blood, and to lay your petition there between the wings of the cherubim where the blood of the accepted sacrifice falls upon it;—if you know all this, you will indeed be strong. He who can vanquish Heaven need never be afraid of anyone or anything on earth; he who has been wrestling with God, and has overcome the covenant angel in importunate intercession, when he comes down among the sons of men, shall be like a lion in the midst of sheep. Strong must he be who knows what it is to be in close contact with his God in prayer.

And next, faith and prayer are much assisted by *the Word of God*. Oh, how much of our strength lies here! Happy is he who knows how to lift the latch, and to enter into this great treasure-house of God. There are, in this Book, precious promises which can give such energy to a man that he can go forty days in the strength of this meat, as Elijah did when he went to Horeb; and not merely for forty days, but for many years. Yes; and if one promise can do this, what cannot all the promises do? He who lives upon this heavenly food by believing and receiving these words of God in his very soul, shall be fully qualified for any work to which his Master may call him. When God says, 'Whom shall I send, and who will go for us?' he answers, 'Here am I; send me;' for he knows that, where God sends him, God will be with him; and though he may pass through the fire, he shall not be burned; and though he may go through the river, he shall not be drowned. Happy is the man who diligently studies the Word, for it is by the Word that his spiritual strength is increased; therefore, 'let the Word of Christ dwell in you richly in all wisdom.' A Bible on the shelf is something, but the Bible in the heart is much more.

Besides this, the strength of our spiritual life is greatly assisted by *communion with God*. Sometimes, we get this in the hearing of the Word; and, frequently,—I may say, very commonly,—we enjoy communion with Christ at his table. But our Master is not confined, in this matter, to the use of any particular means. On a sick-bed, what blessed fellowship we have often had with our Lord! Some of you have rooms in your house where the old arm-chair, at which you have many times kneeled, could tell a wondrous tale of your communion with your God. Again and again have you said, 'He brought me to the banqueting house, and his banner over me was love.' You have, sometimes, been very faint and weary, and have felt that you must fall; but you have fallen into the everlasting arms, and have become strong in a moment. Depend upon it, we shall never be mighty for God except we live near to God. If it is not worth your while to keep close to God, it will never be worth his while to keep close to you. If you do not think it a fit thing to walk with Christ, he will not think it a fit thing to walk with you. So you see that one secret of our strength lies in communion with God.

With all these things put together, I may add that the Christian's strength may often be measured by *his enthusiasm*. That word, long neglected and forgotten until the days of Whitefield and Wesley, and generally held up to scorn by the clergy of their day,—that word 'enthusiasm' is a grand word. It needs to be brought out again, and the thing that it represents to become much more common with us all—that is, burning, passionate love for Christ, that will make us do and dare for him,—a whole-hearted devotion to our Master which will enable each one of us to sing,—

'Through floods and flames, if Jesus lead,
    I'll follow where he goes;
"Hinder me not," shall be my cry,
    Though earth and hell oppose.'

We want the same kind of enthusiasm as inspired the apostles on the day of Pentecost, when some thought they were mad, and others said they were drunk,—a Divine *furore* which takes possession of the entire soul, and carries the man beyond himself. This enthusiasm is both a source and a development of the great strength of the Christian.

But the main source is *his God*. All these things that I have mentioned are only the streams; the great source of strength is God, the ever-blessed One, who makes his people 'strong in the Lord, and in the power of his might.'

III. Our third reflection will be, that IT IS THE GREAT AIM OF THE DEVIL TO DEPRIVE THE CHRISTIAN OF THAT WHEREIN HIS STRENGTH LIES.

You will generally find that the attacks made upon you by Satan are really *attacks upon your God*. Sometimes, it will be Satan's aim to make you doubt the existence of God; at other times, he will seek to make you doubt the revelation of God; while at another time, he will try to make you doubt the truthfulness of God. Or if his temptation does not come in that form, it will be in this: 'If thou be the son of God;'—just as you know that our Lord himself was tempted. You will, perhaps, hear the enemy tauntingly say, 'Where is now thy God?' If he could only cut you off from your God, it would be all over with you; so the main brunt of the battle is to separate the Christian from his Lord. What did the devil gain when he attacked Job? He was allowed to sweep away his family, and his property, and then he touched the patriarch's bones and flesh. Ah! but if God had said to Satan, 'I will leave Job in your hands,' I do not believe the devil would have blown down the house, or taken away the children, or the cattle; he would have felt that he was all the more sure of him if his prosperity continued, and he would have said to himself, 'I have got Job now that God has forsaken him.' But as God did not forsake his servant, the devil was worsted in that conflict; and I think he will wait a long while before he will attack another Job if he should ever meet with such a man; for, surely, he scarcely ever met with a greater and a grander man till he met the Christ of God himself, and was trampled beneath his feet.

Satan will, often, make an attack upon your God *through your faith*. Hence the apostle says, 'Cast not away therefore your confidence, which hath great recompence of reward.' Satan will tell you that you have no right to believe, and that you ought to doubt. He will say to you, 'Look at your many sins.' Ah! that is an old trick of his. 'You have no right to that great shield of faith,' he says, because he hopes that you will drop it, and that then he will be able to hurl his fiery darts at you while you are unprotected. Be not ignorant of his devices; even though sins do prevail against you, still believe that 'Christ Jesus came into the world to save sinners.' If you feel that you are a great sinner, hold on to Christ all the more firmly, for you will defeat the enemy in that way if he cannot make you to be unbelieving. Even in the common trials of life, Satan will try to make you dishonour God by making you to be full of care, and wretchedness, and doubts concerning your God's love and faithfulness.

The devil will also be sure to attack you through *your prayers*. If he can get you to forget to pray, he will have attained his object; but if he cannot do that, he will hinder you all he can. I have known Satan, when I have been praying, suggest all sorts of thoughts to my mind,—vain thoughts, light thoughts, evil thoughts,—to try to stop me from pleading with God. I sometimes think that the devil gets people to call at our houses most of all just when we are praying. We have scarcely begun a season of special fellowship with God before there is a knock at the door, and we hear the message, 'Please, sir, you are wanted.' Of course that is just what Satan desired! The great thing is, if you can, to shut to the door, and get alone with God, and resolve that you will abide with him till you have had true fellowship with him. In some way or other, Satan will, if he can, prevent the prayers of believers from being presented at the throne of grace, for they are his terror. These are the great guns on the battlements of Zion that cause the hosts of hell to tremble. If he can spike these guns, or silence them, he thinks that he can capture the city. So another source of your strength lies in prayer.

I have already mentioned *the Word of God* as partly the source of the believer's strength, so Satan will try to get us to neglect that if he can. Or he will seek to make us merely read passages of Scripture without thinking of the meaning of them; or to look into the Bible to discover difficult points of doctrine, instead of finding the practical, every-day truths about which there can be no mistake. If he can, he will prevent us from getting any profit from reading the Word; and although we may, like Jonathan, walk through the wood, and see every word of Scripture, as it were, dripping with honey, Satan will try to prevent us from putting out our rod, so as to get a taste of it.

And as to *fellowship with Christ,* he cannot bear the thought of it; and when he knows that a believer is walking in the light, he will, if he can, bring him into darkness by leading him to leave the path of holiness, and to withdraw from God.

So is it with *our enthusiasm;* many assaults of the world, the flesh, and the devil, are specially directed against our enthusiastic service for Christ. When a Christian is fully bent on serving God, Satan tries to cool him down by degrees. If he can get him to be like the church of Laodicea, 'neither cold nor hot,' he reckons that to be a great point gained; 'for,' says he, 'if Christ will spue the lukewarm one out of his mouth, then he will be altogether my own.'

So, brethren, rest assured that, wherever your strength lieth, Satan will be certain to bring all his strength and cunning to bear against you. By the long observation which he has had of Christians, he knows well enough that their strength is in their God, so with all his might he will seek to snap the sacred bonds which bind the believer to his God; but blessed be the Name of the Most High, 'neither death, nor life, nor angels, nor principalities, nor powers, nor things present, nor things to come, nor height, nor depth, nor any other creature, shall be able to separate us from the love of God, which is in Christ Jesus our Lord.' This is what Satan is always seeking to do; but, blessed be God, he shall not be able to do it.

IV. So, in the last place, IT BECOMES US, WHO HAVE THIS GREAT STRENGTH, VERY JEALOUSLY TO GUARD IT, LEST WE LOSE IT. We shall never lose our spiritual life, but we may lose spiritual strength, and be brought very low; and what will happen to us then?

First, *we shall be as weak as others are.* We used to endure suffering joyfully, we used to fight our foes bravely, we used to render great service to our Master; but if we lose our strength, we may go out as Samson did, and shake ourselves as at other times, not knowing, perhaps, that the Lord has departed from us; but, when the Philistines come upon us, we shall find out our weakness. We ought to be in such a state that, after having been once strong in the Lord, to come down to be weak as other men would be considered by us to be a great disgrace. In some respects, it would be good for such a man if he had never been born. O Christian, you ought always to be advancing; will you be willing to go back to the beggarly elements of the world? You ought to forget the things that are behind; are you returning to them? It may be pleasant, sometimes, to fall asleep in the arbour on the hill, as Bunyan's pilgrim did; but it is not pleasant afterwards; for, if you drop your roll under the settle, you will have to come back for it with sighs and groans all the way, and it is hard work to have to retrace your steps. A backslider is a most pitiable object. He is to be pitied with true Christian compassion. A Christian cannot look upon him with complacency, he can only look upon him with compassion.

In the case of Samson, after he became weak as other men, there happened to him this great calamity, *he lost his eyes;* and if the believer declines, and loses his strength, he will be likely enough to lose his eyes. His joy will go. David lost his eyes through his great sin, and sorrowfully he prayed, 'Restore unto me the joy of thy salvation.' That was all gone. He had his eyes left to weep with, and that was all the use they were to him; he could not see his God with comfort, and he had mournfully to cry, 'Hide thy face from my sins, and blot out all mine iniquities. For I acknowledge my transgressions: and my sin is ever before me.' It was a great mercy for him ever to have such weeping eyes as he had; but, Christian, you would not like to lose your joy, and your hope, to have to go groping in the darkness, as Samson did, and as some are now doing, who are alive unto God, but not enjoying fellowship with God, and perhaps for years will not do so, because of their sin.

The next thing that happened to Samson was, that *he was bound with fetters of brass or copper,* and led down to Gaza—to the very place where he had aforetime carried away the gates. But, now, the very children gathered around him, and mockingly cried, 'Carry away the gates again if you can;' and they plucked at his robe as they scoffed at the giant, now chained like a lion that has lost his teeth, and is reduced to ignominious weakness. So, many a man, in departing from the living God, has got into the bondage of men, or bondage before God so that he hardly knew whether he was a child of God, or not, for he has spoken and acted like a slave rather than a child. My dear brethren and sisters, whom I love in Christ Jesus, may none of you ever know, by personal experience, what this terrible bondage is.

The next thing that happened to Samson was, that *he had to work for the Philistines:* 'he did grind in the prison house.' That is what the fallen child of God has to do. The enemies roll it as a sweet morsel under their tongue, and say, 'Ha! Ha! so would we have it! Here is another of your Christian men,—another of your ministers,—another of your sanctimonious hypocrites, turned out a scoundrel at the last!' Samson is grinding for the Philistines, while all through the streets of Askelon and Gaza you may hear the uncircumcised go forth, with dance and with song, shouting, 'Jehovah's champion is overcome. Rejoice, ye daughters of Philistia, and bow before your god, for he hath led captive our enemy, and the destroyer of our country, who slew so many of us in the days of his strength.' Oh, how they rejoiced! Philistia was never more jubilant over Israel, nor more blasphemous towards the great I AM than in that unhappy time when the hearts of God's people were filled with mourning and lamentation. There was not a watcher among the children of Israel, who looked toward Gaza from the hill before Hebron, and thought of the son of Manoah, whose wonders had been so many, without feeling sad at heart that the wayward hero was now a slave. It must have struck terror to the hearts of all Israel in that sorrowful day. So is it still when the Christian loses his strength, and falls through sin. According to how much he was known, and his standing in the church, will be the proportionate mischief done by him. Any Christian—though he is the most obscure, and only living in a back street, and having but few relatives,—if he should fall into sin, his enemies are sure to exaggerate it, and make a mockery of it, and say, 'This is your religion, is it?' and lay all the blame to his religion; and, alas! they blaspheme thy Name, O Immanuel, which was, surely, blasphemed enough on the cross, and reviled enough when thou wast making atonement for our sins, without thine own children crucifying their Lord afresh, and putting him to an open shame. The Master shows his hands, and when they ask him what these wounds are, he does not point to those nails on the cross, and call those the wounds,—it is to his honour and glory to be wounded so; but 'these are the wounds,' saith he, 'the wounds that, above all others, I received in the house of my friends.' None can stab Christ as Christians do when they cut at the honour of their Lord. As Cæsar turned to Brutus, and exclaimed, 'And thou, Brutus!' and then his false friend's ingratitude broke his great heart, so, O Christ, if thou wert not what thou art,—God as well as man,—it would be enough to break thy heart to see the dishonour which thine own people have brought upon thee! Watch, then, beloved brethren and sisters; 'watch and pray, lest ye enter into temptation;' beseech the Lord to guard you, for he alone can keep you from falling. Say not that you are able to stand. 'Let him that thinketh he standeth take heed lest he fall.'

Inward fears*

A sermon, preached at Brighton, more than 40 years ago [1861 or earlier] by C. H. Spurgeon

'Within were fears.'—2 Corinthians 7:5.

I T is my desire to address myself, tonight, mainly to those who are seekers after that 'peace of God, which passeth all understanding,'—those who were before careless, but who have been rendered thoughtful, who are no longer loving this world and the things thereof, and sitting down content therewith, but wanting something better, something more satisfactory to their immortal souls. Whilst I shall endeavour to speak to their comfort, I pray that God the Holy Spirit, the Comforter of his people, may bring home the truth of the Lord Jesus to their consciences, and give them 'joy and peace in believing.'

My text is rather the motto of my sermon than the actual text of it. The whole verse runs thus, 'For, when we were come into Macedonia, our flesh had no rest, but we were troubled on every side; without were fightings, within were fears.' The last three words, '*within were fears,*' are to furnish the theme for my discourse.

The apostle would have cared very little concerning the 'fightings' without, if it had not been for the 'fears' within. The sailor will tell us that he has less fear of an ocean full of water without, than he has of the smallest quantity within, when the ship has sprung a leak. So is it with the convinced and awakened sinner,—all the persecution which he could possibly meet with, from the enemies of Christ, would be very little to him, if it were not for the internal fear lest he should not be 'found in Christ.' Neither the stake, the gibbet, nor the rack, could keep back a seeking soul from Christ. There is a thirst so unquenchable in the seeking soul that he would endure all his enemies' torments, if he could but find Christ. But the thing that often staggers him is that he fears, when his soul is cast down within him, lest he should never be 'found in him,' lest he should never be saved through his precious blood.

I no doubt am addressing very many who have fears, and who, perhaps, have been oppressed by them very frequently, having only now and then intervals of comfort. It may be that they have scarcely dared to say they have ever had any solid comfort at all. They are so tried, perplexed, and, as John Bunyan says, 'tumbled up and down in their minds,' that they know not where they are, or what they are; they are like those whom the psalmist describes, who 'reel to and fro, and stagger like a drunken man, and are at their wit's end.'

I purpose to give you, in this sermon, a sort of dialogue. I will first let this poor trembler speak, or I will speak for him as nearly as I suppose in the words he would use; then I will reply to his fears; after that, he shall speak again, and then I will have yet another reply, and may the Master himself reply to the fears which perhaps the evil one has suggested!

'Well,' saith our poor friend, 'I wish that I could "read my title clear to mansions in the skies." I fear that I have no "title," that I have "no part nor lot in the matter;" but am "in the gall of bitterness, and in the bond of iniquity." I think that I am "dead in trespasses and sins,"—that there is no good work whatever in my soul, and I fear there never will be,—that what I am I always shall be, an "alien to the commonwealth of Israel, and a stranger to the covenant of promise." But',—listen to him now, and I hope we can put in the same 'but,'—'I feel that nothing here below can ever satisfy my cravings. I long after something which I cannot find in this world,—either in its amusements, its learning, its pomp, or its promises. I did once build my nest on the trees of this earth, and it was well lined, and I thought I could rest securely there; but now there is a thorn in the nest.— and let me try as I will, and seek where I may,—

> '"I fly, like a bird of the air,
>   In search of a home and a rest;
> A balm for the sickness of care,—
>   A bliss for a bosom unblest."

'I fear that I have nothing to do with Christ, yet I know that I never shall be happy unless I have. I am conscious of a longing within, which I did not know at one time;—for once, if I had only enough to "eat, and drink, and wherewithal to be clothed," I was perfectly content to let heavenly things alone. If my riches increased, and men thought well of me, I was perfectly satisfied; but these things now are poor unction to my heart: they are as songs to one that is sad, they are but mockery to my wounds. The more I have, the more sad I feel, because there is no happiness to be found in them all.'

I answer thee, poor trembler,—Take heart if this be thy case, for already I see signs of the dawn of a better life in thy soul. The first step to wisdom, is to know our folly; the first step to eternal happiness, is to know our misery. I am glad that the Lord hath made thy sweet cups to be bitter, and thrust a thorn into thy nest. I thank him that he has afflicted thee,—that he has taken away one joy after another; and left thee like a childless woman, or like one who hath been bereaved of her husband. I thank God for thy troubles,—not because I rejoice in thy misery, but because these trying experiences are intended to be huge waves to wash thee on the Rock. They are meant to be rods that shall scourge thee to thy Father. Doubtless, the rags and the swine's food, (the husks,) brought the prodigal to his senses; and thy sorrows are intended, in the hand of God, to be the means of bringing thee to thyself, that, afterwards, thou mayest be brought to him.

Now, judge ye what I say, ye who are thus discontented and troubled. Who has made you so uneasy in your mind? Has Satan done it? Indulge not such a delusion; he is too busy rocking the cradles of worldlings, keeping them asleep. Nothing pleases him more than to see men satisfied with his wages. He is a tyrant king; and if murmurings be heard in any portion of his dominions, he immediately lays his heavy hand there. Satan, then, has not made thee discontented with the world, its honours, and its pleasures.

Dost thou think it is thine own heart which has thus troubled thee? If so, surely it would have been so always; but, years ago, thou wert perfectly contented. There must have been some change wrought in thee. Let us hope that it has been wrought by the Holy Spirit; thou shalt know better concerning that matter by-and-by. Already, I think I can say to thee, 'Be of good cheer;' and if I cannot pronounce thee decidedly to be a child of God, yet would I give thee strong exhortations to trust in Christ and in his precious blood, for surely there are designs of love in God's heart towards thee.

Let our tried friend speak again. 'Well,' saith he, 'I think I can go a little further than this. Though it would be presumption in me to say I am a Christian; yet I must say this, I cannot keep it back, I do desire to be a Christian, and there is nothing in the world that is so much the object of my ambition as that I may be saved from sin.'

I am glad that thou hast said, 'Saved from *sin*' for there are many sinners who wish to be saved from hell, who never will be saved therefrom; but to desire to be 'saved from *sin*,' is a blessed mark of the working of the Holy Spirit. The culprit dreads the gallows, but it is a question whether he hates the sin he committed in the murder. Every man, about to be punished, fears the punishment, but very few deplore the sin. But I have interrupted thee, so go on, my friend, with thy story.

'I desire so to be saved *from sin,* that I would give all I am, and all I have, to be able truthfully to say that I am a child of God. Sir, God is my witness, I speak now what I mean, and the tear is in my eye while I say it,—if I had the whole world, I would cheerfully give it up, if I might but know that I am a child of God. Yes, I would live on bread and water, and be willing to be shut up in a loathsome cell till death seized my frame, if I could but call him mine. I have but one desire, "Give me Christ, or else I die." But if once I could say, "My sins are forgiven,"—if I could but say, "He has loved me, and given himself for me," I think the joy would be almost too great for my poor heart, and I should die with excess of bliss.'

Well now, soul, I am glad thou hast spoken like this, for I think I see not only the first rays, but the twilight of the rising sun. I am persuaded that the Holy Spirit 'hath begun a good work in thee.' For where, thinkest thou, did this desire come from? Did Satan see thee longing after Christ? Surely that would be a new business for him to undertake. If he were to do so, that would indeed be Beelzebub divided against Beelzebub, and how then should his kingdom stand? Do you think Satan ever will try to draw souls to Christ? That would be completely changing his nature.

Dost thou think these desires come from thyself? Then, let me tell thee that thy dunghill heart could never have grown such a plant as this, if the seed had not been sown by a Divine hand, stretched out from Heaven itself.

Thou mayest desire morality, and other good things,—for these are within the scope of thy nature; but to be thoroughly desirous to be cleansed from sin, to be made like Christ, to be washed in his blood, to become a partaker of his nature, to be a true child of God,—to these things, nature cannot attain! As soon might swine want to study astronomy,—as soon might a fish wish to become an angel, and join, though dumb, in the song of cherubim and seraphim,—as thine unaided nature might desire to rise above itself, and become Christlike and Divine.

But I say to thee, and I speak by the guidance of the Holy Spirit,—Why hath God given thee these desires? Is it to tantalize thee, to mock thee with wishes he never intends to satisfy? Will God make thee thirsty, and then deny thee drink to quench that thirst? Dost thou think that God delighteth in thy misery so much as to make thee dissatisfied with this world, and set thee longing for another world, and then decline to give it thee? Think not so hardly of him, but believe that, if he had meant to leave thee to thyself, these desires would never have come into thy soul. Certainly, if he makes thee long for him, it is because he longs for thee; and if he sets thy mouth a-watering for the Bread of Heaven, it is because he intends to fill thee with it even to the full. So let thy desires encourage thee, and begin thou at once to hope.

But let me ask thee another question, and do thou honestly answer it,— Does it end in desire with thee? 'Oh, no!' say you, 'it does not end in desire. I pray whenever I can; I often get away alone, and pour out my heart before God; and beg and beseech him to have mercy upon me. I tell him I am a wretch undone without his sovereign grace; but, oh! sir, the heavens are like brass above my head. The door of God's mercy does not open to me; it seems as if, the more I knock, the more tightly the gate becomes closed, and my very knocking fixes it more firmly in its place. I do think prayer is of very little avail for me; I have asked, but the blessing has not been given to me; and, sometimes, I almost resolve that I will give up prayer as hopeless; and then I return to it, and say that I will die praying. If Christ does not hear me, I will never cease to cry unto him. I will be like blind Bartimæus, and say, "Jesus, thou Son of David, have mercy on me;" and if my doubts and fears, like the disciples, should bid me "hold my peace," I will "cry the more," "Thou Son of David, have mercy on me!"'

Ay, poor heart, I know well this state of experience, for I long groaned under it. For many bitter years, I sought for peace, yet found it not; those years were full of the curse and of despair, and my sad spirit lay grovelling in the dust; albeit I can now rejoice with 'exceeding joy.' I thought prayer was a waste of words; I imagined that, in another man's case, it might avail; but, in my case, it was of no use at all,—till I heard a godly woman say, she 'never would believe there was a person, either in this world, or in the next, who would dare to say that he had sought Christ with all his heart, and that Christ had refused to save him.' I determined in my heart I would say that, for I thought it was true; yet I have never said it, for, ere the untrue words could be uttered, I trust I found him,—yea, I know I did.

And so shall it be with you; the time of love shall come. Give one more knock, poor Mercy, though thou art fainting at the gate. Up! take courage! Does the great dog howl at thee? It is not the Master's dog; he is not set there by Christ to frighten thee. Give another knock, and the door shall be opened to thee, and the porter shall say, 'Come in, thou blessed of the Lord, wherefore standest thou without?' Continue in thine expectation of the answer to thy supplication, for it shall come at last. There is not a soul in hell that ever truly sought Christ; never was there one, who truly prayed to him, and who finally said that he did not answer his prayer.

Let our trembling brother speak again. 'Ah!' saith he, 'you put me a little in heart; and since you encourage me, I will speak out once again. Sometimes I have a faint hope of joyous times,—I am able to "touch the hem of his garment" with my finger,—and then I am happy, because I think he may be mine after all. But these seasons are, "like angels' visits, few, and far between;" and they are very short. Yet one thing I know, though I would not be so bold as to say that I really am an heir of Heaven yet, what little hope I have, I would not give up for all the world; and even in my darkest times, I can say, "Though he slay me, yet will I trust in him."'

'Twas bravely spoken, brother; and dost thou not see that thou hast defeated thine own fears by what thou hast just now said? It is strange how, sometimes, the fears of God's people, which are very troublous to them, appear ludicrous to others. Going to see an old lady once, one who had often told me that she had 'no hope of Heaven,' and could not believe herself to be a child of God, I asked her distinctly, 'Do you really mean to say that you have no hope in Christ?' She replied, 'I have not any.' So I took out my purse, and said to her, 'I will give you a five-pound note for what hope you have.' She opened her eyes in astonishment, and said, 'I will not sell it for a thousand worlds.' I enquired, 'Sell what?' She answered, 'My hope.' I said, 'You silly woman, you told me that you had not any;' and still she persisted in saying she had no hope.

I knew a brother in Christ, who was able to get rid of a poor woman's fear when she was dying. 'Sir,' she said, 'I am afraid I am a hypocrite; I have no love for Christ at all.' He said nothing, but he walked towards the window, and took out of his pocket a piece of paper, and wrote on it, 'I do not love the Lord Jesus Christ.' 'There, Sarah,' said he, 'sign that.' She read it, and said, 'Sir, I would be torn in pieces first! I could not sign that.' 'Well, but it is true, isn't it?' he asked. 'No, sir.' 'But you said you did not love him.' She replied, 'I thought I did not; but when you put it like that, I dare not say I do not, for, at times, I hope I do.'

It is a wonderful thing that, when men are drowning, and their strength is almost gone, they clutch with great tenacity the plank that is thrown in their way. So the poor soul, that is sinking into the grave, holds on, with a grasp full of force, to that which before he did not believe he possessed.

In martyr days, those who died the most bravely were often those who thought they could not stand the test; while some who said, 'If Mary burns the Protestants, we can bear the fire,'—recanted. Cranmer who, when he burnt the Baptist maid of Kent, in signing the warrant, told Henry that 'burning was an easy death,' recanted,—though afterwards he also did nobly die for the faith;—while that poor maid did not sink in the fire, though often full of doubts, and vexed with fears. So hath God ordered it that 'when we are weak, then are we strong;' and, sometimes, those who seem to be the strongest prove to be the weakest.

I remember an instance of a young woman, who wished to unite herself with the church, and, according to custom, she was to come to the church-meeting, and give her testimony for Christ. The minister asked her a question, but she could not answer a word. Then he put it in another form, yet still he could get no answer. At last, he said to her, 'My good sister, it is impossible for us to receive you, unless you give us some evidence of your faith in Christ.' As she did not speak, he bade her retire; but as she was doing so, she burst into tears, and exclaimed, 'I could not speak for Christ, but I could die for him!' 'Come back, come back, my sister,' said the minister, 'that will do; that is a good confession.' She was received into the church, and lived consistently with her profession. And many of those, who may not be able to say that Christ is theirs, will be found among those who have the best hold of him,—clasping him most firmly, as a child will cling to the mother's bosom when the night is the darkest, and as our sons, when most in fear of falling over the cliff, tighten their grasp of us. Be not afraid, poor timid soul; these 'fears' are perfectly consistent with the existence of faith in thy soul.

Let us hear our trembling friend again. 'Well,' saith he, 'now you are getting my secrets out of me, I must say, once again, I dare not take all this comfort to myself, for I feel myself so unworthy, and so full of sin; and one thing makes me think I cannot be a partaker of the life of God,—it is this,— I am not what I could wish to be. Do you know, sir, I strive to keep from sin, yet I cannot? I am anxious to keep from it. "To will is present with me; but how to perform that which is good I find not." Often do I pray to God, and struggle in prayer, and think I never will sin again; yet I go out, and sin just as I did before; then am I grieved and pained to the very quick, so that I cry out, "O wretched man that I am! who shall deliver me from the body of this death?" I feel like two men,—one good, the other evil. I seem as if I had within me both an angel and a devil. There is a stern struggle as to which of these two shall get the upper hand; there is a perpetual warfare. My heart is like a case of knives, cutting each other. My soul is like a battlefield, rent, and torn, and covered with blood. There is a conflict of two armies within me; can I really be a living child of God if I feel like this?'

You have asked a question which is very easy for me to answer. Would you feel like this, if you were not a living child? Would it be possible for a dead man to know anything about a conflict? Do you imagine, if your body were dead, that you would feel pain? There must be life where this conflict is going on. I tell thee, man, this contrast was not always there. Once the tide ran in one direction, now the two tides meet, and there is a desperate whirlpool in thy spirit, sucking down thy comfort, and seeming to drag thy soul to the lowest hell. The language I used just now is thine, and it was the language of the apostle Paul; and as he used it, and thou dost not doubt that he was a true believer in Christ, surely thou mayest use it, and be a believer, too.

These conflicts are not only consistent with grace, but they are the results of grace. Dost thou think that darkness shall be driven out of thee without an effort? Will Satan lose a soul without a struggle? Did not even the Bourbon king, when he had gained a little courage, seek to release a liberator? And dost thou imagine that thy sins will give up their throne without disputing, inch by inch, for the mastery? In every Christian, it is a hand-to-hand conflict. Sin proclaims 'war to the knife' with grace; and, on its part, grace has drawn the sword, and flung away the scabbard. None are so much like reprobates as those who have religion in their heads, but who never know the conflict that the godly experience. 'Moab hath been at ease from his youth, and he hath settled on his lees, and hath not been emptied from vessel to vessel.' These are the careless ones, concerning whom it is said, 'Woe to them that are at ease in Zion;' but blessed is the man who feels a conflict raging within his soul, and who longs for the time when sin shall be overturned, and Jesus Christ shall be all in all in his heart. I say, then, that these conflicts should be a ground of joy and comfort to thy soul.

'Well,' saith our friend, 'though I have thus talked of conflicts, it is but fair to say, as I am unburdening my heart, that sometimes I have little gleams of joy,—like lightning flashes across a black tempestcloud;—and sometimes I see a great light, which dazzles and confounds me; and when I look again, it is quite gone.'

Will you tell me, from thine own honest heart, when do these joy-flashes come?

'They come, sometimes, when hearing a comforting sermon; when sitting in the house of God, and listening to the voice of the man who preaches "Jesus Christ, and him crucified," I feel that the Gospel is the only balm for my wounds;—and, sometimes, when the good Samaritan pours in oil and wine, and binds them up, I do indeed feel great joy.'

And dost thou think this would be the case if thou wert not being dealt tenderly with by Christ himself? Thou dost rejoice in the very things in which God's people rejoice,—when Christ crucified is lifted up; but thou wouldst never rejoice in this if there were not in thine heart some secret love towards him. When else art thou glad?

'To tell the truth, I am very glad when I see others converted. If I never shall be saved myself, I do rejoice that Jesus Christ is being glorified in the salvation of others. Nothing pleases me more than to hear of some being "plucked as brands from the burning." I sometimes pray that God would bless others; and if I never go to Heaven myself, I feel that I must praise Christ for what he has done for others. It is so gracious on his part to bleed and die for rebels, who did not love him, that I must admire him for that, even if I have no share in it myself.'

My brother, you are indeed getting on; you have let out a secret, this night, showing that you are akin to the angels of God, for they 'rejoice over one sinner that repenteth.' Thy heart is in tune with the harps of angels; and if so, will God send thee down to howl with devils? It cannot be. He that hath taught thee to praise his love and grace, in the conversion of others, will teach thee to run up the higher notes of the scale, and thou shalt yet say, 'He hath loved me, and given himself for me.' In thy personal interest in Christ, thou shalt soon rejoice; this I do verily believe. When else are you glad?

'I am glad, sometimes, after overcoming a temptation. When I have come home, and thought I have lived as I ought to live; when I have checked my hasty temper,—when I have not spoken harshly to someone who has spoken harshly to me,—when I have gone out of my way in order to do a kindness to others, who have done no kindness to me,—when I have schooled myself to be like Christ, and in the effort have felt glad,—not as the Pharisee, who thanked God that he was not as other men are,—I was not thinking of other men just then, but I felt glad because I thought, perhaps God the Holy Spirit has wrought this work in me, and possibly it is a proof that he is dwelling in my soul; and, O sir, when I do but think that Christ loves me, my soul is all on fire! If I have even a faint hope that he loves me, I am filled with joy,—though, when that hope is crushed, I go back to dust and ashes.'

Poor soul! I see no reason why thou shouldst go back to thy sackcloth and gloomy dungeon, if ever thou hast had a victory over sin, and if grace has ever helped thee to overcome thine infirmities. Has God begun a work, which he will not finish? Has he laid the first stone of an edifice which he will never complete? Has he cast the shuttle over the web, and will he ever leave that fabric till he has finished it in the loom? Oh, no! believe that the first work is the pledge of the last work, that he who hath commenced the work will continue it until it is finished. Rejoice, then, if God has begun to be merciful unto thee.

Our friend shall speak once more, and when he has done that, I think I shall turn to the congregation generally, and preach the Gospel with all simplicity.

'Oh!' saith my poor friend, 'I can scarcely dare to hope that what I have said is true. I feel very miserable lest I should never read my name in the Lamb's book of life; but I know this, if my name is not in the family register of God, I do love his people; and I love them as his people. The conversation of the wicked, I detest; and their lascivious songs and oaths, I cannot away with; even the talk of the light and frivolous, I cannot endure, it vexes me; but put me with two or three of the people of God, and I rejoice to hear them speak about Christ. I am like John Bunyan, of Bedford, standing behind the door, listening to three old women, who were talking of the things of God and the world to come. I love best the company of God's people. I can truthfully say that I am never ashamed of any of them; let them be ever so meanly dressed, I think they are all princes, and I only wish I was worthy to sit at their feet. If only I could have my name in the Lamb's book of life, I would not mind if it were next to the meanest, ay, the vilest sinner, that ever was saved by sovereign grace.'

Well, friend, thou hast spoken so freely, that I must speak plainly to thee. The apostle John says, 'We know that we have passed from death unto life, because we love the brethren.' I have in my mind's eye, at the present moment, a person who often comes into contact with me. He is one of the most generous souls living. Sometimes, when I have met with him, and asked him why he does not 'make a profession of religion,' he blushes, and says that he is 'not fit to join the church.' Yet I have known him often feed the hungry, and clothe the naked, and never a tale of distress comes to him, about a child of God, but the tear of sympathy is in his eye in a moment, and his open-handed liberality is ready to help. I happened, a few Sunday evenings ago, to mention that I had met with the widow of that famous Welsh preacher, Christmas Evans, and that I had found her absolutely in want. My friend came into the vestry, after the service, and said to me, 'Do let me know where that poor woman dwells; she shall have five shillings a week from me as long as she lives.' He cannot bear that God's people should be in need, yet he will persist in saying that he is 'not worthy to be called a child of God.' But if you questioned him as to whether he would live without Christ and without prayer, he would say that he loved prayer, and that he trusts in Christ.

If such a man as that is not a true Christian, I know not where to look for one in the whole world. I cannot understand what our Saviour says, in the twenty-fifth of Matthew, if that man has not the grace of God within his heart, for Christ there says, 'I was an hungred, and ye gave me meat: I was thirsty, and ye gave me drink: I was a stranger, and ye took me in: naked, and ye clothed me: I was in prison, and ye came unto me.' These things being done to disciples, as disciples, and for Christ's sake, are marks and evidences of grace, so sure and certain that they are mentioned in the judgment-day in preference to any others; and true and unfeigned love and sympathy with the tried and tempted people of God, are marks of grace, so indisputable, that I wonder at the impudence of Satan in endeavouring to make any, who possess them, doubt their interest in Christ.

And now, turning from our trembling friend, I wish to say that there is one evidence of salvation which he, doubtless, would have mentioned, if he had spoken longer. He would have said, 'I have no hope in anything that I am, or in anything that I do, or in anything or everything that I feel, as a ground of my salvation. My hope, if I have any, is fixed on Jesus Christ, and him crucified, and on him alone.'

And if our friend had said that, I would have replied that it was not only an evidence of salvation, but it was an expression of salvation itself. The way of salvation is so plain, so clear, that, as we preach it, we are compelled to say that we wonder how men ever could have so muddled it, and made it such a mystery as some of them have.

Here is one man, who will have it that the way of salvation has a dozen things in it. It begins with the sprinkling of water, and even that must have the sanctity of the apostolic succession of the dispenser. That being done, salvation is not sure even then. There must come, after this, certain forms and ceremonies,—none of which have been commanded by God. Then there must be constant 'sacraments' to renew the sacramental efficacy once given. At no single period in the transaction, can a man say it is done, for it is not; and even when he comes to the grave, there remains, according to some, an imperfection in his salvation. He is to be followed by prayers for the dead, and masses for his soul's repose. Indeed, to know the whole plan of salvation, as taught by so-called priests, it would be necessary to buy a library, and read it through; and when you had done so, you would not know what you were to do.

Many Christian ministers make a great mystery of the plan of salvation; it is very complex, according to their explanation. It is something like good Mr Mason's notes on Bunyan's *Pilgrim's Progress*. He asked one of his parishioners once, 'Have you ever read Bunyan's *Pilgrim's Progress*, and do you understand the volume?' 'Oh, yes!' was the reply, 'I understand the book well enough; and I hope, by the grace of God, one of these days, I shall be able to understand your explanations of it.' So, I doubt not, many hearers could say to their ministers, 'We understand the text, "Believe on the Lord Jesus Christ, and thou shalt be saved," and no doubt, one day, we shall understand your explanation of it.' Really, according to some, salvation is made such a long task, such a difficult thing; and after being once complete, it may be made all null and void; a soul once saved, after having gone through a kind of new birth, which does not ensure eternal life,—for this sort of spiritual life may come to an end,—that sinner may, through the power of his lusts, be lost seven times, and seven times be saved, and then be finally lost after all! I do not believe there is anything in the Scriptures to warrant such teaching as that.

When you go to hear some preachers, it is necessary to take your dictionary, to enable you to understand them. Other preachers will give you the title of a huge book, and tell you that you must read it before you can understand what they mean. Sometimes, when I wish to understand some new theory, I ask, 'What is the best book on the subject?' I am informed, 'There are fifty-four volumes of a work, at, say twelve shillings each, and cheap at the price!—and if you read them through, you will get the gist of it!' You will see, at once, that this cannot be the Gospel that is meant for the poor.

I go into a church, and see a number of boys dressed up, and I see somebody decked out in fine trappings, which must have cost a large sum, and I say, 'Well now, if this be the original worship of the Church of Christ, a person must have had a good haul of fish, for a year or two, before he could save enough money to fit himself out in that style. If this be the religion of Christ, he must have contrived (as was once done) to bring all his fish to land with thirty pence in each of their mouths.' These brethren cannot preach without gown, and cassock, and altar, and all sorts of frippery. Anyone who chooses to reason will say, 'This cannot be the religion of Christ's open-air sermons on the mountain-top; this cannot be the religion of the dozen poor fishermen who "turned the world upside down;" this cannot be the religion of Paul, who, dressed in common garb, preached the Gospel of Christ, with no altar, or vestments, but simply used his tongue, and so won souls for his Master.'

What, then, is 'the Gospel of Christ'? I reply,—The way of salvation is just this,—trust Christ, and you are saved. Christ Jesus, the Son of God, became the Son of Mary,—he lived a life of holiness, he died a death of unutterable agony. In that life, he obeyed the law of God, and wrought out a perfect righteousness. In that death, he made full atonement to God for all the sins which his people had committed. The way to realize this righteousness, and the merit of this blood, is to trust Christ.

'But,' says one, 'may I believe that Christ died for me?' That is not the question I am speaking about now; trust Christ, and you shall find that out. Some men teach that Christ died for everybody; and if he died for everybody, then he died for me. Yet I may believe, in that general sense, that Christ died for all, and find out, after all, that I am not saved. Christ's blood is not efficacious for any man but the believer. Christ hath bought some good things for all men,—the common mercies of life. He has bought all good things for some men, and they are known by this mark, they trust Christ; and if you trust Christ, that must be an evidence that he died for you, that he was punished for your sins; and certainly the righteous God cannot punish two persons for one offence. He has punished your Substitute, and therefore he cannot punish you. Christ has wrought out a perfect righteousness. You trust him, and that righteousness is yours, and you stand before God as if you had kept the whole law, and never committed a sin. Trusting Christ puts you where he is, just as Christ's love put him where you are. Christ voluntarily placed himself where those who now trust him once were. They were sinful, so he took their sins upon himself; they deserved punishment, so he bore it all in their place. He emptied the cup which they ought to have emptied; and—

'At one tremendous draught of love,
    He drank damnation dry.'

He gave to God all he demanded on behalf of his people. God needed not to be made loving, 'for he was love before.' It was a proof of his love that he gave Christ to die for the ungodly. It was the Divine plan that God should be just, and merciful. He is just, for he punished Christ to the utmost rigour of his law. He is just; he required a perfect righteousness from Christ, and he abated none of the demands of his law. But he is also merciful; and, thus, believers are made to stand where Christ did. God looks on them as if they had kept all his law. He gives them Heaven as a reward. He looks on them as if they had never sinned, and he gives them full pardon.

'Well, then,' someone may ask, 'May I trust Christ without hesitation?' I say,—Yes, be you who you may.

I must say a few words here, not by way of apology,—for I never apologize for preaching the Gospel freely,—but to put aside what some brethren say. Some of my brethren hold strong Calvinistic doctrines; but not stronger than I hold, yet, they think that, to preach the Word indiscriminately, in a Gospel sense,—is not Calvinistic; and some say it is not Scriptural,—for Calvinism to some, by the way, is of more importance than Scripture!

I think I know better than most men what Calvin taught. His works consist of fifty-six volumes, or more: I do not say that I have read them all through; but if any man ever has, I have. I never read a chapter through for exposition without consulting John Calvin, because he is the most consistent commentator I know. Sometimes he is inconsistent with himself

310 C H Spurgeon's forgotten early sermons

in his Institutes; but they were the production of his early youth, when he had not fully mastered the Word of God. He is not to be judged by them, but by his expositions, which are the ripe fruit of his later life. There is not a single word in the whole fifty-six volumes that gives the slightest warrant for preaching a limited gospel.

Now, my dear brethren, allow me to say that there are no brethren in the world I love more heartily and sincerely than you, who are so particular upon this point; and it is because I so love you, that I am going out of my way to show you that you are wrong. You dare not preach Christ to sinners till you see some good in them. Brethren, this is rank Popery! It is contrary to that Gospel which you so much love. You tell the sinner, when you preach, 'If you are a sensible sinner,—if you are this or that,—you may come to Christ.' Then a sinner must look to himself to see whether he is this, or that, or the other; but that is just what you do not want him to do. You are not making him look to Christ, but to himself. In the course of a very extensive pastoral experience, I certainly have met with hundreds of persons who have been troubled with fear upon this point. 'Oh, sir!' says such an one, 'I do not think I am a sensible sinner; and my minister has told me that the promises of the Gospel are not made to me, unless I have felt my need.' So, all the while, they are looking to themselves, and not out of self to Christ. The fact is, this kind of teaching is sheer legality; it is making a part-christ out of the sinner's sense of need; so I say, 'Away with it!' I care not from what lip it comes,—whether from a Calvinist or an Arminian,—nothing must be put between the sinner and Christ. While I say to the Puseyite, 'Down with your drapery, sir!' I say to these legal preachers, 'Away with your qualifications, if they prevent any sinner from coming to Christ.'

The truth is, that the Word of God *commands* sinners to believe. 'This is his *commandment*,' says John, 'That we should believe on the name of his Son Jesus Christ, and love one another, as *he* gave us *commandment*.' 'Then,' saith one, 'if he commands men to believe, they can do it of themselves.' I believe they can do no such thing. Still, I am to command them to do it.

Look yonder, at Peter and John going up into the temple, and finding there a man who had been lame from his birth. Now, Peter and John, do not tell him to rise up and walk, for that would be duty-faith. But supposing that man had possessed power in himself to leap up, and walk, and enter into the temple with the apostles, anyone might have told him to do so; but as he had not the power, it took an inspired Peter and John to do it effectually.

Look again! There are the dry bones in the valley. If there were any power in them to make themselves live, any simpleton could tell them to do so; but as they had no power, it needed a God-sent Ezekiel to say, 'O ye dry bones, hear the Word of the Lord.'

I do not preach the Gospel because there is any power to will in sinners; but because God makes them believe just as they are. You may say, 'I do not feel this or that;'—away with your feelings! It is not what you feel that will save you; you are to trust Christ. If you do trust Christ, you are saved; and all the devils in hell cannot rob you of your salvation.

But why does God command men to believe? I think it is in order that a poor sinner, if he could not get comfort from an invitation, might get comfort from a command. If any qualification were appended to it, he might say it was not for him; so it is put thus broadly, 'He that believeth and is baptized shall be saved;' or in the form of a command with a threatening appended to it, 'Believe on the Lord Jesus Christ, and thou shalt be saved;' 'but he that believeth not shall be damned.'

I will show you the working of this truth upon the conscience of a sinner. Supposing an order comes that I am to go, just as I am, at once to Windsor for an audience with the Queen. (I will imagine myself to be miserable, black, and ragged.) If the Queen sent such a command, (supposing her to have absolute authority over me,) if I did not go, I should be punished. Therefore I go,—not because I have any garments fit to go in, but because I am ordered to do it. I arrive at Windsor, and a big grenadier says to me, 'What are you up to here? You have no right to be in such a place as this.' 'I was ordered by the Queen to come,' I reply. 'Then,' says he, 'you must pass, for the Queen's commands must be obeyed.' A little further on, a footman in livery says, 'What's your business here? I am surprised the porter should allow a person like you to pass; you are filthy, sir!' I answer, 'I was told to come, and to come just as I am.' I go a little further, and another official says, 'According to the laws of this Court, you cannot possibly enter.' I am abashed; but I show him the royal command, and he permits me to pass. I go into the ante-room, and sit down there, and say to myself, 'I do not feel, after all, that I have any right here; I do not think I will go in.' Why, I should be guilty of disobedience! But if, instead of so acting, I walk straight up to the throne on which the Queen is sitting,—though I break all the laws of etiquette,—though I am dressed just the reverse of what one should be on such an occasion,—though I blunder out bad grammar, or utter no words at all,—I have done what I was told to do.

This is how God deals with you, poor sinners, for he knows that you will not trust Christ unless he does so; therefore he gives you this plain command, 'Believe on the Lord Jesus Christ, and thou shalt be saved;' that command is addressed to you. Trust Christ, and you will be saved. I tell you, sirs, I will be responsible if I preach not the truth;—at the judgment-day, I will bear the responsibility if this be not the way of salvation. If this is not the Gospel, I am not saved. If the devil tells you that you are not a sensible sinner, say, 'I am a stupid sinner;' if he says you are not alive, tell him you are dead; but tell him that you are obliged to say, 'Dead or alive, I cling to Christ.' If you cannot find any qualification, you can still lay hold of his cross,—sink or swim. I know no other hope for you; I had no other qualification myself. I sighed and groaned for five long years; and when at last I came to Christ, I was obliged to leave all idea of qualification behind me; I am sure I should never have come to Christ at all if I had not come just as I was. Believing he was able and willing to save me, I cast myself upon him, and he did save me there and then.

'But still,' says someone, 'suppose I were to trust myself on Christ, and yet I were to be lost.' Sir, that can never be! I will make my bed in hell, side by side with you,—I will bear with you the indescribable pangs of the eternal fires, and you shall taunt me as a deceiver, and mock me as a liar, throughout eternity, if ever you perish after trusting in Christ. You would be the first, you would be the only one who had perished like that; but, if you trust Christ, you will not be lost. Heaven might sooner reel, and pass away, and angels lose their first estate, and God himself lose his throne, than ever one, trusting in Christ, should perish.

'But I am not the right man;'—but you are the right man. 'But I am not qualified;'—but you are qualified. If you think you are, then you are not. If you think, 'There is an invitation, and I am the character referred to in it,' probably you are not therein described; for, generally, those who are included in the invitations of the Gospel think they are not.

'Well,' says one, 'there is the invitation, "Come unto me, all ye that labour, and are heavy laden."' Yes; that is directed to the labouring and the heavy laden; but there are tens of thousands who are heavy laden, who are addressed like this, 'Whosoever will, let him take the water of life freely.' As Mr Brooks truly says, 'While the invitation there is given to the labouring and the heavy laden, the promise is to those that come: "Come unto me, all ye that labour and are heavy laden, and I will give you rest."' It has no limit.

'Don't you believe in God's election?' somebody asks. Of course I do; and the very fact that I do believe therein, makes me preach a free-grace Gospel. I cannot see any use in preaching to sinners that they must have something preparatory done to them to bring them to Christ. I marvel how any, believing in God's electing love, out of pure grace, and in Christ's redeeming blood, should have thought the calling of God needed something in the sinner to make it efficacious.

Poor souls! I pray you, whatever may be the teaching to which you listen, do not permit it to get the mastery over you, so as to prevent you from casting yourselves on Christ. Black, filthy, lost, ruined souls, trust Christ, and you are saved. Will any of you accept that great blessing? No; not one of you unless the Spirit of God shall humble your pride, and bring you to the feet of Jesus as true penitents. You would accept the Gospel if it had qualifications in it; but it comes to you as unqualified sinners. It tells you to come to Christ just as you are,—not as sensible sinners, or awakened sinners, or any special sort of sinners,—but simply as sinners, without any qualifying word added to your name; and if you do come like that, I know why you will come,—because the Lord hath 'made you willing in the day of his power.' You will find that truth out by-and-by; you will discover that you never would have come if he had not drawn you by his grace.

I wish I could spread my net so far that the Lord would bring many of you therein. I remember reading about old Mr Flavel, who preached on what was called 'The Soul's Preparation for Christ.' An excellent man (Mr

Richards) invited Mr Flavel to preach for him; and he preached the Gospel to sinners simply as sinners; and about a dozen persons met him outside, when the service was over, and said to him, 'This day, we have been set at liberty.' Poor Mr Richards had for years preached only part of the truth; he had always held up Christ to sensible sinners, but they were afraid they were not sensible enough; yet, when Mr Flavel preached to them simply as sinners, they found Christ. Then they discovered that they were sensible sinners, but they did not know it before. I think they were very 'sensible' sinners indeed not to look at their sensibility, but to look to Christ.

I have often been pleased in reading the works of Tobias Crisp. Dr Gill made a few notes thereon; he somewhere says, 'that a drunken man, on seeing a drunkard saved, may have as much reason to believe that Christ died for him as for that other man who had sinned in a similar fashion; he may come to Christ on that warrant.' I think he may come on the other warrant; simply because God bids him to come.

I have been astonished, sometimes, to see how a solemn doctrine, which teaches that the work of salvation is all of grace, is consistent with the broad invitation, while the other kind of teaching is not, but is positively Popery wearing a mask. Down with qualifications, and up with the finished work of Christ. Down with all preparations for Christ, and come to Christ just as you are,—sinner as you are,—hardhearted, sinful, full of vileness, and beset by all that can damn thy soul. Come as thou art; and if Christ reject thee, then is his Word not true where he says, 'him that cometh to me I will in no wise cast out.' 'All that the Father giveth me shall come to me,'—and none beside these will come unto him.

I know, and rejoice in knowing, that some will 'come' as the result of this sermon; and I will put the truth of my doctrine to this test—that some souls will be brought to Christ by it. Look and see, dear friends, if some men and women are not saved through this discourse. I never knew the plan of salvation so clearly, as when I found that nothing was wanted from a sinner but to trust in Christ.

Spirit of Christ, set thy seal to this message! If it be not thy truth, teach us our error. But if this be the Word of God, thou must bless it. Now, Spirit of the living God, own it. Let the trembling heart find peace; and may some, who have been hovering about the camp, come near to thee; and though they think themselves to be only like dogs, let them say, 'Yes, Lord; yet the dogs under the table eat of the children's crumbs.'

God bless you, and bless the Word I have spoken, as far as it is consistent with his will, for Jesus Christ's sake! Amen.

Note

* This is probably the sermon preached in Brighton in about 1859 which gave rise to the allegation that Spurgeon had abandoned Calvinistic doctrines—See G.H. Pike, *The Life and Work of Charles Haddon Spurgeon,* vol. 2, p. 327. Published in *The Sword and the Trowel,* July and August 1901.

About Day One:

Day One's threefold commitment:

• TO BE FAITHFUL TO THE BIBLE, GOD'S INERRANT, INFALLIBLE WORD;

• TO BE RELEVANT TO OUR MODERN GENERATION;

• TO BE EXCELLENT IN OUR PUBLICATION STANDARDS.

I continue to be thankful for the publications of Day One. They are biblical; they have sound theology; and they are relative to the issues at hand. The material is condensed and manageable while, at the same time, being complete—a challenging balance to find. We are happy in our ministry to make use of these excellent publications.

JOHN MACARTHUR, PASTOR-TEACHER, GRACE COMMUNITY CHURCH, CALIFORNIA

It is a great encouragement to see Day One making such excellent progress. Their publications are always biblical, accessible and attractively produced, with no compromise on quality. Long may their progress continue and increase!

JOHN BLANCHARD, AUTHOR, EVANGELIST AND APOLOGIST

Visit our website for more information and to request a free catalogue of our books.

www.dayone.co.uk
www.dayonebookstore.com

C H Spurgeon's sermons beyond Volume 63

TERENCE PETER CROSBY (EDITOR)

640 PAGES, HARDBACK

978-1-84625-145-0

C H SPURGEON'S
SERMONS BEYOND
VOLUME 63

An authentic supplement to the
Metropolitan Tabernacle Pulpit
Forty-five forgotten sermons compiled from the
Baptist Messenger by Terence Peter Crosby

Here are 45 sermons which were awaiting publication in the *Metropolitan Tabernacle Pulpit* when it came to an abrupt end in 1917. The 63 volumes and 3563 sermons of Spurgeon's *New Park Street* and *Metropolitan Tabernacle Pulpits* were a remarkable achievement, and it was only on account of the shortage of paper and metal caused by the First World War that publication ceased on 10 May 1917.

Many hundreds of sermons were ready and waiting for their weekly publication and notices in the last two sermons indicated that it was the intention to resume publication once peace had been restored. However, only twenty hitherto unpublished sermons were to appear in 1922 in a volume entitled *Able to the uttermost.*

It is the purpose of this volume to bring to light the sermons which probably would have appeared in the remainder of Volume 63 and at the start of volume 64 of the *Metropolitan Tabernacle Pulpit*, sermons which originally appeared only in magazine format from 1877 to 1881.

Terence Peter Crosby holds a PhD in Classics (Greek and Latin) from London University and was for some time Secretary of the Evangelical Library,

London. He is the compiler of Day One's volumes of daily readings *365 Days with Spurgeon, My book of hobbies* and *God's Book, the Bible*, and the author of *Greek to the Rescue.*

Charles Haddon Spurgeon (1834–92) was England's best-known preacher for most of the second half of the nineteenth century. In 1854, just four years after his conversion, Spurgeon, then only 19, became pastor of London's famed New Park Street Church. The congregation quickly outgrew their building, moved to Exeter Hall, then to the Royal Surrey Gardens Music Hall. In these venues Spurgeon frequently preached to audiences numbering more than 10,000—all in the days before electronic amplification. In 1861 the congregation moved permanently to the newly constructed Metropolitan Tabernacle. Spurgeon's printed works are voluminous.